Authentic Assessment in Social Studies

This engaging book will show you how to move beyond tests and essay writing to implement authentic assessments in your middle or high school social studies classroom. Award-winning teacher David Sherrin explains the value of authentic assessments and offers practical ways to get started and dive deeper in your own practice. You'll be encouraged and inspired by the real-life stories of classroom successes and failures that illustrate the points throughout the book. The chapters cover a range of categories, including different types of written, creative, and civic action assessments. The book includes:

- ◆ planning charts and rubrics showing how to use, grade, and give feedback on assessments so they truly aid student learning and progress
- ◆ specific examples, useful tips, and ready-to-go instructions that you can use immediately with your class
- ◆ open-ended assessments encourage scaffolding or adaptation for individual or group work to fit your classroom needs

You will learn how to personalize instruction and provide students with avenues for creativity and the types of learning experiences they need to be prepared for a complex world.

David Sherrin is a Social Studies teacher at Scarsdale High School. Previously, he was a department chair and a New York City Master Teacher at Harvest Collegiate in New York City. He is the author of *The Classes They Remember: Using Role-Plays to Bring Social Studies and English to Life* and *Judging for Themselves: Using Mock Trials to Bring Social Studies and English to Life*. David was the recipient of the 2014 Robert H Jackson Center National Award for Teaching Justice.

D1597076

Also Available from Routledge Eye On Education
(www.routledge.com/k-12)

**Judging for Themselves:
Using Mock Trials to Bring Social Studies and English to Life**
David Sherrin

**The Classes They Remember: Using Role-Plays to
Bring Social Studies and English to Life**
David Sherrin

**Authentic Project-Based Learning in Grades 4–8:
Standards-Based Strategies and Scaffolding for Success**
Dayna Laur

**Authentic Project-Based Learning in Grades 9–12:
Standards-Based Strategies and Scaffolding for Success**
Dayna Laur

Rigor in the 6–12 ELA and Social Studies Classroom
Barbara R. Blackburn

Rigor Is Not a Four-Letter Word, 3rd Edition
Barbara R. Blackburn

**Creating Citizens:
Teaching Civics and Current Events in
the History Classroom, Grades 6–9**
Sarah Cooper

**History Class Revisited:
Tools and Projects to Engage Middle School Students
in Social Studies**
Jody Passanisi

**Close Reading the Media:
Literacy Lessons and Activities for Every Month
of the School Year**
Frank W. Baker

Authentic Assessment in Social Studies

A Guide to Keeping it Real

David Sherrin

Routledge
Taylor & Francis Group

NEW YORK AND LONDON

First published 2020
by Routledge
52 Vanderbilt Avenue, New York, NY 10017

and by Routledge
2 Park Square, Milton Park, Abingdon, Oxon, OX14 4RN

Routledge is an imprint of the Taylor & Francis Group, an informa business

© 2020 Taylor & Francis

Library of Congress Cataloging-in-Publication Data
Names: Sherrin, David, author.
Title: Authentic assessment in social studies : a guide to keeping it real / David Sherrin.
Description: New York, NY : Routledge, 2020. | Includes bibliographical references.
Identifiers: LCCN 2019050305 (print) | LCCN 2019050306 (ebook) |
Subjects: LCSH: Social sciences—Study and teaching—United States. |
Educational evaluation—United States. | Curriculum planning—United States.
Classification: LCC H62.5.U5 S5187 2020 (print) | LCC H62.5.U5 (ebook) |
DDC 300.71/073—dc23
LC record available at https://lccn.loc.gov/2019050305
LC ebook record available at https://lccn.loc.gov/2019050306

ISBN: 978-0-367-20365-8 (hbk)
ISBN: 978-0-367-20366-5 (pbk)
ISBN: 978-0-429-26111-4 (ebk)

Typeset in Palatino
by Swales & Willis, Exeter, Devon, UK

Dedication

To Ariel, Gabby, and Daniel – I try to teach students to find joy in learning, but it is you who teach me to find joy in life. May you always discover ways to add sparks of love and creativity to the world.

In memory of Marta Meacham, whose passionate teaching of Spanish led to my journey to Chile, and then to Brazil, and thus to the elevator where I met my wife, and finally to my own career as an educator.

Contents

Meet the Author

David Sherrin is the father of three young children. In his spare time, he also teaches Social Studies at Scarsdale High School. He is the creator and curator of a unique educational resource on the Holocaust: the *Joseph & Myra Brandman Virtual Holocaust Memorial Museum*. Previously, he was a department chair and a New York City Master Teacher at Harvest Collegiate in New York City. He is the author of *The Classes They Remember: Using Role-Plays to Bring Social Studies and English to Life* and *Judging for Themselves: Using Mock Trials to Bring Social and English to Life*. In 2014, David was the recipient of the 2014 Robert H Jackson Center National Award for Teaching Justice. David's passion is to make education Joyful, Authentic, Dynamic, and Effective, and thus he regularly updates his JADE Learning website to provide tools for educators.

Bonus eResources

Find more rubrics, discussion protocols, role-plays, and other strategies for social studies on David's website: JADE Learning. Go to davidsherrin.net to locate the resources.

Acknowledgments

Rather than include a lengthy list of acknowledgments here, throughout the book, I have recognized and appreciated the contributions of countless colleagues as they pertain to particular projects or assessments. This way, it will be even clearer the extent to which I am fortunate to have worked with and learned from such smart and dedicated teachers. Also, now those teachers are more likely to read the rest of the book.

I do want to give my heartfelt thanks to the educators (and friends) who took the time to read draft chapters of this book and provide expert feedback: Emily Block, Ken Bonamo, Andy del-Calvo, Shira Epstein, Maggie Favretti, Emily Haines, Bishop Sand, Andy Snyder, and Lisa Yokana. Your insights made this into a better book. Thank you to all my students who have challenged themselves with creative work and who always keep me smiling.

I am grateful to have worked again with my wonderful editor, Lauren Davis, and her top-notch team at Routledge. Thank you, Lauren, for your positivity, wisdom, and expertise in steering me in the right direction. And a final thank you to my wife, Lea, for patience and support through the lengthy and sometimes tortuous writing process.

Introduction

The Art of History

My favorite historical source is about the Spanish Civil War. It describes the tragic devastation inflicted on ordinary men and women by the Italian and German air forces. Like all great historical texts, its argument is vivid and persuasive: the war was calamitous and the indiscriminate bombing campaign led to inhumane suffering. The source focuses on the experience on the ground – the mothers who have lost babies, terrified people attempting to flee, the agony of injured animals, and even hopeless individuals who throw their hands up in despair.

This source is so influential because for many people it is the only connection they have to the Spanish Civil War, a topic that is rarely studied in schools, discussed in popular histories, or made into period films. It is also available to the public, since it is easy to access online or, if one is fortunate, in person at the Museo Reina Sofía in Madrid.

The historian who produced this text is Pablo Picasso and the work I am referring to is the painting *Guernica*. We tend to think of Picasso only as an artist. And we think of historians only as scholars who sift through dusty archives in order to *write* about the past. While Picasso was not a trained historian, in *Guernica* he was engaging in much of the important work of a historian. Historians do more than tell a story. The work of a historian is to put forward an argument about the meaning of our past. Picasso's *Guernica* is so vital to the world's cultural heritage not only because of its immense artistic value, but also because for so many individuals it has become the cornerstone that supports our rather feeble historical memory of the Nazi bombing campaigns against Republican resistance in the Basque Country.

I remember standing in front of *Guernica* at the Reina Sofía. While sometimes Picasso's cubism just seems strange, the style worked perfectly to illustrate the despair and tragedy of the bombings. I was a 22-year-old student of international affairs, learning about this event for the first time. My teacher was Picasso. In the decades that followed, despite becoming a social studies teacher, I have never read a book about Francisco Franco or the Spanish Civil War. Without this historical work, so many people like me would lack any gateway into this event.

Pablo Picasso was a precocious artist. His father was a successful painter and art instructor, and Pablo must have earned his 10,000 hours of practice early on. By age 13, he was enrolled in advanced classes in Barcelona's School of Fine Arts. By age 16, he had gained admission to Madrid's Real Academia de Bellas Artes. He was fortunate to have opportunities to pursue his artistic passion in school.

I wonder, however, the following: if Picasso wrote the way he painted, in a cubist style, what type of feedback would he have received in a traditional academic setting? Probably, something like this:

> *Pablo,*
> *This is an interesting piece. You have the beginnings of an argument here but your organization is sloppy and difficult to follow. Instead of your topic sentence being at the head of the paragraph, for some reason it is at the tail. It is unclear how the different pieces fit together to support your points. You need to stick to three major points, separate them clearly into sections, and make it easier for your reader to connect your evidence and to follow your argument. Grade: B-*

I don't know whether Picasso was a cubist writer, but given the fact that he eventually dropped out of art school because he found it too restrictive, I can only imagine the torment he might have faced in a traditional academic setting. Picasso, we must infer, would have emerged from high school with the takeaway that he was a dullard, incapable of making a historical argument or participating in the intellectual world. My dream is to contribute to an educational system in which even people as creative and unorthodox as Pablo Picasso can experience success in an academic setting.

Any student, in his or her K-12 education, will have about six elementary school teachers, and 30 or more middle and high school teachers, with at least seven of these being social studies teachers. I can say, with confidence, that plenty of those educators will provide the traditional guidance, insisting that the student draws within the lines and checks-off all the boxes. My question is this: will that same student have at least one teacher who encourages her to blur the lines and erase the boxes? Each student really only needs one such teacher. Will it be you?

All of us are part of a larger educational system and none of us are completely responsible for educating any one child. That fact should provide us with some freedom, the ability to take solace in what we do best, and to take advantage of what makes each of us unique as teachers. As an educator, I can think of three things that set me apart: (1) my passion for developing Dungeons & Dragons style historical role-plays; (2) I once got mugged by two youths wielding machetes in Brazil; and (3) I have spent a considerable chunk of my career thinking about and implementing authentic assessments in my classes, thereby making it a purposeful and consistent core of my educational philosophy.

Probably only the latter factor qualifies me to write *this* book.

During this fortunate career I have taught just about every type of student imaginable, at least in the diverse New York City metro area. I began teaching at a private Jewish high school where my students' skill levels ranged widely. I then moved on to the Facing History School, a NYC public school whose student population in 2016–17 was 69% Hispanic, 26% Black, 16% ELL, and 23% special needs. Many of the students were motivated and engaged while many others presented the academic, economic, and social traits that make urban education so challenging. I helped found my third school, Harvest Collegiate, a non-selective NYC public school that serves a more diverse student body: in 2016–17 its students were 45% Hispanic, 26% Black, 19% White, 7% Asian, 2% ELL, and 29% special needs. It was as wide of a swath of New York City that one can find in terms of race, social class, and skill-level.[1] Finally, I moved on to teach at Scarsdale High School whose students, 72% White, 15% Asian, and 7% Latinos, come mostly from affluent families and are often highly motivated and high-performing.[2]

There are very few commonalities between all of those teenagers. But here are two: nearly all of them thrive and do better work when we provide them with authentic assessments and all of them find joy and meaning when we provide them with their rightful opportunity to choose their own questions, to write meaningful texts, to engage in civic action, and to produce authentic historical art. Authentic assessment has worked in three of the most distinct public schools imaginable.

I hope that what I've learned on my path, which I describe below, will help you on your own journey, whether you are already an experienced teacher who occasionally uses authentic assessments and wants to expand your toolbox or whether you are a student-teacher first considering the possibilities of your future classroom.

Aim of This Book

This book is partly a call to my fellow educators to allow our next generation of artists, singers, poets, activists, web designers, museum curators, historians, and non-profit leaders to make their arguments in social studies classes using a wide and rich array of mediums: the same mediums through which people actually produce history (and political action) in our world. It is also a guide for how to successfully do so in your classroom. For some of our students, this may take the form of traditional writing, for others it may be painting, and for others it may be dance, video, discussion, podcasts, poetry, narrative perspective pieces, or even civic action. Providing opportunities for authentic assessment is not just about putting on an "innovation" badge; instead, it is a teaching and learning strategy grounded in educational theory and research that will lead to deeper learning and a fairer and more democratic educational system.

As a high school social studies teacher perhaps the most frequent compliment I receive each year from students and parents is that what I do in the classroom is creative (I've noticed the compliments are never about my shoes). One of the ways that I "create" for my students is by developing role-plays in which I design an immersive historical world and experience for the students. I wrote about this strategy in *The Classes They Remember: Using Role-Plays to Bring Social Studies and English to Life*.[3] I'm not the only teacher who practices creative pedagogy that goes beyond lecture or even seminar discussions. Yet, it seems far more uncommon for secondary teachers to provide our students with the same avenues for creativity that we allow for ourselves.

Following my work on role-plays, my focus in teaching and learning has shifted toward the imperative to provide options for student expression, especially in the area of assessment. Would it not be tragic if I were innovative in my pedagogy and used teaching as my own outlet for creativity but I did not allow my students the opportunity to cultivate their own imaginations and voices? Assessments drive much of what we do in class; when we limit those assessments to tests and writing, we therefore stymie the possibilities for our students to express what they know, to create, and to discover new talents and passions.

JADE Learning

Much of the answer to this problem lies in authentic assessment and what I call JADE learning. In Chapter 1, I delve deeply into the nature of authentic assessment. For now, I will briefly define it as the practice of having students engage in "real-world" tasks and consequently evaluating, or grading, students on that type of work. Educators and authors, unfortunately, have often truncated the nature of authentic assessment until it has become almost synonymous with formal writing. This is a problem. My assertion, instead, is that we need to breathe-in three more elements so that authentic assessment becomes synonymous with JADE. JADE is my own acronymic concept for what our ideal assessments ought to be; it is a broadening of our mission and values to include four crucial criteria: Joy, Authenticity, Dynamism, and Effectiveness.

Joy

We don't normally equate assessments like tests with joy. In fact, traditional assessments are some of the primary causes of academic anxiety for students. Many students find some pleasure in the day-to-day of school, but dread the test-taking experience. Yet, we can provide assessments that actually add joy to education, increasing the sense of positivity that students can attribute to learning. We can simultaneously evaluate students' learning and allow them to have fun. Painting, civic action, museum galleries, digital history, dance, leading lessons, oral communication, and even inquiry research papers can serve as play for students. The fun does not need to end with assessments; that is when the fun can really begin.

Authenticity

Much of Chapter 1 deals with the concept of authentic assessment so I will not belabor the point here other than to emphasize that there is more to authentic social studies than formal writing. Perhaps the best evidence to support this claim is that the American Historical Review declared in December 2018 that the journal is "open to historical writing and presentation in new formats."[4] With its broadened view of authentic history, the AHA's journal now reviews films, documentaries, museums, websites, graphic histories, podcasts, and historical fiction – much of what is at the core of this book. If professional historians get to work in those formats, why not our students?

Dynamism

Tests and most formal writing are rather static processes. Students respond to teacher-directed questions in stratified and fixed ways. There is little room for student voice to enter into the product. A dynamic assessment is about the student's creativity, voice, interaction, energy, motivation, and interests. Any art that a student creates is dynamic because the student is the primary mover. Civic action gets the student interacting with society and other activists and oral histories can allow students to connect deeply with family members. Oral communication, such as fishbowl or panel conversations, allows students to engage with other learners. Some assessments like dance can let students literally get up, move, and share their knowledge through dynamic kinesthetics. We know about student-centered learning that puts students at the heart of lessons; we need to also cultivate how we get students fully engaged in the experiences that we value enough to assess.

Effectiveness

Tests and formal writing only shed light on a slice of what our students understand and who they are as learners and as people. I do use quizzes, tests, and essays regularly to capture that slice of students' learning for which they function best. A teacher-crafted test that explicitly targets knowledge and thinking skills that students ought to have mastered in the course is a strong evaluation tool. But for assessments to be effective at capturing the rest of the pie, they have to communicate what students know, what they can do on a real task, and what they care about. Tests and formulaic writing can only go so far. We need a wider repertoire to effectively assess the complex people we have in our classroom. Assessments ought not be effective only for the teacher's evaluation, but also for the students' learning and growth. They can provide an added layer of effectiveness when they are meaningful enough that they contribute additional learning experiences for the students. Through projects, students can gain exposure to real-world tasks, learn about their passions and interests, and develop a variety of skills that are useful in a complex and ever-changing world. The assessment need not be the endpoint of learning; rather, they can be the apex of the educational experience and a bridge for future growth.

We can and should go beyond formal writing to include JADE assessment tasks that add deeper meaning, reality, joy, and interactivity. When we open the gates of social studies, we consequently treat our students as unique individuals, we cultivate some of the wide range of skills students need to learn to prepare for an increasingly complex world, and by doing so we cleave more faithfully to the meaning of history and social studies as a discipline.

My Path Toward Authentic/JADE Assessments

My passion for integrating art and other authentic assessments into my social studies practice is not an obvious one. I am traditionally academic; I love to read and write and I always loved school. I am writing this book because I can't paint it, sing it, or film it. I am not actually "artistic" other than having written a few mediocre poems and one that was good enough to get a second date. I have no background in visual arts and I don't play any musical instrument. As a child, my family implored me to sing more quietly at the Passover Seder. I can somewhat dance a samba although each step propels me slightly backwards until eventually I bang into a wall (best case) or trip and fall (worst case). I have thought a few times about doing stand-up comedy although, as you will quickly see, such an endeavor would be futile.

My path (other than when dancing samba) has not been linear and, until somewhat recently, was not a conscious pedagogical choice. I am sharing a brief overview of my career trajectory here to show: (1) if I can integrate art into my social studies teaching career, anyone can do so; (2) having worked with an extremely wide range of students, my assertion that authentic assessments are vital for all students is based on experience; (3) the surprising and somewhat coincidental twists and turns that led me to adopt authentic assessments.

The Mariner's Gaze

I attended a typical high-performing suburban high school in the 1990s and my education followed the standard academic path. In social studies, we took tests, which often included in-class essays. The only experiences I remember now were the few times I was afforded choice and an authentic task, such as my 10th grade research paper on *The Communist Manifesto*, my 11th grade research paper on Chief Joseph, a physics project in which my partner and I decided to analyze whether the video game *Goldeneye* followed the laws of Newtonian physics, and my final project in Marta Meacham's Spanish class in which I chose to watch, review, and analyze a handful of Mexican films such as *Como Agua Para Chocolate*. I never had a teacher who asked me to produce an artistic argument about history or any authentic product other than an essay. In my history classes, I never wrote a song, filmed a movie, engaged in civic action, wrote a historical fiction story, or sculpted a memorial.

My trajectory veered slightly in the fall of my senior year at Georgetown University. I was taking a popular course called *Explorers, Warriors, and Statesmen*, taught by a beloved and well-respected professor named Peter Krogh, a former dean of the School of Foreign Service. After class one day, I hesitantly approached him and meekly asked if I could write a poem, instead of an essay, about our topic of early modern Portuguese explorers. He agreed.

The topic had stirred something inside me about exploration, possibly because I had recently returned from a year-long study abroad program in

Santiago, Chile, which had allowed me to venture off to remote locations in Patagonia and the Atacama Desert. I sensed that I needed a creative outlet to express my thoughts. I don't believe that I had written a poem since middle or high school, and my own proposition made me nervous.

I wrote a lengthy poem called "The Mariner's Gaze." It was one of the only pieces that I wrote in college that I still remember today. I spent days on it, carefully considering every word and line break. I was thrilled when Dr. Krogh returned it to me with raving feedback and the word "Bravo!" I still use the exclamation "Bravo!" on occasion with my own students when I am floored by their work. His confidence in my artistic production of history gave me enough confidence a year later to read it to my future wife on our first date. Somehow, she still married me.

"The Mariner's Gaze" taught me something essential about myself, about my creativity, and about education. To write the poem, I had to ponder deeply the mechanisms of a different medium, tone, word choice, my fundamental argument about exploration, and how to portray a sense of awe through language. When Dr. Krogh afforded me the chance to communicate history through poetry, it began a journey of thought and expression that I could never have embarked upon by filling in a bubble or even writing a prose essay. In slightly more confusing words, my poetic exploration about exploration became a personal and educational exploration.

Arts Education in Brazil

After my traditional academic studies, which culminated in a degree in international affairs, I began my teaching career in 2002 with a two-year stint as a street educator in Brazil. I joined an organization called Projeto Axé, which is probably the most influential non-profit for street children in Brazil. Projeto Axé is based in Salvador, the largest city in northeast Brazil, one of the poorest regions of the country.

My role in the organization was minimal. In addition to teaching some very basic computer skills to students, I participated in street education, in which I walked around downtown Salvador with my partner, Junior, who grew up in one of the city's *favelas*. We were an odd couple, to be sure. When we saw street children we talked to them, tried to understand their situation, and worked to gradually convince them to get off the streets and join Projeto Axé or to get help from one of the city's services. He, of course, was more effective at the job, but my accent and my sincere desire to speak with the kids we met at least interested some of them.

Once the young people made the choice to join Projeto Axé, they integrated into one of the organization's arts education programs, such as dance, visual arts, Brazilian music, and capoeira. Projeto Axé's mission was not to provide a traditional academic education but rather to use art to build up the children's self-image and to make them want to do something different with their lives. Art led to motivation, introspection, learning, and life changes.

Students in the organization were required to attend a public school, but arts served as the core of the program. Despite my relatively recent penning of "The Mariner's Gaze," this emphasis on art was outside of my experience. My inclination at the time was that Projeto Axé was doing something wrong by focusing on art rather than the "traditional" core academics that young people would need for "traditional" success. I understand it differently now – the founders of Projeto Axé fully grasped the transformative power of art for young people and its role as a crucible of learning.

The Heschel School

After returning to New York in 2004, I began my official classroom teaching at a non-denominational and progressive Jewish private school, the Abraham Joshua Heschel School. I taught Spanish and social studies, and while the challenge of teaching two disciplines at the start of my career was daunting, it also gave me a sense of the different ways that students learn. When teaching language, I really needed to consider engagement and multiple forms of learning (and communicating) since the normal verbal/intellectual dialogue of education is off the table.

I was extremely fortunate to begin my career in a school where high-stakes tests did not exist, thereby allowing me free reign to experiment. I was also lucky to start out under a confident department chair, Lisa Cohen, who called me the "young whippersnapper" and trusted my instincts and good intentions enough to let me try to figure out who I was in the classroom and what I could do.

My lessons integrated art, music, clock-throwing, and silly theatrical performances (from myself). Thankfully, this was before cell phones. I could change the time on wall clocks and then throw the clocks like a frisbee at students. This worked back then because they could still tell time on a wall clock. And, nowadays, a student would record it on a cell phone and that video would get me on the cover of the New York Post (headline: "Spanish teacher clocks student in class!"). Whomever caught the clock had to tell the time.

I thought I was a pretty great teacher. But at the end of all that really dynamic teaching, the students were doing pretty traditional learning and showing me what they learned in pretty traditional ways: tests and essays. I was creating and they were regurgitating. We had fun and I made them think, but I didn't have the tools to put more of the learning in their hands.

Graduate School

In 2006, I entered a graduate program in education so that I could pursue my next dream: teaching in a New York City public school. I don't remember much from my master's program, which unfortunately is often the case for teachers. I'm not sure that in my classes I fully developed my sense of what education could be for students. One book, however, stood out among all those that I read and did influence my practice: Howard Gardner's 1993 book *Multiple Intelligences*, which elaborated on a theory that he first propounded in his 1983 book *Frames of Mind*.

I recall reading Gardner's theory that intelligence is about much more than doing well on tests; more than what he calls "logical-mathematical intelligence." It made sense to me. Humans are complex and varied beings who bring to the table a wide array of knowledge, skills, and domains. In the book *Multiple Intelligences: New Horizons*, Gardner's 2006 revisit of his masterpiece, he maintains that multiple intelligences is about developing "a pluralistic view of mind, recognizing many different and discrete facets of cognition, acknowledging that people have different cognitive strengths and contrasting cognitive styles."[5] His original set of intelligences included: musical, bodily-kinesthetic, logical-mathematical, linguistic, spatial, interpersonal, and intrapersonal.

When I first read Gardner's work, I wondered whether those were truly the only intelligences. Was this the definitive list? Indeed, much critique of his work has involved arguments about other possible intelligences, such as spiritual and naturalist. In his later writings, Gardner addresses some of those concerns and makes it clear that there is space to identify more intelligences.

I also wasn't sure, after reading his work, whether people have innate differences in types of intelligence or whether being a "kinesthetic" person or a "logical-mathematical" person came out of experiences. The important point I took from Gardner's text was the idea that whatever the cause, students are different and various types of intelligences need to be valued in our classrooms. In other words, I'm not sure that we need to see one kid as intrinsically "kinesthetic" and another as "naturalistic" and I don't believe that is really Gardner's argument either. Doing so might put them in simple and restrictive boxes, and I'm not in favor of teachers or students determining that a 15-year-old is, necessarily, a "musical" learner. Rather, to me it meant that there were myriad ways students could express their understandings and all of them were intellectually valid.

His work raised many questions for me. To what extent was I overemphasizing just a couple of intelligences, especially logical and linguistic, over all others? Should we try to identify the key intelligence of a particular student and cater to the corresponding domain? What does this mean for the types of assessments that I used to evaluate my students: tests and essays?

As Sir Ken Robinson, a former professor of arts education and a leading advocate for educational transformation, has synthesized nicely, what we know about education is that it is diverse, dynamic, and distinct.[6] It exists in different forms, all of which are important; it changes as we interact with other people and across disciplines; and individuals have their own unique combinations of intelligence.

Gardner recognizes that his theory has considerable educational implications and his more recent work addresses assessment and alternatives to standardized testing. Not surprisingly, he argues for thinking about assessment rather than testing and for developing assessment strategies that are "intelligence-fair" and that use multiple measures to tap into the complexity of student understanding and mastery.

My own experience has been that elementary and middle school teachers, who do the bulk of the actual teaching of skills to our children, have a stronger grasp of the complexity of learning and children's minds than do most high school teachers. Elementary school teachers very often integrate project-based learning into their curriculum and assess their students in a variety of ways, whereas many high school teachers focus solely on tests and writing. Elementary school is where the most profound learning happens so high school teachers ought to keep an eye on what K-5 educators are doing.

My first foray into using multiple intelligences as a framework for thinking about assessment was in my final project at the Heschel School. I was teaching a course on world religions and decided to open the possibilities for my students. The project essentially asked them to make an argument about religion, and they could use any medium of their choice. I was blown away by what I encountered; a spectrum of voices and thoughts that I would have never seen if I had restricted the format. Students produced songs, artwork, movies, and more. I knew that Gardner had pointed me in the right direction.

The Facing History School

When I began teaching in public school, at the Facing History School (FHS) in New York City, I was now working with a very different group of students. FHS generally serves high-needs teenagers, many of whom recently arrived to the United States. They are often far behind grade level in reading and writing. During my five years there, I learned much about real teaching and what it means to build skills and engage students as people and learners.

Moreover, during my first year at the school, FHS gained admission into the New York State Performance Standards Consortium. This was a prized moment for the staff – it meant that we had earned a waiver from the high-stakes Regents exams and instead could do the work with our students that really mattered: performance assessment. In the discipline of social studies, this meant that students needed to show proficiency in an authentic task, a research paper, in order to graduate.

As is often the case for teachers in tough urban environments, I began to focus my thinking on the nitty-gritty of teaching writing, on scaffolds, and on backwards planning that would allow my students to work on their writing in steps so they could compose a full essay. Together with my colleagues, we spent countless hours thinking about writing instruction and I learned a tremendous amount from a group of smart and dedicated teachers about scaffolding to support young writers.

However, many of my students spent a whole lot of time failing because they had no interest in writing about what I had required. I spent a lot of time working with them on what they disliked, which they probably loathed because they were rarely told they were good at it. To be sure, the teaching of writing was crucial, as the students needed to be able to write. But at what cost?

Like many small schools, at FHS we lacked a traditional arts program but we participated in Urban Arts Partnership, which brought teaching-artists, who were exponentially cooler than I was, into the classroom. People like Fabian Saucedo, the spoken-word poet and current director of The Hip Hop Re:Education Project who helped my students craft an identity poem and Monique Schubert, the visual artist who worked with my geometry class on geometric art and cubism. I taught one geometry class for one year to help out with a scheduling snafu; I was pretty incompetent other than that art project and one activity I made that involved complementary and vertical angles and X-wing fighters.

However, I used less art in my classes with students who really needed more artful learning. I faced a common dilemma. So many students were struggling with their writing, so how could I afford to spend much time on art? While we did not face the Global and American History Regents exams, our work with performance assessment meant that students needed to pass a Performance-Based Assessment Task (PBAT) to graduate: essentially a mini-dissertation and oral defense of their culminating research papers. When working with students who were struggling to meet the basic writing competencies necessary to graduate from high school, it was difficult to maintain the long view that art, music, and dance in social studies classes were beneficial. The PBAT became the new high-stakes assessment that drove teaching, and writing became the one ring to rule them all.

The shelving of art and other JADE assessments in my teaching, I believe, revealed a common and tragic problem. We need to see art and writing not as zero-sum trade-offs. Integrating more art into my curriculum could have engaged more students, allowed more students to succeed by providing them with better means to express what they knew, and it could have been used as a method of teaching argumentation in a more accessible way. Time spent on art does not necessarily weaken writing; if used thoughtfully it can strengthen it.

Harvest Collegiate

After five years at the Facing History School, I moved on to help found a new public school in Manhattan called Harvest Collegiate, which also ended up gaining the coveted Regents waiver. Harvest's student body was more diverse, with a wider mix of high-, middle-, and low-achieving students. I was also surrounded by an incredibly brilliant faculty who had read and thought a great deal about writing and assessment. At Harvest, I had to consider how to really support a diverse student body in their written work. Much of what I discuss in the writing chapters of this book came out of rich collaboration with colleagues at Harvest.

As a Consortium PBAT school, writing was also the cornerstone of Harvest social studies education, but at times I branched off on my own. I increasingly began to try to match my assessment format to the topics and periods we were studying in class. I developed the mock trials on Galileo and on the Julius Streicher's Nuremberg Trial that led to my book *Judging for Themselves: Using Mock Trials to Bring Social Studies and English to Life*. When I taught a class called *Sports, Fashion, and Politics* I had the students design colonial resistance fashion and then put on an actual fashion show.

It was this propensity to design learning experiences outside of the traditional curricular bubbles that led me to think about the ways that social studies intersected with other disciplines, especially art. I was accepted as a member of the first cohort of New York City Master Teachers, and thus had the opportunity to mentor biology, music, English, and Special Education teachers at my school. By doing so, I had the chance to further see the ways that our work intersected across disciplines and the commonalities of our mission as educators.

One of my closest colleagues at Harvest Collegiate was my former student-teacher, Andy del-Calvo, whom we all called ADC. ADC is a stocky, energetic millennial who wears vibrant socks and combines a sharp intellect with a deep care for students. He is also one of the most annoyingly multi-talented people I know. He happens to be an incredible drummer, a superb marathon runner (he took 512th place in the NYC Marathon in 2016, which is way more impressive than it sounds), and an avid kite-flyer. The only thing that makes me feel better about myself is that he's a terrible speller, which he has proven on the blackboard multiple times.

Once he joined the faculty, Andy and I co-planned a semester-long course on colonialism, together with a fantastic student-teacher who worked with me named Bassem Elbendary. We chose to organize the class around one to two week case-study modules on topics like Aztec-Spanish colonialism, Dutch New York, British Egypt, British India, and the Mau-Mau in Kenya. At the end of each module, students had a content quiz and an authentic or artful assessment. Here we unleashed students' creativity for the first time and the rewards were astonishing. Bassem put together an assessment about the role of cotton in British colonialism in Egypt. It required students to create a fashion design about colonialism and colonial resistance that they drew on a white cotton shirt. One student wrote and drew a graphic history on her shoes (I'm not sure what her mom said about that). Another student created a 3D model of an Ottoman marketplace and the various nationalities and ethnicities that became part of the Ottoman Empire.

After that, I knew I was onto something.

Scarsdale High School

In 2017, my wife and I made the major decision to leave Brooklyn for the suburbs of Westchester due to difficulties with our commutes. I not only left the city, but also made the excruciatingly painful decision to end my career as a New York City public school teacher and to say goodbye to a tremendous school that I played some part in founding. I also entered into an existential crisis when I purchased a mini-van. Not only was I heading to the burbs, but also I ended up in a pretty legendary place: Scarsdale High School.

I had no idea what to expect. I had never taught in a large institution, let alone a suburban school. I expected an emphasis on the Regents exam, traditional pedagogy, and a cold and impersonal environment. Somehow, I was lucky enough to stumble into a large suburban school that was warm, collaborative, and dedicated to pedagogical excellence and innovation. Scarsdale is a community of incredible resources and it is imbued with a true dedication to education.

My department chair, John Harrison, has a gregarious personality, a hearty laugh, and insatiable curiosity about people. He also knows more about the minutiae of life, history, and culture of Westchester than anyone I've met. He welcomed me to a special place, "Shangri-La," as he called Scarsdale. He was right. Whereas most teachers at most schools get a sense of what education really is, Scarsdale gives you a sense of what education *can be*. Here, you have all the necessary resources, supportive parents, a smart and dedicated faculty, and motivated students. The limit to what we can achieve, to some extent, is only the limit we place on ourselves and time. Scarsdale allows you to dream, to think big, and then to actually put that into practice with students who will follow you wherever you take them.

In Scarsdale, there is a mentorship program for all new teachers to the district regardless of their experience. As an experienced teacher who had previously mentored over a dozen educators, suddenly I had a weekly meeting with a wonderful teacher named Fallon Plunkett who guided me through the new culture and expectations. I had a weekly meeting with John to help me in my transition as well. And I found a friendly and supportive departmental and faculty culture.

As I describe in various parts of the book, my experience in Scarsdale has been another transformation in my work. In some sense, given the community's demographics and the high level of student achievement, it was like a return to my first gig at the Heschel School. However, in Scarsdale, most students in the high school have reaped the benefits of the district's schools for their entire lives. All students can read, all students can write, and all students are striving for a strong college placement. This environment forced me to rethink what the students and I could do in partnership over the course of a year.

Such a context means a considerable emphasis on assessment and the idea of rigor. It also meant that I encountered insightful questions about JADE assessments from John, and from my principal Ken Bonamo, that sharpened my thinking and practice. In Scarsdale, we need to carefully consider not only what the students do, but also how we assess it in a reliable way. Grades matter here a lot. As Ken, John, and I have talked about, since most Scarsdale students can succeed in a traditional educational structure, when we shift over to something new we need to really consider the rationale and the benefits and drawbacks that it may bring.

At Scarsdale High School, I have also been fortunate to work closely with a number of motivated teachers who pushed me to expand my vision of civic education. As I describe in the Civic Action chapter, the methodology of Design Thinking plays an important role in Scarsdale's educational philosophy, and the creators of a course called City 2.0, Maggie Favretti, Fallon Plunkett, and Emily Block, were extraordinarily generous with their time and expertise to teach me the ins and outs of Design Thinking when I took on teaching City 2.0.

My experience at Scarsdale has fleshed out my emphasis on authentic assessment, the connections I have made between art and historical arguments, and my firm belief that all students (whether from advantaged or disadvantaged backgrounds) ought to benefit from JADE assessments. I learned that those students who are strongest academically also flourish when doing creative assessments, and they crave that intellectual liberty. And I've learned that students who struggle in traditional contexts flourish even more when given the chance to show what they know and can do in a different format. They, of course, need authentic assessment as well.

Unfortunately, while students from all walks of life would benefit from authentic assessment, opposing pressures make it difficult for educators serving both the most advantaged and the most high-needs populations to provide such opportunities. In underserved urban areas we often see a laser-like focus on content acquisition and basic literacy skills in order to meet graduation requirements. In practice, this can mean drill-and-kill test preparation along with formulaic, unimaginative, and highly scaffolded writing. In elite environments, concerns about preparing students for traditional success on the "path" and fulfilling notions of academic rigor can make people nervous about authentic assessments. Moreover, the importance of grades can lead teachers to fear veering off into an unknown territory that is open-ended and leaves more room for ambiguity. Each of these environments have their own stresses and pressures for teachers and administrators that make the implementation of JADE assessments complicated.

The disjuncture between school and preparedness for a complex future certainly is not limited to social studies. Jo Boaler, a professor of mathematics education at Stanford University, explains that she would:

> change the curriculum to really reflect real mathematics, and [she] would also change it to reflect the 21st century, because maths still looks in classrooms pretty much as it did in Victorian days ... high school in particular

has lots of antiquated methods that students sit and work out by hand. They will never do that again in their lives. What kids can be doing that computers cannot be doing is creative, flexible thinking.[7]

A book about authentic assessments and JADE learning could encompass the entire school system and all of the disciplines, but my view is that the need for practicality in a book like this one is essential so that teachers have something real to use, and that only happens when we get specific, targeted, and concrete. For that reason, and because of my own specialized expertise, I have chosen to focus my writing on social studies.

Some of the impetus for writing this book actually came out of an invitation from Ken Bonamo and our Assistant Superintendent for Curriculum, Edgar McIntosh. They asked me to present my assessments at an annual district-wide professional development day for all Scarsdale K-12 educators. It was the start of my second year in the district and I was nervous. I tried out a few of my introductory jokes with my wife. None even broke a smile. So instead of mediocre humor, I just laid out a bit of what I do and showed a few student examples. The response from other educators was extremely positive, and it was also clear to me that many of them really wanted to hear more, think more, and learn more about authentic assessment.

Much of *Authentic Assessment in Social Studies* is about my own work and my own vision about why and how we need to overcome our fears and habits and take a deep plunge into the world of authentic assessments. However, just as much of it is a collaborative process that came out of working with extremely dedicated teachers across four excellent schools. These teachers brought in the experience and expertise that they had gained from a few dozen of their previous institutions and their former colleagues. In other words, I am standing on the shoulders of a few generations of very ordinary folk, mostly about 5'5" in height, who happened to be talented and knowledgeable teachers committed to their vocation. Their lower backs must really be aching after I put on my "Westchester 15."

In other words, I am by no means the only social studies teacher amongst my colleagues or across the country who uses authentic assessments in my class. I do believe that most teachers at some point utilize an authentic assessment. At Facing History School, my colleagues like Emily Haines, Crystal Gifford, and James Grey had students write Identity Poems and historical newspaper articles. At Harvest Collegiate, Steve Lazar's classes conducted oral history interviews of their families for an immigration unit, Andy Snyder's students marched at the post office for a civic action project, and Nitzan Ziv's students engaged in Constitutional law moot court cases. At Scarsdale

High School, in addition to those working on Design Thinking and civics, my colleagues Andrew Morgan, Brendan Lee, Christopher Paulison, and Andrew Morgan put together an incredible United Nations Climate Change conference; Nicola Minchillo has her students create board games; and a cohort of 9th grade teachers collaborated to create a museum of the Age of Exploration. The 3rd grade team, with collaboration from the librarian and Literacy Coach, at Dows Lane Elementary School, for example, collaborated on a project in which students researched biographies, role-played their characters in a wax museum, and then came to life to describe their historical importance. Here we see a role-play assessment that is dynamic and joyful while requiring students to make an effective argument. If this is all happening at just a few schools, I know many great authentic assessments exist in social studies classes across the United States.

I have taught for about 15 years and I am nearing the midpoint of my career. I don't have all the answers nor will I ever. I am not the best teacher out there, if such a thing exists, and I have not perfectly mastered assessment. Once we reach a certain level of proficiency in teaching, we should realize that we have good days and bad ones; moments of excellence and mediocrity; and that we all bring different attributes to the table. I tend to get bored and fidgety while students are doing groupwork, I struggle to get kids to peer-edit writing, my classroom is a visual wasteland, and I'm home cooking for my own kids at 4pm rather than putting in late nights advising a club. There are exceptional teachers out there from Los Angeles to Baltimore who are staying in the classroom until the custodians kick them out in the evening just to help a kid finish one essay. That level of educational heroism isn't my reality at the moment, or perhaps ever, but I hope this book can be my contribution to the field beyond the everyday joy and dedication I bring to my classes.

In this book, I am not arguing that we ought to abandon tests and formal essays. I certainly have not. Rather, my purpose is to help social studies teachers think about how and why we might go beyond those formats at some points in the year to really develop JADE assessments: once, twice, or a handful of times. We ought not make our goal the training of a generation of academic historians, but rather a generation of thoughtful, flexible, and creative individuals who can contribute to our society's most important conversations about the past and present in unique ways. It is time we recognize that art is not for elementary school while writing is for high school. We need to incorporate more creative and meaningful options into our assessment strategies, such as film, podcast, poetry, leading lessons, painting, songwriting, panel discussions, civic action, documentaries, and children's books.

These are the forms of intellectual communication that actually have an impact in our world, and thus they are ones we should encourage our students to use. Steve Levitt, a professor of economics at the University of Chicago, described in the Freakonomics podcast his existential frustration at having poured his heart and years of his life into producing academic journal articles that have only been cited, and apparently read, by six other scholars. The host, Stephen Dubner, responded by remarking, "nobody reads academic journals. People listen to podcasts. So if you want to reach the people, and make change in the world, I suggest you get on this podcast a little bit more."[8] Steven Levitt guest hosted the episode, and his ideas consequently reached six million people.

This book will teach you how to take a similar leap in your classroom and make it into a more vibrant and relevant environment for everyone in the room. It will transform your experience as an educator and your students' experiences as learners.

A Note on Reading This Book

I wrote this book for a few reasons. First, I hope the annual windfall can go a ways toward offsetting the purchase of a package of diapers for my one-year-old. Second, I hope to convince you of the wide range of authentic assessments available for social studies, as well as to provide useful tips and ready-to-go assessment instructions that you can use immediately with your class. It is not meant to convince you to do everything in this book. I haven't even reached the Jedi level in all, or most, of these areas. I could never do all of the assessments I describe here each year. This is a half-career's worth of thinking and designing authentic assessments, not something I do all the time or all at once. If I did, my students would probably revolt. When you read the book, think about what could work for you and your learners, and remember that not only are our students still works in progress, so too are we as teachers. Due to my own experience, I've written this book from the vantage point of high school, but I have no doubt that most of these ideas and assessments, when modified, can succeed in elementary and middle school.

I've divided this book into chapters based on types of assessments, from writing to art to civic action, and each individual chapter includes a number of specific examples of assessments that fall within those categories. I have not described every possible authentic assessment in social studies; I tried to emphasize those with the widest range of utility and those that I've actually done successfully in my own class. As such, I left out ones like board games, moot court, and creating role-plays. Just like the Ninth Amendment says (more or less), just because an assessment isn't written down here doesn't mean it doesn't exist. I did not include a section on mock trials, for example, which are incredible assessments, because I already wrote about those in *Judging for Themselves* and writing about them again would be boring (for me).

I've attempted to demonstrate that each specific form of assessment, such as music, dance, or podcast, is indeed an authentic medium for knowledge communication in the discipline. So, I begin by providing examples and stories to show you how historians use these various formats to discuss history. Then, each section includes suggestions of ways in which you could integrate that particular type of assessment in the class.

Finally, each part of the book includes an actual assignment that you can use as a template, which you ought to modify, of course, based on your students' needs. I have tried to really break down the task to the bare minimum so you can add scaffolding when necessary and not get bogged down in details that you have to remove. From my viewpoint, when we ask students to create and to act outside the box, then we shouldn't box them in with overwhelming requirements. If we do, is it still art? That being said, my confidence is in each teacher to modify and adapt to meet the particular needs of classes and individual students. Before we begin, let us look to the horizon.

The Mariner's Gaze

Steely Gaze of the Mariner,
Lofty and austere, fuerte y estoico.
How I hark back to thee!
Vanished like the very heavens
That you bind to the soul.

'Tis not the heroic conqueror I seek;
Columbus or Drake, Cortés or Magellen.
True vassals of power and pride,
Prideful schemers of wealth and glory.
Supreme doppelgangers, eternally present.

No, 'tis the humble and lowly mariner.
The thirstless guide on camel,
Sturdy porter in snow and wind.
Forgotten but in the starry eyes
Del cielo, jahua-pacha, sama'

Bottomless Gaze of the Mariner,
Adoration of the universe, its simple and wondrous harmony;
Endless stars, a child's giggle, crashing waves,

Café with friends, a candlelight's flicker, a pregnant woman,
Clouds at sunset, a surprise hug, warm water.

Sublime Gaze – annihilated by progress,
Butchered by enlightenment.
Simple "L" of the languid, the listless
Deforms you into a "Glaze"
Empty and edgy in stillness.

Blank Glaze of the modern man
Mistress only to the pixel
Drugged by the decibel and ambition.
Homeric in darkness, deafened in silence,
Blasé with friends, family and lover.

Awakened only by a flash, by a burst!
Mariner on a cruise, RV wanderer.
Explorers on a guided tour.
Cool ice water? Plain white rice?
No, fluorescent "Mountain Blast" Gatorade.

I plead to oracles above:
Resurrect the gaze,
And the simple mariner.
Reveal our destiny,
Bestow hope!

The stars respond to my call,
Eternally faithful and diligent.
But the arrow never reaches my flesh.
Smothered beneath a bright haze of city lights
The answer disappears in a bright flash.

Notes

1   NYC Department of Education: School Quality Snapshot. (2017). Retrieved December 13, 2019, from https://tools.nycenet.edu/snapshot/2019/02M534/HS.
2   Scarsdale Senior High School in Scarsdale, NY. (n.d.). Retrieved December 13, 2019, from https://www.greatschools.org/new-york/scarsdale/3555-Scarsdale-Senior-High-School/.

3   Sherrin, D. (2016). *The classes they remember: using role-plays to bring social studies and English to life*. New York: Routledge.

4   What form can history take today? New voices in the *AHR*. *The American Historical Review*, 123(3), June 2018, page xviii, https://doi.org/10.1093/ahr/123.3.xviii.

5   Gardner, H. (2006). *Multiple intelligences: new horizons*. New York: Basic Books, 5.

6   Robinson, K. (2006). Do schools kill creativity? Retrieved from www.ted.com/talks/ken_robinson_says_schools_kill_creativity?language=en.

7   Levitt, S. D., & Lapinski, Z. (2019, October 2). *America's math curriculum doesn't add up* (Ep. 391). Retrieved from http://freakonomics.com/podcast/math-curriculum/.

8   Levitt, S. D., & Lapinski, Z. (2019, October 2). *America's math curriculum doesn't add up* (Ep. 391). Retrieved from http://freakonomics.com/podcast/math-curriculum/.

Part 1
Authentic Assessment

1

Authentic Assessment Q&A

What Is Authentic Assessment?

Thoughtful decisions about assessment should lay at the heart of all teachers' practices since assessment ought to drive many of our instructional choices. Much has been written about assessment over the past decades as many schools and educators have moved, thankfully, away from test-taking to an emphasis on writing. Writing, especially in the Humanities, forms the basis of authentic assessments – a concept that is the centerpiece of this book and my work as a teacher.

Before we dive into the idea of authentic assessment, it is worthwhile to consider the very nature of assessment itself. Why do we assess students? There are at least seven reasons why teachers commonly assess their students: (1) to stratify them (for college placement) and report cards; (2) to prepare students for standardized tests; (3) to determine what they know; (4) to determine what they can do; (5) to evaluate their growth; (6) for the teacher to evaluate his or her own practice; and (7) to determine student mastery while simultaneously providing an additional rich learning experience.

The stratification outlook often drives much teaching and assessment, leading to an emphasis on tests that can easily differentiate students according to traditional understandings of intelligence and ability. I do value content knowledge, and when we are interested in measuring what content students have learned in a unit, I actually believe that a well-crafted multiple-choice quiz that is geared toward evaluating what students specifically learned in a unit and certain thinking skills serves as a valuable targeted assessment. I use multiple-choice quizzes in almost all of my content-heavy units.

Nonetheless, this ought to be only a small part of teaching and assessment. My former colleague Emily Block, who is clearly brilliant because she fled Westchester for Madison, Wisconsin, pointed the following out to me:

> *If an assessment is a way for students to demonstrate competency or mastery of "x" – then consider all of the things "x" could represent: content knowledge, certainly, but also academic skills and habits of mind like empathy, perseverance, and civic engagement.*

When we think of assessment in this manner, then it is clear that tests and formal writing cannot fully encompass all of what we care about when engaging in meaningful learning. In this vein, as Emily thoughtfully explains, "many of our learning goals *demand* an authentic assessment because there is no other way to effectively gauge student success."

In many schools, including my own, educators think about and discuss "project-based learning" and "authentic assessment." It is not always clear, however, what some of those terms even mean. Judith T.M. Gulikers, Theo J. Bastiaens, and Paul Kirschner wrote a 2004 article in *Educational Technology Research and Development* that sought to lay out the nature of authentic assessment. They argue that when students engage in authentic assessments they are practicing the type of tasks that mirror what happens in professional practice.[1]

Fred Newmann and his colleagues at the University of Wisconsin-Madison have produced some of the best work on authentic assessment. A 2002 article called "Developing Authentic Instruction in the Social Studies" in the *Journal of Research in Education* describes Newmann's framework as consisting of "student construction of knowledge through disciplined inquiry that has value beyond the classroom."[2] According to the authors, we can see the authenticity in assessment tasks, instruction, and student performance.

Newmann's Center for Authentic Intellectual Work composed a guide for the Iowa Department of Education in 2007 called "Authentic Instruction and Assessment." Newmann and his fellow writers argued that "the usual work demanded in school is rarely considered meaningful, significant, or worthwhile" and in order to correct course, they analyzed what type of mastery was needed for successful adults who continue to work, in a variety of fields, with knowledge. As they maintain:

> *authentic intellectual work involves original application of knowledge and skills, rather than just routine use of facts and procedures. It also entails careful study of the details of a particular problem and results in a product or presentation that has meaning beyond success in school.*[3]

Denise Pope, a professor of education at Stanford University, and her colleagues at Challenge Success, Maureen Brown and Sarah Miles, describe two threads of authentic assessment in their book *Overloaded and Underprepared: Strategies for Stronger Schools and Healthy, Successful Kids*. One is the idea that it "must be an actual task done in the real world, such as painting a mural" in which the students have real audiences and they leave a mark on their communities. They explain that other educators, such as McTighe and Ferrara, argue that authentic assessment can instead be a simulation of tasks that take place in the real word; for example, in-class debates or writing newspaper articles.[4]

It is clearly the case that for decades social studies teachers have integrated some level of authentic assessment into their classrooms; almost any piece of writing is authentic to the discipline even if it is in a traditional essay format. However, it is my assertion that social studies teachers can and should do much more to increase the authenticity of our assessments both in terms of the various types of tasks we ask (or allow) students to do as well as the format and context in which they do them.

The term "authentic assessment" derives from the premise that most people in their careers, no matter what the field, do not take tests on a regular basis. Tests are artificial creations that exist almost solely in the classroom. Pope, Brown, and Miles provide a wonderful illustration of the absurdity of tests:

> *Imagine if, in the working world, your boss told you early in the week that you would have a test later that week. He couldn't tell you exactly what would be on the test, but it would definitely be timed, and you would not be allowed to use any of the typical resources on which you were used to relying, such as your working notes, your colleagues, the Internet, and so on. He would be the sole designer and assessor of this test; there would be no ability to ask questions or retake the test, and your score would greatly impact your next pay bonus. Sounds crazy, right? But in schools, this scenario may take place multiple times per week, and the students are suffering because of it.[5]*

In higher education and in the professional world, people produce real artifacts of far greater complexity than tests. They write, present, film, record, and create. Even in my graduate program in history, I never took a test. I wrote and I presented. As a teacher, I took a couple of exams for certification and the rest of my career has involved creating written artifacts (worksheets, PowerPoints, role-plays, mock trials, and lessons) and about five presentations a day. We know teaching is a challenging profession because no other job asks people to give five presentations a day to an audience that really doesn't want to be there! Even my professional evaluations have been based on observations, conversations, and my portfolios. Thankfully, never on my capacity to keep my shirt tucked in. I hope.

The term "authentic" is useful as a barometer for valuable tasks. While I will continue to use the phrase "authentic assessment" throughout this book, given its wide acceptance in the field of education, I hope to expand our thinking around assessments to include the four main criteria of the acronym JADE: Joyful, Authentic, Dynamic, and Effective. When we connect students to tasks that are student-centered, interactive, fun, and real, then the end result is that we achieve that final criteria of effectiveness. Formal essay writing might be authentic, to some degree, but my claim is that poems, civic action, mock UN conferences, museum galleries, monument-building, and historical fiction are the types of assessments that truly shine like JADE.

Perhaps the educators whose work most closely aligns with my expanded notion of authentic assessment are Jal Mehta and Sarah Fine. Mehta is a professor of education at Harvard University and Sarah Fine runs a teacher preparation program in San Diego. Together, they authored the book *In Search of Deeper Learning: The Quest to Remake the American High School*. The concept of Deep Learning looks at six core competencies: content mastery, effective communication, critical thinking & problem solving, collaboration, self-directed learning, and academic mindset.[6] In their *New York Times* article "High School Doesn't Have to be Boring," Mehta and Fine argue that in schools boredom is rampant and "in lower-level courses, students were often largely disengaged; in honors courses, students scrambled for grades at the expense of intellectual curiosity."

Not surprisingly, they found core academic courses to be intellectually stultifying whereas "powerful learning was happening most often at the periphery – in electives, clubs and extracurriculars … [the] lively, productive places where teachers and students engaged together in consequential work." Deeper learning asks us to invert our notion of authentic education. We need to look at clubs as the model for learning since, "the truly powerful core classes echoed what we saw in extracurriculars. Rather than touring students through the textbook, teachers invited students to participate in the authentic work of the field." Instead of rote memorization and formulaic learning, Mehta and Fine recommend that schools deepen their attachment to the outside world and that "high school students need to be granted much more agency, responsibility and choice." Assessments need to be authentic, but they also must fight the boredom and apathy by bringing joy, meaning, and leadership into the experience.[7]

What Are Authentic Products or Tasks in the Field of Social Studies?

If we look at any terminus field for social studies: historian, teacher, sociologist, policy maker, lawyer, human rights activist, anthropologist, artist, or filmmaker – we can identify a plethora of authentic products those professionals create. Authentic assessment is about starting students down this path of engaging in a rich array of real-world tasks, about providing them with the opportunity to sense the joy and achievement of making something that is real, and about respecting their intelligence and capabilities enough to put that power in their hands.

The bulk of the literature and practice in authentic assessment revolves around writing. I care deeply about formal writing and have worked throughout my career to support students in their writing, and I devoted two chapters in this book to that process. Writing is the foundational authentic assessment in history and in the larger field of social studies. Most of the formal academic work in the discipline still appears to take place within the somewhat strict confines of the book, journal article, dissertation, and essay.

Writing, however, is by no means the sole format that academics, artists, and laypeople use to teach and communicate historical understanding. We know that for most of human history and, until recently, in most cultures oral communication was the predominant form of passing down history. Moreover, historians are increasingly searching out alternative means to reach larger audiences. We see esteemed historians like Trevor Getz and Laurent Dubois producing graphic histories. We see experts on the French Revolution like Lynne Hunt sharing her expertise in History Channel documentaries. We see the top academics in American history like Eric Foner on YouTube panel discussions. And we see respected historians like Joanne Freeman and Ed Ayers on podcasts like *Backstory*.

Perhaps the best illustration of the changing nature of how we communicate history is to consider how we have learned about the Founding Fathers. For centuries, historians cultivated our understanding of the founders through the traditional means: paintings, books, and journal articles. We know what Alexander Hamilton and George Washington look like from portraits composed by artists like John Trumbull and Gilbert Stuart. We may know of their policies through journal articles like a 1961 piece by Jim E. Davis entitled "Alexander Hamilton: His Politics and Policies." In the later 20th century, a number of historians of the American Revolution began to skirt around this obsession with the founders and instead focus on the role of women, Native Americans, African Americans, and ordinary citizens. Some academic historians like Joseph Ellis continued to produce high-quality biographies of the founders, such as his Pulitzer Prize winning book *Founding Brothers*. Popular historians, such as David McCullough, have never lost their love for the founders, and his book *John Adams* was truly one of my favorites. The conversation changed, however, in 2005 when another popular historian, Ron Chernow, published his riveting biography *Alexander Hamilton*.

I should say, rather, that everything changed when Lin-Manuel Miranda read the 818 page book and transformed it into one of the most unique and powerful Broadway shows ever put on stage. I have not actually seen *Hamilton*, but from being alive and living in Brooklyn in 2015, I know enough to be certain that the use of hip-hop, brilliant lyrics, rapping cabinet duels, and a multi-racial cast all served to provide a new meaning to *Hamilton*'s legacy and to the entire American Revolution. Broadway shows, of course, meld artistic genres and include theater, dance, and song into their productions. With the play, Miranda entered the historical conversation about the Revolution, the historiography, and took it by storm. Now we have to consider: who has told the most important story of Alexander Hamilton to shape people's historical memory, Jim E. Davis, Ron Chernow, or Lin-Manuel Miranda? Certainly, at least among wealthy socialites without the time or patience for Chernow's masterpiece, the answer is pretty clear and it begins with "How does a bastard, orphan, son of a whore ..."

This is not just the case with *Hamilton*. For instance, how do we really understand the Holocaust at any depth? For most people, it is not by reading journal articles or important historical works like Lucy Dawidowicz' *The War Against the Jews*, Christopher Browning's *Police Battalion 101*, or Daniel Jonah Goldhagen's *Hitler's Willing Executioners*. We need to feel the Holocaust before we can understand it. We begin learning with some historical fiction children's books, such as *The Devil's Arithmetic* or *Number the Stars*. We move onto films, perhaps *Schindler's List*, *Defiance*, *The Pianist*, or *Life is Beautiful*. We may read a memoir like *Night* or *All But My Life*. We visit brilliantly designed museums such as the United States Holocaust Memorial Museum or Yad Vashem and we gain a physical, visceral experience; we hear, see, touch, and cry. We watch testimonies, such as my own video of my grandfather, Joseph Brandman. Hopefully, we view the haunting art of a concentration camp survivor, such as Jan Komski's *Eating and Starvation*, or even more painfully, the images made by Jewish children in camps. We may look at art made by a victim like Felix Nussbaum, whose beautiful and tragic piece *Threesome* shows himself, his wife, and son in hiding. The painting's style seems to merge Renaissance sacral art with surrealism, producing a poignant image of despair. The music of *Schindler's List* evokes some sense of the suffering and we can hear Yiddish protest music from the ghetto, such as the Lodz Ghetto's call to survival, *Men Darf Tsi Kemfn*. There is, of course, poetry; most famously we have "First They Came for the Jews" by Martin Niemoller and we can also delve into various pieces from famous survivors like Primo Levi and more obscure ones from poets like Samuel Menashe.

Formal academic works do not own our memory of the Holocaust. Thus, there is no reason why a student's description of her understanding of an event like the Holocaust should or must be in the form of a five-paragraph essay or multiple-choice questions.

Why Do We Need to Create Authentic Assessments?

There are at least five principal reasons why we need to integrate authentic assessments into our teaching of social studies: authenticity, equity, future opportunity and preparedness, joy and play, and wellness.

The Argument from Authenticity

It seems a bit redundant to argue that we need authentic assessments because they are more authentic, but I have never been too concerned about being redundant. I am, after all, a history teacher.

It is still worth clarifying, though, that if we are teaching history then we want students to learn to do what historians do. If we are teaching sociology, they should do what sociologists do. And if we are teaching civics, they should do what engaged citizens and activists do. And in all those fields (as well as in the bizarre variety of other disciplines included in social studies, such as psychology), experts do far more than take tests. Although psychologists, I must admit, do love to give tests; at least the psychologists who write for *Cosmopolitan* magazine.

We know that historians don't sit around taking tests all day. Most historians don't even write tests, since history tests are pretty rare in higher education. But we need to recognize that even writing is no longer the sole means of publishing history.

Those who produce history have always used multiple mediums to express their perspectives and arguments. Think about Homer's *The Iliad*, Jose Clemente Orozco's *Cortez and the Cross*, Steven Spielberg's *Schindler's List*, Neil Young's *Cortez the Killer*, and Schoolhouse Rock's *I'm Just a Bill*. Many of these works not only tell what happened in the past but also engage in historical argumentation about meaning. *Cortez and the Cross* is a work of art deeply critical of Cortez' conquest and exploitation of the Aztec empire.

Schindler's List is, of course, an exploration of the meaning of resistance and morality during genocide.

We can read historical children's books like *The Soccer Fence* about apartheid or *Stepping Stones* about Syrian refugees. College students now read graphic histories, such as *Abina and the Important Men*, in their classes. And public artists and historians have always taught us about the past through museum exhibits, sculptures, and the monuments that we take pride in or try to tear down.

Historian Laurent Dubois of Duke University maintains that historians often rely too much on text in their work, ignoring other important forms of knowledge transmission. He writes in a wonderful piece called "Why Haiti should be at the Centre of the Age of Revolution":

> *Although they [historians] are increasingly incorporating other materials into their analysis, archives remain largely textual. This can lead to a kind of distortion: because we use texts to access the past, we can sometimes overestimate the centrality of those particular texts within that past. But, as when we study the Haitian Revolution, we need to constantly remind ourselves that these texts are mostly traces of a much larger set of conversations that did not take place through writing, but rather through speaking, organising and debating in the midst of military and political action.*[8]

If texts are only a small part of the conversations humans have used to understand and remember their history, why is it often the only product that we deem acceptable for our students to produce?

In today's world, new technologies have resulted in history emerging digitally through written, visual, and oral means. We hear history podcasts like *Backstory, Revisionist History, Revolutions,* and *Moonrise.* We see online panel discussions involving historians like Eric Foner discussing the Emancipation Proclamation. We watch short online documentaries or video essays like *The Guardian*'s "War in Syria Explained in Five Minutes." More and more full-length historical films and documentaries of superb quality are released each year, far too many to name. Hence, when we talk about providing students with the opportunity to engage in real history, and to provide the first touches for skills they may discover, love, and use later on in their college and professional lives, we must allow and encourage them to produce their own work using this wide array of mediums if we truly seek authentic assessments.

The point here is that if we want to coach our students to do what historians do then we need to think far beyond tests and even far beyond traditional writing.

The Argument from Equity

A brilliant cartoon in the book *Overloaded and Underprepared* perfectly depicts the absurdity of standard assessment practices. A man who looks somewhat like me (so he is clearly a history teacher) sits behind a desk. He declares to the onlookers "for a fair selection everybody has to take the same exam: please climb that tree."[9] This is the epitome of testing as "fair" assessment – everybody does the same thing. The only problem? In this cartoon, the onlookers include a bird, monkey, penguin, elephant, fish in a fishbowl, seal, and dog.

I have not done the proper research to determine whether penguins can climb trees. Based on how they walk and their lack of hands, I assume they can't. But in a social studies class based on authentic assessment, the penguin actually has a fair chance of succeeding. Penguins have incredible skills, and I love that male penguins actually take care of the egg. In a swimming test, the penguin might even do as well as the fish (especially if the fish is still in the bowl). But in school, so many of our wonderful, adorable, and brilliant penguins are not succeeding because we are constantly insisting that they climb trees.

We all know those people who struggle taking tests and in some classes tests are the main forms of assessment. In other classes, writing is the main form of authentic assessment, which is certainly better. But we know, of course, that some students are just not writers (sometimes due to learning disabilities and sometimes just due to proclivities) and that when we assess writing we are evaluating not only their knowledge and understanding, but also their organizational structure, style, syntax, and ability to formulate or defend their arguments linguistically. Many students understand things that they can't put in writing in the way they'd like. This is especially true for recent immigrants who are just being introduced to English.

When we only assess writing we unfairly penalize those who know and understand (and can "do" through other formats) but struggle to express their thoughts in writing. I sometimes think: if school success were based on the ability to put together furniture, where would I be now? I'd only graduate high school if I were teamed up with my wife and she were doing the work and I were cheering her on and handing her the tools. Mounting furniture, like writing, is essentially just a puzzle in which we are fitting together different pieces to create a larger whole. Yet, since writing and carpentry exist in different realms and utilize different skills, we rarely place the same value on them in school or in society, even though no one has ever broken a bone because of a poorly constructed paragraph.

I began to consider this cost when I stumbled upon and watched Ken Robinson's beautiful 2006 TED talk called "Do Schools Kill Creativity?" Robinson makes a robust assertion about education:

> *My contention is that creativity now is as important in education as literacy, and we should treat it with the same status. I believe this passionately, that we don't grow into creativity, we grow out of it. Or rather, we get educated out of it.*[10]

Erika Christakis, a former preschool teacher and educator at the Yale Child Study Center, similarly argues that young children are far more capable, more intelligent, and more interesting than is typically understood. In her book *The Importance of Being Little*, she explains that "getting out of the way is often the best thing we can do for a young child."[11] We need to transfer some of this wisdom to the later years of adolescent education. Adolescents are curious, multi-dimensional, and creative; we need to sometimes step aside so that when they leave our care they still have those attributes.

Robinson's lecture was one of the first handful of online TED talks, and it is the most watched of all time, with over 5 million views. This fact alone tells us that Robinson is speaking to something many of us have experienced and intuitively know to be true. And, his humorous and eloquent talk reminded me that there was more to my students, and more to my students' ability to communicate knowledge, than their test-taking and formal essay writing.

In one of his subsequent books, *Creative Schools*, Robinson explains that

> *we're all born with immense natural talents, but by the time we've been through education far too many of us have lost touch with them. Many highly talented, brilliant people think they're not because the thing they were good at in school wasn't valued or was actually stigmatized.*[12]

For Robinson, opening up our notion of education and assessment is actually a matter of equity and justice; we are treating our children unfairly when we equate intelligence solely with traditional academic traits.

If students struggle to demonstrate what they know through writing it is only fair and equitable that we provide them with alternative authentic formats to demonstrate their knowledge, such as paintings, podcasts, films, panel discussions, poetry, debates, activism, children's books, etc. Failure to do so unfairly handicaps them in a field in which there are countless real products that they could produce. We should not, hopefully, train a whole generation of university historians. But I would be thrilled to train a whole generation of writers, artists, poets, activists, policy makers, and architects.

Over the past years, I've had students create remarkable pieces: silent films on urbanization, stop-motion animation on the Constitution, performances of *Hamilton* songs rewritten to be about MLK and Malcolm X, poems on Ghanaian independence, beautiful paintings and drawings rife with symbolism about the French Revolution, and children's books using colored pencils as characters to illustrate the complexities of race. Each of these projects required argumentation, symbolic thinking, and the use of evidence to support their claims. Each of them left me in awe of my students' ability to use art as a medium to express deep understanding and complex arguments.

A young person who can do something artistic, such as painting or filmmaking, and wants to demonstrate her knowledge through that product should have the opportunity to do so at various points throughout the year. We must be willing to recognize not only what students can't do but also actually emphasize what they can do. Otherwise, we are abdicating our responsibility to see our students as individuals and to cultivate fair learning environments.

The Argument from Future Opportunity

There are two reasons for believing Ken Robinson's argument that we do not actually want to train a generation of academics. First, it would be catastrophic for society. Second, broad opportunity simply does not exist in the ivory tower, and if the only products we ask for from our students are traditionally academic, then the only destination we are leading them toward is academia. Yet, a 2016 report on faculty diversity from the TIAA institute highlighted that "the opportunity structure for academic careers has been turned on its head."[13] While about 80% of faculty positions were tenure-tracked in 1969, the number has been reduced to about 25% today. Instead, as an article in *The Atlantic* called "The Death of an Adjunct"[14] describes, adjunct and visiting professors with prestigious degrees experience professional lives that are tenuous and often leave them in abject poverty, earning only a few thousand dollars per course while going without health insurance.

When I was considering a doctorate in history years ago, a thoughtful professor warned me about the paucity of jobs in the field. Do it for the intellectual adventure, he advised, but not for the employment. The jobs in the Humanities aren't there anymore. There are two possible interpretations of that advice. One is that he recognized my intellectual limitations for this type of work and was just being kind. The other is that he was concerned about encouraging me to pursue a field with little opportunity. I really can't do the mental calculations to understand which of those is correct, so I will assume it was for the latter reason.

Indeed, a *New York Times* article "Without Tenure or a Home" depicts the struggles of homeless adjuncts living in cars or squatting in their friends' homes. For one adjunct with a master's degree from Middlebury College, whose reality is by no means unique, the "professorial lifestyle has meant spending some nights sleeping in her car, showering at college athletic centers and applying for food stamps and other government benefits."[15] Certainly many professors have wonderful and meaningful careers and a PhD normally is by no means a path to poverty. We must recognize, however, that it is also by no means a path to opportunity.

The push to rethink educational assessment and how we provide diverse opportunities for our learners comes not just from educators, but also from journalists, organizational psychologists, economists, authors, artists, and historians. Those who are thinking about the world from other angles recognize its incredible complexity and the current system's failure to prepare young people for the challenges of a dynamic 21st century environment. The main career options are no longer to be a farmer, factory worker, lawyer, teacher, merchant, or doctor. Since we are not even sure what the future options will be they maintain that creativity and flexibility are crucial.

The world, as David Epstein describes it in his masterful book *Range: Why Generalists Triumph in a Specialized World*, is a wicked learning environment. There are no clear rules. Historian Yuval Noah Harari agrees, maintaining that there are fewer and fewer guidelines for life and professional success than ever before.[16]

Insisting that all students learn the same thing, do the same thing, and check off little boxes (on a test or in formulaic writing) might help them achieve very immediate success in the class and it might make it easier for teachers, schools, and colleges to sort and rank them, but it will not provide the most help for the learners in the long-run.

David Epstein presents a fascinating study conducted by the Air Force Academy to look at the short- and long-term effects of different teaching styles in a Calculus I class. The study found that the professors whose students did best on short-term learning measurements (i.e. the final exam) actually did notably worse in future courses that required them to use the calculus they had learned in that course. The teachers "who were the best at promoting student overachievement in their own class were somehow not great for their students in the long run."[17]

Why? The professors who forced their students to struggle with the material made fewer short-term gains. They engaged in slow constructivist learning, the type that included experimentation, mistakes, and reflection. They weren't learning for the test. But then those students ended up with deeper understanding. And those professors, ironically, ended up with worse reviews from the students.

Adam Grant, a psychologist at the University of Pennsylvania's Wharton School, published *Originals: How Non-Conformists Move the World* in 2016. His book, of course, is about the nature of originality and how people generate novel and useful concepts. Why and how do certain people reject the default and look for another solution?

This is a question we should ask ourselves as teachers and ask our students to consider. As teachers, why do we so often go with the default: teaching the same content that we learned in high school and assessing that content in the same way? What does it take to become an original teacher? And, perhaps even more importantly, what can we do to help our students develop their originality? Do we want a society where all our young people go for the default, know the same information, and all produce five-paragraph essays? Will such an approach actually help our students in the long-run?

In his *New York Times* article, "What Straight-A Students Get Wrong," Grant explains that academic excellence does not function as an indicator of career excellence. Partly, this is because, as he states,

> *academic grades rarely assess qualities like creativity, leadership and teamwork skills, or social, emotional and political intelligence. When we reward students only for cramming for tests and mastering the checkpoints of the five-paragraph essay, we are not actually helping them develop the varied and complex skills they need for later career success.*

As Grant points out, career success is not only about finding solutions to problems, it is even more about finding the "right problem to solve." This is why inquiry education, the strategy in which students are involved in defining the questions and problems that they answer, is so crucial to strong learning and why I will argue so fervently, later on, for having our students write their own research paper questions. Students generating questions for their writing is not only a matter of choice, but also of increased rigor. In our current context, Grant maintains that "getting straight A's requires conformity" but that "having an influential career demands originality."[18]

Hugh Howey, the award-winning author of the WOOL and SILO series, describes in an interview on *The Knowledge Project* how his most important creative tool for writing, daydreaming, is exactly what got him in trouble in school:

> *If someone saw me as a kid, they would have said "give this kid implements of art, let him draw and paint, and make up stories, because we need storytellers.*

Having a school system that had more diversity in our expected outcomes would be a great thing."[19]

Historian Yuval Noah Harari, author of *Sapiens* and *21 Lessons for the 21st Century*, has an intellectual gaze that is now focused on the short- and long-term future, especially around such issues as nationalism, artificial intelligence, and climate change. He recognizes that we are in the midst of great societal change and his goal, it appears, is to try to get us to think about those major transformations and what we can do to be ready for them.

In *21 Lessons*, Harari shares important insights about the possibilities for education. He reminds us that "humankind is facing unprecedented revolutions" and he asks us: "How can we prepare ourselves and our children for a world of such unprecedented transformations and radical uncertainties?" Harari has the ability to write with great confidence about his vision while at the same time reminding us that we really don't know what the world will be like in three decades when our current babies become full-fledged adults. Throughout human history, we more or less knew what the near future would look like. Now we don't. We don't know what the United States will look like, what China will look like, what people will do for a living, or to what extent computers and humans will merge.[20]

This uncertainty should lead to an existential crisis for education; but for most schools and teachers it hasn't. Most continue to go by what Adam Grant calls the "default." We still cram information into kids' brains even though we have more information than we could ever use at our fingertips. And we evaluate students by how much of that information they can remember (or at least whether they can remember what we choose to ask them on a particular Thursday). Harari argues that in our world, "the last thing a teacher needs to give her pupils is more information." Instead, we need to help them figure out true from false and to decide what is important.

Ken Robinson also argues that we wrongly focus on the goal of providing all students with the same set of predetermined skills; given the uncertainty of the world, we don't actually know what skills they will need as adults. "I have a big interest in education, and I think we all do," Robinson says in his TED talk.

We have a huge vested interest in it, partly because it's education that's meant to take us into this future that we can't grasp. If you think of it, children starting school this year will be retiring in 2065. Nobody has a clue what the world will look like in five years' time. And yet, we're meant to be educating them for it.

For Harari, the goal of education needs to be to prepare students for a world of flux, to be able to reinvent themselves. We need what he calls "mental flexibility." Now, Harari might be the first to admit we don't fully know what all of this looks like in practice. But we do know that traditional lecture classes that culminate only in multiple-choice question tests will not get us where we need to go.

David Epstein's book *Range* challenges the status-quo approach in sports (and school) that takes kids as early as possible (and seemingly earlier each year) to train them in a very specific skill, whether golf, chess, math, violin, or tennis. While this approach might offer some benefits in learning environments that run by fixed rules, such as chess, he provides ample evidence that the world, and most complex professions like medicine, are wicked learning environments with constantly changing rules and a malleable playing field.

Social studies classrooms often appear to be environments in which there is a clear playing field in which hyper-specialized practice can do wonders. This is where multiple-choice tests and five-paragraph essays allow the motivated achievers to "do school" and appear to have achieved great success. In the world, though, he reminds us that "nobody has shared the rules. It is up to you to derive them, and they are subject to change without notice."[21] Real-world success values flexibility and interdisciplinary capacities; when traditional interdisciplinary work can't happen in schools because of scheduling, we can still bring other subjects like art, poetry, dance, literature, and filmmaking into a history class to blur the boundaries.

In our complex world, those who practice narrow specializations over and over again have difficulty adapting to any change. Typical learning in social studies involves what Erik Dane, a Rice University professor who specializes in organizational behavior, terms "cognitive entrenchment."[22] Students practice the five-paragraph essay and then cannot adapt their argument structure to any other format. Dane's recommendation for avoiding cognitive entrenchment is to switch-up the types of challenges you present students within a domain. This is why, Epstein argues, scientists are far more successful when they are also artists. Those who are creative often have broad interests or, to put it bluntly, a "range."

This is also why classes that include a wide range of authentic assessments are serving our students' interests in the long-term. But the issue of future opportunity is not just about what is best for students, but also for society. We live in complex, rapidly constantly changing times. As of this writing, we are only 12 years into the iPhone era and the world is now completely different. We face looming catastrophes in climate change, the rise of authoritarian nationalism, surveillance, cyberwarfare, and an unknown future of artificial intelligence.

How ought we educate this generation amidst so many unknowns? Should we teach them all the exact same thing? Ask them all the very same questions? Have them all write the same essay? What will be best for the success of our society in dire times?

As Ken Robinson points out, since we are facing major problems as a species in the 21st century, especially new problems like climate change, we just can't do what we've always been doing before. It is a disastrous approach for society if we all learn the same things in the same way. "We now have limitless opportunities to engage young people's imaginations," he explains, "and to provide forms of teaching and learning that are highly customized to them."[23] We don't need uniformity; we need creativity. Not just for the students, but for society and for our very complex 21st century problems.

The Argument from Joy and Play

At the end of my first year of teaching at Scarsdale High School, together with my cohort of freshmen educators, I was asked to put together a portfolio with a cover letter answering the question: why do I teach? This is how I began my letter:

> Teaching and learning, for me, are paths deeply linked to the goals of joy and authenticity. My students and I walk down this path together because I make every attempt to turn education into an experience. I cultivate a classroom culture that allows all students to find joy in their learning and to pursue authentic forms of expression of their historical knowledge. The result is that students recognize that joy and authenticity actually bring more rigor to their learning. When they are engaged in true historical work they strive to reach for more and to excel in ways that they had not previously imagined. In other words, I teach so that students and I find joy in our work together, creating real historical products, and consequently reaching higher-levels of achievements.

I was not thinking of writing a book at that time about authentic assessments. I was barely even thinking. I had just had my third child. But it is clear that I connected three ideas that are central to this book: authentic assessments are joyful, joy helps to make learning deeper, and joy makes for more effective education. When I once asked Scott Storm, a brilliant English teacher at Harvest Collegiate whether my work counted me as a "social justice educator" he answered in an email:

> *I actually think of your class as most closely linked to the Ted Sizer progressive movement. The ideas of art-based lessons and of fun and joy are all part of this and connecting it with a text like Les Mis is situated right in that school of thought.*

Joy has always been central to my practice. It is no surprise that when I considered a name for my teaching website I ended up with the "J" in JADE learning. Joy has led me toward role-plays, mock trials, and chucking clocks at students. Joy led me to run around the room 24 times in imitation of the Battle of Marathon and to the use, whenever possible, of Legos and Indiana Jones clips in my classes. But joy has also been so important to me because it helps learning.

Andy del-Calvo, my colleague at Harvest, also recognized that joy was at the heart of what we were trying to build together in the classroom. After I left the school, he wrote to me:

> *Fun remained a critical aspect of EVERYTHING we were doing. How can we make reading fun? How can we make talking about cricket fun? Joy was at the heart of it all and has continued to be an important impetus for everything I try to design.*

The research is undeniable that kids learn through play, kids learn better with play, and kids need play. As the authors of *Overloaded and Underprepared* explain, "research suggests that play – especially when it is freely chosen, unstructured, and kid-directed – is linked to a wide variety of positive outcomes including increased cognitive skills, physical health, self-regulations, language abilities, and social skills."[24] These social skills are not "soft" but rather crucial for later success, and they include the ability to collaborate, compromise, and fail forward. Entire schools, such as Quest to Learn, in Manhattan, are built around the incredible value of play for learning.

Forms of play change over time for people. My three little kids think fun play is to climb on top of me, jump up and down, and poke me in the eye while I am lying on the floor desperately trying to nap for four minutes. I don't advocate for that type of play for high school students, especially with me. Denise Pope and her colleagues remind us that for older students, just spending time with friends counts as play, as well as activities like sports, arts, community service, and journalism.

Thus, the link between authentic assessment and joy is clear. Group projects mean that students get to be with each other, talking, face-to-face. This is especially important in the era of social media when so much interaction happens behind a screen. While some authentic assessment, such as digital history, may include screen time, the work they are doing, whether creating artwork, writing a story, or filming a movie together, really feels like play to them. They enjoy it. They smile. And that matters.

The Argument from Wellness

Right next to the great cartoon in *Overloaded and Underprepared* of the soon-to-be unsuccessful tree climbers there is a quotation, source unknown, that rightly connects the issue of assessment to student wellness: "Everybody is a genius, but if you judge a fish by its ability to climb a tree, it will live its whole life believing that it is stupid."

The next step on the ladder of inequity in assessment that I discussed previously is the effect of our educational structure on student self-image. The stories of people who thought they could do nothing right (or were told they could do nothing right) in school only to achieve great success later on are numerous. Jonathan Mooney describes this dynamic well in his book *Normal Sucks*. He writes that "from my first day in kindergarten at Pennekamp Elementary School, me and school just didn't get along. It started with the desk. My relationship with my school desk was fraught." Then, he continues by explaining the long-lasting implications for his self-esteem of being placed in the "dumb" group for reading, a practice which he eloquently calls a "crime of good intentions."

In his book, Mooney frankly discusses how differences, including learning differences, are treated as deficiencies and how those with ADHD, depression, dyslexia and other differences are "dehumanized, victimized, and wounded" in school. He shares a letter he received from a nine-year-old boy, who is dyslexic, explaining how his teacher tells him he's not good at spelling and so he is waiting for school to finish so he never has to learn anything ever again.[25]

Unfortunately, we only know the stories of people like Jonathan Mooney because those individuals achieved success and got to tell their stories. But how many people get failed by the system and then just end up failing in life as well?

The standard assessment system often destroys smart people's sense of themselves as intellectuals. Ken Robinson maintains that if we consistently "punish" students who fall outside the traditional box of academic intelligence with poor grades, we consequently limit their ability to value themselves and to become productive, active, and compassionate citizens. This reality takes place in high-performing environments where academic success is linked to self-image and in struggling communities where failure on tests could mean the closing of their school. We are essentially restricting a future generation's capacity to find themselves and how they can best contribute to our society.

An overemphasis on box-checking hurts struggling students and it also hurts high-achievers and the types of schools and students depicted in *Overloaded and Underprepared*. There is a reason that Pope and her colleagues connect student wellness problems and stress not only to homework, social media, and excessive extracurricular problems but also to assessments. Those who really want to learn deeply can't do so because they have to cram for a test they don't care about; those who study hard for a test or write the formulaic paper realize they have learned nothing and forget it all soon afterwards; those who know so much about the topic do poorly if they don't respond correctly to the particular question the teacher asks on the test. It is a treadmill on which some fall off and those who stay on realize they are going nowhere.

One of Denise Pope's educational slogans she teaches at Stanford is to give students "voice, choice, revision, and redemption." Those ideas are not just helpful for learning, but also for adolescent well-being. A traditional assessment structure allows students no choice in how to be assessed. They take a mandatory test. They answer a teacher's prescribed question on an essay. None of it matters much. And they know it. A quiz or test can be useful as an assessment for the teacher, in the sense that it provides concrete information about what a student knows about a topic, such as the French Revolution, at one point in time. While it may crystalize content for students and contribute to learning in the short-term, the experience does little in meaning-making for students and we know that students cram and then forget soon after.

Authentic assessments work differently since they are really about both the teacher and the student. The experience holds meaning for the students because they recognize the growth and learning that accrued as a result of engaging in the process. In other words, the assessment becomes part of the whole learning process, an activity of additional learning, not simply a marker of termination.

Additionally, the nature of JADE assessments allows students to develop deeper personal connections to the content. This is not a small matter. Facing History and Ourselves' philosophy of teaching history, a crucial one in our discipline, is geared primarily toward the goal of cultivating an empathetic link between the content and the students' realities, thereby creating meaning. When assessments inject meaning into the students' educational experience, the consequent increase in well-being can be remarkable.

Teenagers today, as always, are chafing hard for some freedom. Lenore Skenazy points out in *Free-Range Kids* that our young people have far less freedom than ever before and far less than their peers in most of the rest of the world. Our adolescents want our trust, they want responsibility, and they want freedom. Children are incredibly competent, but they can only really be as competent as we allow them to be. Unfortunately, at home, many can't leave their own block, they have to be driven everywhere, and they must be accompanied at all times by adults.[26]

In the classroom, where teenagers could have some intellectual freedom, at least, they are told what to read, when to read it, what to write, what format to use, and what question to answer. It is no wonder so many of our young people are bored, stressed, and angry. Without student agency in co-creating their life experience at home or their educational experience in school, there are precious few opportunities for self-efficacy to grow, leading to increased anxiety and dependence.

David Brooks perhaps best illuminates the contrast between the box-checking world of school and the flexibility of the adult world. In his book *The Second Mountain*, Brooks writes poetically that

> when you're a student, life is station to station. There's always the next assignment, the next test, the next admissions applications. Then, from the most structured and supervised childhood in human history, you get spit out after graduation into the least structured young adulthood in human history. The average American has seven jobs over the course of their twenties.[27]

His book, in many ways, is an exploration of the emotional and moral complexities of living in a cloudy age; preparing students for flexibility is not just giving them more chance of professional success, it is also providing them with some of the emotional resilience and bounce that they need for the future.

When I left Harvest Collegiate a few years ago, one of my students wrote me a special thank you note, which I think most poignantly reveals the connection between the encouragement of creativity and student wellness. He wrote:

> I took your colonialism class, and I ended up writing one story that would forever change how I wrote. It was a story about a Janissary boy, and the first paragraph I wrote has been the best intro I have ever written in my life. I try to make every paragraph exactly as good as that one. I never would have written that story if it wasn't for you.
>
> You inspire me to continue to grow my creative side. That means a lot to me. In the final project for english, I revealed that I was struggling with

depression the last few months. Writing stories is one of the only things that makes me feel okay again. When I write stories, it's exactly like theatre. I become enveloped in a completely new world. And i'm a part of it. Not just like reading where you're observing their world, while writing, I am actually structuring their world, becoming part of it. It distracts me from all my problems at home, and because of my creativeness, I'm already working on a movie idea.

As educators, it is our obligation to unleash our students intellectually, provide them with the choice of what to produce, and the voice to express themselves. Let them make mistakes and learn. They will be happier, smarter, and better off because of it.

When Should We Implement Authentic Assessments into Our Curriculum?

One of the key attributes of successful teaching involves carefully laying out our curriculum in a way that makes sense to ourselves and our students. We ought to consider our larger goals for the course, the themes and questions we wish to emphasize, the skills we hope to build, and the things we imagine our students might do. This is the essence of Backwards Planning, a strategy through which we envision the endpoint before we plot out the daily lessons. A strong practice of Backwards Planning might make use of Wiggins and McTighe's *Understanding by Design*[28] framework or it might exist in a loose and organic process.

One of the challenges of Backwards Planning is the contradiction between setting out a clear path of study while also leaving room for the twists and turns that emerge when working with real students. Almost invariably, if we are doing it right, the lessons and units take longer in reality than we had penciled into our calendars. Students raise new questions, we encounter new resources, and we adjust to some of the formative feedback that tells us that the students need a review session or a primer on writing an introduction.

Thus, when we develop our assessments, which ought to be one of the first stops in our planning trajectory, we should think about how each piece fits into the larger map of our course. Or, using another analogy, creating a course is like planning a holiday meal in which we imagine how the ingredients will form dishes but then when we get to the stove we inevitably make adjustments. In my case, poorly. As I'm writing this, I just realized I forgot to buy the lemon for my salmon dish. Yes, I'm writing while I cook salmon. Either the writing or the salmon will surely turn out dry.

I don't think I need to explain where to put writing into the curriculum in order to begin your work with authentic assessments. Most social studies teachers at this point, I would hope, have their students write, and we should have them write as much as we can feasibly read and grade their work. At Harvest, we had one course called *Looking for an Argument* in which students wrote weekly essays. Personally, it became difficult for me to stay on top of the grading and feedback, but the course itself produced some of the strongest short-term growth in writing I had ever seen. It makes sense – if we want students to get better at writing they ought to do it as much as possible and we ought to give them immediate and targeted feedback.

The question, then, is not when to have them write. We should have them write as much as possible in whatever form: in-class essays, take-home essays, historical fiction, civic action plans, or research papers. The question is how and when to incorporate JADE assessments: the poems, films, dance, civic action, paintings, perspective pieces, panel discussions, and web design.

I have developed two separate strategies for successfully integrating authentic assessments into my course plan: the "click approach" and the "menu approach."

The Click Approach

The click approach is when an assessment perfectly matches the instruction of the unit. In this case, all students should engage in the same format because it matches (or clicks) with the content, period, or theme of the unit.

One of my goals as a social studies teacher is to have students express their knowledge using a medium that was prevalent during the time period we are studying. So, when Andy del-Calvo and I planned out a Cold War unit, we asked students to create a *radio* propaganda piece from the Soviet or American perspective.

When we studied the use of homespun clothing in India and kente cloth in Ghana to protest colonialism, my class as a whole designed anti-colonialism clothing, together with a local fashion designer, and then put on an actual fashion show. It might be the case, similarly, that your unit on Gandhi and Indian resistance is when you want to work on a civic action piece, your unit on the American Revolution is when you want them to build a memorial to the American Revolution that honors an ignored historical figure, or that when you teach early 20th century America and the Progressive Era you ask students to create a silent film. Those are some artful projects I've done that have "clicked" with the content, themes, and periods of study.

With the click approach, I set aside certain units as JADE assessment units. In this case, you may want to consider how many assessments you hope to do over the course of the year. If you choose to engage in two or four of them, decide which units will best match the type of assessment you hope that they will produce.

If all students are doing one type of art, then you do want to find some way to teach them a bit of the medium. Consider whether you can partner with an art teacher or bring in a local expert or artist (who are usually thrilled to partner with schools). Here, we want to value craft, mastery, and the intricacies of each genre. You can show them models from that genre to discuss and dissect. Providing a rubric, such as the ones I've included in this book, can help students understand the specific language, terminology, and expectations within a particular medium. And, it is helpful to provide logistical suggestions to help students succeed in a task, such as web design sites, templates for a civic action plan, online programs to make a newspaper format, etc.

The Menu Approach

The menu approach is the epitome of Denise Pope's "voice and choice" mantra. In this format, which I currently use, students have to do a specific number of project assessments each quarter. So for example, in the second quarter they must complete two projects. One must be an essay and the other a JADE assessment. Here's the catch, it doesn't matter which project is which.

So, for example, some students might write an essay on the Russian Revolution while others do a piece of visual art, or a group film, or a podcast. In the next unit, on Germany and Holocaust, those who did the essay now produce a piece of historical art. And whomever previously made art now write an essay. And, in each case, the student chooses the focus of the project and the historical question and argument.

The menu approach is fantastic for student voice and choice, and it is fantastic for me. When I teach two to three sections of a course, it means that I grade different types of work, mediums, questions, and arguments. It makes the assessment more meaningful for them and more enjoyable and thought-provoking for me.

That is why I require students each semester to produce JADE history for some units, and to do traditional essay writing for others. An inquiry research paper and some traditional argumentative essays remain as the foundation of the course but they are bookended by song, poetry, paintings, and film. Teachers have had to take difficult and important steps to move beyond test-taking into writing as a centerpiece of assessment. Now it is the time to take a second step in which we maintain writing's importance but elevate art to be a valued mode of communicating real historical understanding.

When students choose a JADE format for a menu assignment, I feel less need to teach each student the particularities of the medium for a few reasons. First, they have chosen that genre as the format that will best allow them to communicate their understanding. Hence, given the choice, they now have the responsibility. Additionally, here I'm often more concerned with them having the chance to communicate their understanding and argument through the means that works for them, and less about the necessary mastery of the craft. For example, if they choose to create a podcast audio production, I really care more about the knowledge and argument they convey, rather than the particular sound effects and musical background they are able to integrate into the product.

How Should I Begin to Implement JADE Assessments?

Throughout the book, I provide guidance on how to specifically incorporate different types of assessments. I categorize my suggestions as: apprentice step, samurai step, Jedi step. Here is an overview of how that might look for a course:

An Apprentice Step

Decide on one unit to "click" in one authentic assessment that the class completes together. For example, after a unit on Indian independence movement, the entire class could design (individually or in groups) an Indian independence memorial and decide where to place it. Or, all students could organize a new protest movement (a new Satyagraha campaign) during World War II. Or, all students could write a two-part perspective piece from the viewpoints of two people during the Indian independence movement.

A Samurai Step

Choose one unit during the year in which all students can select the JADE project that they wish to produce. For example, during the Indian independence movement unit, all students do a JADE authentic assessment other than formal writing. But, each student gets to choose the specific format, such as a dance, civic action, speech writing, or building a monument.

A Jedi Step

Develop a menu approach in which students determine the unit in which they will do a formal essay and the unit in which they will do a piece of art. So, everyone is really on their own path (unless they choose to work in groups). In my class, all students do an essay for the first project of the year and an art project for the second project during quarter one. For the second and third quarters, however, they each need to complete one art project and one essay (per quarter). They have the right to choose the topic for each as long as they meet the requirements. I keep track to make sure if a student writes an essay first, then she produces art next and vice-versa. In the fourth quarter, we culminate the year with mandatory projects, such as a research paper and a final civic action piece.

What if JADE Authentic Assessments Don't Seem as Rigorous as Tests or Formal Writing? What if People Think Authentic Assessments are Softballs that Mean Kids Won't Actually Need to Know Anything?

Since I began teaching at Scarsdale High School, one of the main questions surrounding my work has been about rigor. The thoughtful questions raised by John Harrison, my department chair, and Ken Bonamo, my principal, have sharpened and deepened my thinking and practice in this area.

A sad truth in many high-needs educational settings is that rigor gets sidelined and proficiency gets highlighted. In other words, we need to move kids forward toward graduation and to do that we need to ensure that all students show basic understanding and proficiency. This isn't ideal, but it is reality. In those contexts, the pursuit of "rigor" or "high expectations" doesn't have the weight it ought to in our practice. If art gets used, it becomes a mechanism to show student understanding of the content but not necessarily student mastery.

At Scarsdale, just as in many high-performing districts, most of the students demonstrate proficiency in understanding and skill. Thus, assessments serve the function of driving their learning to higher levels and ensuring complete mastery of the material. Given the importance of college placements, grades also have a very high symbolic value. In short, it becomes extremely important to the department and to the school that in the case that one teacher is assessing the French Revolution through a test and another through an essay, while the third is using an art project, all of the teachers require the same level of mastery or rigor.

This is probably the area in which my teaching and assessment practices have grown most significantly since joining Scarsdale. I want to make sure that all historical art, action pieces, or other authentic assessments still address a real historical question, use evidence to support that argument, and demonstrate a grasp of the complexity and nuance of the issue. For example, we can't settle with a lovely depiction of the Storming of the Bastille. Instead, students need to explicitly use a piece of visual art to answer a question like "How did the Storming of the Bastille change the power dynamic between the three estates?" Students perceive JADE assessments as driving them deeper than they would have gone otherwise; by playing with allegory and symbolism they have added intellectual depth to their work.

Some educators, parents, and even students might doubt that art can be as rigorous as writing. The truth, however, is that artful assessments can be as rigorous as writing as long as we hold them to the same expectations, define those expectations in the assignment, and identify those expectations in the rubric. This is the reason why the wording of the task is so essential. Students must know that the purpose is not to just create something beautiful; they need to answer a question, make an argument, use evidence to support their argument, and explain their choices in the artist statement.

The relative "newness" of artful assessments is also why using a strong and thought-out rubric is so crucial. Can we actually give a student a B for a beautiful piece of artwork that she worked extremely hard on? As my students will tell you, the answer is surely "yes" since the assignment and rubric are quite clear. Students work hard on writing all the time and yet they still know that they don't always earn perfect grades. The artwork formats leave their creative possibilities open but do not reduce their need to think deeply and communicate effectively to earn an A. After their work is complete, students most often realize that they had to dig deeper than they would if they did the essay. Symbolic representation of an argument is tougher in many ways.

Given the importance of rubrics in helping us show students how to achieve higher-level products, I have included at least one authentic assessment rubric in each chapter of this book.

If we require argumentation and evidence from the art, and we develop rubrics that support those expectations, students will often submit art that far exceeds in effort and output what they may have produced had they been required to write a formulaic essay to answer a prescribed question. Rigorous rubrics can assure we hold students accountable for delivering products with strong and complex arguments.

What if Doing Artwork Takes Away from Crucial Practice with Writing?

One of the tensions of teaching is the appearance of a zero-sum game with our time. We have a finite amount of time with our students that never gets extended. We have a limited time allotted for homework and in certain contexts, in my experience, few students complete the homework. Either the students are in overstressed academic environments in which we need to reduce the homework load for their well-being or we are working in difficult circumstances in which students' home lives often prevent them from completing homework. We mostly need to rely on the time we have in class to do what is most important.

With only 180 days of school, and fewer class periods of actual instruction, every choice we make seems crucial: do we show a movie or read a text on Tuesday? Do we do a role-play or practice reading on Thursday? Do we practice discussion skills or note-taking on Friday?

These are real choices and they are never easy. When we pack too much into our lessons we actually achieve little. Since we can't overload, when we think about assessing student knowledge we often revert to tests and when we want to develop a practical and authentic skill we work on writing.

If classes have time for two large summative assessments in a quarter, can we afford to dedicate one of them to art? In high-performing schools the emphasis is on writing to prepare students for college success. In struggling schools, the emphasis is on basic writing skills to prepare students for graduation and hopefully for college and career success as well. In each of those cases, relinquishing writing time in favor of artwork may appear to be a problematic choice.

Nonetheless, we should not consider the use of JADE assessments to be a "loss" or a "waste." We need to consider the collaboration, creativity, and connectivity that comes out of art and action projects, and that the long-term benefits of slow learning are quite difficult for us to measure. Equally important, we ought to remember that writing and art are both forms of communication and argument. In an age where symbolic language is languishing, art is a social necessity. Artful language is far more nuanced than most youthful (or adult) communication and it requires deep symbolic analysis and "linguistic" flexibility.

Our goal should not be simply to make students into the best writers they can be – we need to make students into great communicators who can engage in nuanced arguments. Even traditional teachers in my schooling days realized that idea, often asking students to present in front of the class and grading "oral communication." But now we must go further and recognize the plethora of legitimate ways that students can communicate what they know. Providing students with a broader range of experiences prepares them for a future in which flexibility is crucial.

Moreover, we must consider cognitive load of tasks on our young learners. Writing is often the most demanding form of communication for many students. If we truly want to teach them how to develop nuanced, thoughtful, and complex evidence-based arguments, then writing is likely not the best (or only) medium to do so. So much of the students' cognitive load gets caught up in the difficult task of composing the written word that they cannot devote any of it to the thinking. For students who struggle with formal writing, we can, and should, use art, painting, dance, podcasts, and panel discussion, among other options, to teach communication and argument; they can use these friendlier formats to try, to critique each other, and to learn. Finally, we can have students apply all of that to their written arguments.

What if I'm Not Good at Art and Other JADE Assessments? How Can I Grade Students at It?

As I mentioned previously, by no means do I have any credibility in the world of art. I never played a musical instrument other than my middle school recorder and I haven't painted anything since 9th grade studio art. The absence of artistic development in my own life perhaps explains my passion for seeing it flower in my students.

When I evaluate their writing, my mindset is almost always about *deficit* since I'm better at the task (usually) than they are. I'm thinking about what they are not doing well or what else they could have included rather than appreciating what they actually achieved in the piece. This is a common problem, I have noticed, about how teachers view students' written work.

I often think of the students who do not shine at formal writing. When those students produce art and other authentic assessments, however, I get to appreciate them and the talent, skills, and attributes they have that so often go overlooked and unacknowledged in schools. The experience of assessment becomes more positive – I see them as more fully rounded people, I see talents and passions that had been hidden. Most importantly, I experience a sense of awe at the sight of teenagers producing work that far exceeds my own capabilities. I can still make critiques and suggestions about their argumentation, symbolism, and overall artistic choices but I do so while also taking joy in their creation.

The question of assessing work outside our area of expertise is a common comfort-zone question for teachers. Social studies teachers familiarize themselves with the language and norms of our discipline and we rarely if ever grade work in science or math. How can we grade a painting, song, or video if we are not experts in those fields?

First, we need to remember that critics are rarely experts in creating the types of work that they review. Art critics are rarely artists, film critics are rarely filmmakers, and literary critics are rarely novelists. That might be a reason for resentment among artists who receive poor reviews but it isn't a reason to delegitimize the process. The truth is that we can learn to appreciate quality in disciplines outside our own and we do that all the time. We are all, in a sense, restaurant critics every time we eat out of the house.

Once we begin to ask an entire class to produce a non-traditional authentic assessment, it is also an opportunity for us to learn and grow as teachers. We should learn some of the basic elements of the craft and teach them to the students if we want them to compose a painting, a historical fiction piece, or a poem. We become more confident, they become more confident, and the assessment works even better.

One point that we need to remember is that when students use art to express historical arguments, only one factor (or standard) that we grade needs to involve the artistic quality. We are actually evaluating historical argumentation, evidence, and analysis similarly to how we do it with writing. Most of us can differentiate between high and low artistic quality and we get better at that over time. Grading historical art is like grading writing in that it is hard at first (and anyone who has worked with a student-teacher will be reminded that assessing writing is excruciatingly difficult at first) but we learn to recognize argument, symbolism, and analysis in the artwork over time. Finally, one of the roles of the artist statement is to ensure that we see the art as the student does and really grasp the symbolism, evidence, and argument that it puts forth.

What if There Is a Student Who Isn't Good at Art or Other Authentic Assessments, Isn't It Unfair to Grade Her at It?

I sometimes hear this question not just from teachers, but also from students; how can we grade them through a medium that they aren't "good" at? Isn't that unfair?

Unfortunately, we do this to those students who are not strong writers or test-takers all the time. We take those penguins and make them climb trees. But then for some reason we have a problem evaluating the monkey on his flying.

We evaluate student understanding through tests and writing, ignoring the fact that they are not the ways that those students would choose to demonstrate their knowledge. Many students know a whole lot of history, but not the specific questions we ask on tests (or how we ask them). Many students have deep knowledge, but not the skills to articulate it on paper. How many people protest the unjust nature of solely evaluating those students through writing and test-taking?

We can't even argue, legitimately, that writing is a more authentic form of historical expression than, let's say, oral communication. If we look at one profession that communicates historical knowledge regularly (teaching) we see that the teacher relies far more on oral communication than the written word. So if we were to choose only one "fair" method, wouldn't it be a presentation, panel discussion, or podcast?

Hence, even if a student is not strong at art I do not consider it unjust to evaluate him or her on an artistic project. It is actually more equitable in that it puts strong writers, test-takers, and artists on a more even playing field for once.

I also rarely demand that students produce a specific art form. My art projects tend to exist as "menus" in which students get to choose from a wide spectrum of artistic formats that include much of what is in this book: poetry, perspective pieces, board games, podcasts, filmmaking, etc. I've been hard-pressed to identify a teenager who can produce nothing authentic outside of an essay. Those who are strong writers can still revel, normally, in one of the creative writing options mentioned above or one of the audio-visual mediums. At times, I have worked with students who struggle considerably on tests and writing but who can produce superb historical art. I've never met a student who can write an essay but suffers to create one more form of authentic history.

The following section includes a generic rubric that can be used to evaluate all authentic and artful assessments. Throughout the book, I provide additional rubrics geared toward specific forms of assessments, such as discussions, leading lessons, civic action, and design thinking.

What if Some Authentic Assessments are Spectacular, but Others are Subpar? Won't the Subpar Pieces Mean that Art and Civic Action as Assessment Isn't Working?

This is a strange question. But for some reason, teachers try something new and if the students produce subpar work they assume there is a fundamental problem with the assignment. Think about if you've ever assigned an essay. Aren't some of the pieces excellent and others mediocre? When that happens, we don't toss aside the idea of having students write. Instead, we just recognize it is the nature of working with diverse individual students and that there are areas in which our instruction could be better. And then we try again. JADE assessments work the same way. Don't give up just because a few students produce simple, basic pieces of art.

Notes

1 Gulikers, J. T. M., Bastiaens, T. J., & Kirschner, P. A. (2004). A five-dimensional framework for authentic assessment. *Educational Technology Research and Development*, 52(3), 67–86.

2 Avery, P. G., Freeman, C., & Carmichael-Tanaka, D. L. (2002). Developing authentic instruction in the social studies. *Journal of Research in Education*, 12(1), 50–56.

3 Newmann, F. M., King, M. B., & Carmichael, D. L. (2007). *Authentic instruction and assessment: common standards for rigor and relevance in teaching academic subjects*. Des Moines, IA: Iowa Department of Education.

4 Pope, D. C., Brown, M., & Miles, S. B. (2015). *Overloaded and underprepared: strategies for stronger schools and healthy, successful kids*. San Francisco, CA: Jossey-Bass.

5 Pope, D. C., Brown, M., & Miles, S. B. (2015). *Overloaded and underprepared: strategies for stronger schools and healthy, successful kids*. San Francisco, CA: Jossey-Bass.

6 Mehta, J., & Fine, S. (2019). *In search of deeper learning. The quest to remake the American high school*. Cambridge: Harvard University Press.

7 Mehta, J., & Fine, S. (2019, March 30). High school doesn't have to be boring. *New York Times*. Retrieved from www.nytimes.com/2019/03/30/opinion/sunday/fix-high-school-education.html.

8 Dubois, L. (2016, November 7). Why Haiti should be at the centre of the Age of Revolution. Retrieved from https://aeon.co/essays/why-haiti-should-be-at-the-centre-of-the-age-of-revolution.

9 Pope, D. C., Brown, M., & Miles, S. B. (2015). *Overloaded and underprepared: strategies for stronger schools and healthy, successful kids*. San Francisco, CA: Jossey-Bass.

10 Robinson, K. (2006). Do schools kill creativity? Retrieved from www.ted.com/talks/ken_robinson_says_schools_kill_creativity?language=en.

11 Christakis, E. (2017). *The importance of being little: what young children really need from grownups*. New York: Penguin Books.

12 Robinson, K., & Aronica, L. (2016). *Creative schools: the grassroots revolution that's transforming education*. New York: Penguin Books.

13 Study finds gains in faculty diversity, but not on the tenure track. (n.d.). Retrieved from www.insidehighered.com/news/2016/08/22/study-finds-gains-faculty-diversity-not-tenure-track.

14 Harris, A. (2019, April 8). The death of an adjunct. Retrieved from www.theatlantic.com/education/archive/2019/04/adjunct-professors-higher-education-thea-hunter/586168/.

15 Kilgannon, C. (2014, March 28). Without tenure or a home. Retrieved from www.nytimes.com/2014/03/30/nyregion/without-tenure-or-a-home.html.

16 Harari, Y. N. (2018). *21 lessons for the 21st century*. New York: Spiegel & Grau.

17 Epstein, D. (2019). *Range: why generalists triumph in a specialized world*. New York: Riverhead Books.

18 Grant, A. (2018, December 8). What straight-A students get wrong. Retrieved from www.nytimes.com/2018/12/08/opinion/college-gpa-career-success.html.

19 Parrish, (n.d.). Hugh Howey: winning at the self-publishing game. Retrieved from https://fs.blog/hugh-howey/

20 Harari, Y. N. (2018). *21 lessons for the 21st century*. New York: Spiegel & Grau.

21 Epstein, D. (2019). *Range: why generalists triumph in a specialized world*. New York: Riverhead Books.

22 Dane, E. (2010). Reconsidering the trade-off between expertise and flexibility: a cognitive entrenchment perspective. *The Academy of Management Review*, 35(4), 579-603. Retrieved from www.jstor.org/stable/29765006

23 Robinson, K., & Aronica, L. (2016). *Creative schools: the grassroots revolution that's transforming education*. New York: Penguin Books.

24 Pope, D. C., Brown, M., & Miles, S. B. (2015). *Overloaded and underprepared: strategies for stronger schools and healthy, successful kids*. San Francisco, CA: Jossey-Bass.

25 Mooney, J. (2019). *Normal sucks: how to live, learn, and thrive outside the lines*. New York: Henry Holt and Company.

26 Skenazy, L. (2010). *Free-range kids: how to raise safe, self-reliant children (without going nuts with worry)*. San Francisco, CA: Jossey-Bass.

27 Brooks, D. (2019). *The second mountain: how people move from the prison of self to the joy of commitment*. New York: Random House.

28 Wiggins, G. P., & McTighe, J. (2008). *Understanding by design*. Alexandria, VA: Association for Supervision and Curriculum Development.

Part 2

Written Assessments

2

Formal Essay

Formal writing is the cornerstone of authentic assessment in social studies. This chapter provides a variety of practical tips and strategies for improving student writing and making it more authentic both for high-skilled and struggling writers. I delve into techniques for teaching students to write dynamic introductions and conclusions, as well as for scaffolding body paragraphs. I also raise a number of questions about writing that defy a simple and definitive answer. Writing is complex, so it is okay to be in doubt about how to teach it, but it is important to think and talk about that process to plant that doubt.

After reading the chapter, use the following chart as a plan to "keep the learning real"

How will questions be developed for your essays: teacher-produced, a menu of options, or student-created?
How will you first teach students to hook their reader in their introductions?
To what extent will you use a structure for body paragraphs? If so, what type?

The Teaching of Writing

It was early autumn, about 15 years ago. I plopped myself on the couch, put my feet up, and opened a folder of papers that I had brought home. I grabbed a blue pen. I was incredibly eager to see what my students had written, which means, of course, that it was my first year of teaching. My 10th graders had engaged in fantastic discussions of ancient Greek politics in class, so I was intrigued to discover what they would say about Pericles' funeral oration.

Five papers into the pile, I was baffled. Some of the essays had no clear arguments, while others had claims that were nearly impossible to decipher amidst convoluted sentences and grammatical errors. And this was in an elite private school! My mind drifted between confusion and annoyance. And soon, in my first great awakening as a teacher, I realized I had about 45 more of these to read, edit, and grade. I took the right decision, at that moment: I went down to the local corner store and grabbed some ice cream.

Looking back, I understand the situation better. In those first years of teaching, I was flummoxed when I came across student writing that was jumbled, rambling, and bordering on incomprehensible. At the time, I had not yet studied education, but, more importantly, I hadn't engaged in discussion, professional development, and problem-solving with a wide-range of experienced teachers. I hadn't looked at examples of student writing with colleagues, debated the wording in rubrics, co-planned scaffolding or engaged in any of the collaboration that helps us grow as teachers of writing. I know, now, that the students had not failed me in their writing; I had failed them in not teaching them strategies to communicate their ideas effectively.

As a more experienced teacher, there are still times when I am baffled about what to do to improve student writing. After years of working in schools where it seemed that every student required intensive writing support and many students struggled to put any words on paper, now I am in a setting in which many students can just go at it and produce magnificent pieces, while others still benefit from scaffolding. Working on skill-building in a heterogeneous context can be even more difficult, in some ways, than in one where every student needs support.

I am not a researcher in the teaching of writing. True scholarship exists on this topic and is worth exploration. This chapter, instead, is a bridge into my mind; into the mind of one experienced social studies teacher who has spent what seems like eons thinking and talking about the teaching of writing.

Writing Essays: The Question

The first step for any teacher embarking on an essay must be deep consideration of the question or prompt. There are good historical questions and there are bad ones. There are also different ways to think about how to structure the choice of a question.

Educators generally sort into three camps in terms of developing an essay question. The default is to compose one question that all students answer. This is what most of our teachers did for us and what most of us do for our students. Some teachers write out a few questions, thereby allowing each student to choose the one s/he wants to answer.

A few daredevils allow students to compose and then answer their own questions. This is true student inquiry and the epitome of Denise Pope's mantra of "voice and choice."

Teacher-produced Question

There are clear advantages to choosing one question for the entire class. First, you can ensure that the students will engage with a strong, complex question that has multiple possible answers and that is answerable given the available resources for the students. This approach allows for true backwards planning, which is especially helpful for struggling writers. By knowing the question ahead of time the teacher can organize the process so that students work individually or in groups to gather evidence throughout the unit, thereby getting a headstart on the planning. The hope is that the structure, scaffolding, and chunking will allow them to complete a piece of writing that meets standards.

There are, however, disadvantages to this approach. It means that all students are doing the same teacher-directed project, ridding them of any agency or individual curiosity and most likely of motivation. Everyone is in the same box; no one is innovating or doing something unique. It does not matter if a student finds the question uninspiring; she still needs to spend significant time on it. The work becomes a bit more rote and less authentic. It also means that you, the teacher, need to read and grade the same paper time and time again.

This was my typical structure when working in schools with students who needed significant support. Structure and backwards planning was reassuring for both the students and for myself. It gave us the sense of a clear process, checkpoints, and direction. In the best cases, students produced solid and coherent arguments that utilized a clear organizational structure. In the worst cases, students did not submit the papers.

Multiple Teacher-produced Questions

As I mentioned, a second option is for teachers to identify roughly two to six possible questions to answer. Here, the development of the question may still originate from the teacher, ensuring that students are pursuing legitimate historical questions that are answerable based on the resources at hand. Alternatively, an entire class can engage in inquiry, together producing a menu of possible questions to choose from, which might also include a few of the teacher's own questions. Students can even still work in groups to prepare their writing, preferably according to the question each has chosen. This format has the obvious advantage of providing more agency for the students and more of a sense of buy-in; students are more likely to end up writing about something of interest to them. It also means that we have more variety in what we read and grade. This process, as a whole, is more authentic in that students are engaged more completely in all the steps of writing, including the selection of a question.

The downside of this structure is that it adds a bit of complexity for the teacher. Now, depending on the amount of scaffolding and support your students require, you must keep track of a few different questions and the corresponding resources and evidence that students might use to support their arguments. It is a bit more weighty of a process, and requires more flexibility and nimbleness on the side of the teacher. This has been my go-to format for the past few years.

Student-produced Questions

Consider a third format: allowing students at some point in the year to compose and answer their own questions. Doing so is more time-consuming since in many settings you might need to dedicate a day or two for students to write their questions. The upshot, of course, is that such a move increases authenticity, motivation, and student buy-in. Now, students are really taking ownership of their writing from start to finish. It also means that we are reading and grading unique pieces of writing that may often surprise and teach us something.

The problem, though, is that this format makes it really difficult to provide clear structure, backwards planning, and class-wide or group support. Without check-ins about the question, it is also possible students may end up choosing a question that is simple, vague or large, or unanswerable. When I've taken this approach, I make sure to keep a shared spreadsheet (best if it is a shared Google Doc that students can edit) of student questions so I can track them from the start. This way, I can catch early on if a student has written a question that, from my experience, just won't work.

My students have written their own questions for essays at times over the past two years and I swear by the outcome. They also recognize the importance of this freedom in the learning. One student wrote that the most important thing she or he had learned was "to create well thought out questions based on what we were learning." Another student remarked that she had learned that "I never thought that choosing your own question could be so beneficial to producing a relevant essay." I read fascinating and unique papers that feel like first steps to historical scholarship.

Admittingly, I now work with a pretty high-skilled group of students. I do believe, however, that as my former colleague at Harvest Collegiate, Steve Lazar, maintains, all students can do this type of inquiry with the right support. I have learned as much about teaching from Steve as from anyone. Steve has taught social studies education at City College and was one of four teachers chosen to testify before the United States Senate on No Child Left Behind in 2015. Steve has a gruff exterior that hides an extremely compassionate heart, and the students love him for it. He is like the teacher in *Dangerous Minds*; not the terrible protagonist played by Michelle Pfeiffer who knows nothing about what she is doing and then quits after one year, but rather the wise veteran who gives her the answers, stays in the background, and continues in the classroom for decades. He has one of the sharpest minds of anyone I know; he's the type of person who I love to ask a question just to see his mind work out the answer.

Steve was fundamental in teaching me that we are better off moving students toward authentic inquiry than boxing them in. I regret that in my years teaching in urban public schools I so often drove down Default Route 1 by having all students answer my question. I wonder whether more students would have produced work that they cared about if I had allowed more choice, as I currently do. This seems to be one of the cases where students from elite socio-economic backgrounds are more likely to get the kind of engaging educational experience that education we want for our own kids than those in high-needs schools.

Writing Introductions: The Magical Camera

I walked around the room, fluorescent lights ablaze, as students began working on their essay. A few furiously scribbled down ideas. A couple of them put their heads down in despair. One boy called me over. "David," he asked in what I would soon learn was a common question, "how do I start my essay?"

I thought for a moment and then answered: "you need to hook your reader! Get the reader excited about reading the essay."

"How do I do that?" he responded.

I was stumped. Not for the last time. My pulse quickened and I felt a knot in my throat. I resorted to a traditional stalling tactic like a politician deferring the resolution of the problem for the next generation to take care of. "Go write the rest of the essay and then come back to the hook at the end," I replied. "Maybe then you'll figure it out." My stall was not even creative; I've heard countless teachers say the same thing.

How do we teach students to write introductions? Emily Haines is an incredible educator who was the lead teacher at the Facing History School when I taught there and who now teaches at the Laboratory School for Finance and Technology at the Bronx. Emily is extremely smart, soft-spoken, and humble, but when you're in her presence you know you're around educational mastery, even if she'd never say that. She was one of my first mentors, as she coached a group of teachers in my early years at the Facing History School. Emily came up with a great acronym for the structure of writing an introductory paragraph, which she called HITT. It stands for: Hook, Introduce Topic, Topic, Thesis. That being said, even that structure doesn't solve the problem of teaching students how to create a hook that really has pizzazz.

I needed to come to grips with the fact that I had no teaching tool to actually tell the student how to start an essay with a bang and hook a reader.

When I began my graduate program in history, I realized that I had my own strategy for beginning my essays and hooking the reader. I dissected what I was actually doing so then I could teach my students to do it. I came up with a name in a moment of inspiration, which has stuck ever since: the Magical Camera.

Everywhere I have gone as a teacher, the Magical Camera has trailed along beside me. It has been a fantastic teaching tool to share with other educators. In fact, it has probably been one of my best contributions as a colleague. Many of my colleagues might say that my creation of the Magical Camera is one of my best characteristics. Others say it is my set of stainless steel lunch tins.

Last year, when I asked students about the most important thing they learned in class, about half the students said it was to learn how to really write an introduction using the Magical Camera. This means either that the Magical Camera really works or that the rest of my teaching is pretty uninspiring. I didn't ask them for clarification on that question.

Here is an example of one Magical Camera hook that I wrote in graduate school for a paper on the British anti-slavery movement. As you're reading, try to determine the writing strategy that is making this introduction pop.

In Jamaica, late in the evening on July 31st, 1838, a group of black slaves gathered around a coffin filled with whips, chains, and an iron punishment collar. Their white minister, William Knibb, led them in prayers of thanks. The church walls were lined with pictures of famous abolitionists, such as Thomas Clarkson and William Wilberforce. Together, they lowered the coffin, inscribed with the words "Colonial Slavery, died July 31st, 1838, aged 276 years," into the earth. At midnight, Knibb called out "The monster is dead!" and the congregation applauded and cheered. After a fifty year struggle, slavery was abolished in the British West Indies and they were free. The cry of liberty was also one of gratitude to white Englishmen like Clarkson and Wilberforce – who had worked most of their lives to lead a mass movement in Britain to break the chains holding strangers across an ocean. In that church stood other men and women, black slaves, who had fought equally hard, albeit in a very different way, to bring the same struggle to fruition.

The Magical Camera technique asks writers to imagine the most powerful or gripping moment of the historical story that serves as the background or context of their piece. If the essay is about the French Revolution, the moment could be an execution during the Reign of Terror, the king arriving at the guillotine, or the parade of citizens at the Bastille proudly displaying the governor's head on a pike. If the story is the Holocaust, the moment could be when a Jewish mother is making the anguishing choice to send her children away on the kindertransport.

Now, imagine that you, the writer, were there at that moment, camera in hand. You took one picture. But this is a "Magical Camera" and it records every sense of that instant: the sound, smell, taste, emotion, touch, etc. Describe that moment in a few sentences or more. Describe all that the camera captures in minute detail. Focus on the sensory detail, including even metaphorical description, such as the "scent of despair." This writing strategy not only works beautifully to improve the vividness and quality of student introductions; it also makes the writing process joyful for the author.

One crucial characteristic of the Magical Camera is that the writer must describe the scene in the third person. The technique does not work in the first or second person, using "I" or "you" … it has to be about someone else, even if that someone else is imaginary. Additionally, the writer should not use quotations unless they are direct quotations from a source. After the Magical Camera hook, the writer then needs to transition into the essay's larger topic, question, and thesis.

Once I developed the strategy and began teaching it, I realized that this is really how many historians (and journalists who write history) begin their books. Consider this hook by Edwin Burrows, a Pulitzer Prize winning historian. It is from his book *Forgotten Patriots: The Untold Story of American Prisoners During the Revolutionary War*:

The biggest battle of the Revolutionary War began at the Red Lion Inn at around two o'clock in the morning of August 27, 1776. A passing cold front had put an unseasonable chill in the air, and the handful of American pickets posted nearby, sprigs of green tucked into their hats in lieu of proper uniforms, shivered and yawned while they watched for the enemy. Maybe they heard something beforehand – a muffled cough, horses blowing, the metallic ring of a sword being drawn from its scabbard …[1]

Or this hook, in Russell Shorto's wonderful book *The Island at the Center of the World*, the book that convinced me to write my master's thesis on Dutch colonial history. Shorto has perfected the art of journalist histories in which a superb writer unearths a somewhat ignored story and brings it to life. He opens his book with a vivid description of what must have been one of Henry Hudson's walks:

On a late summer's day in the year 1608, a gentleman of London made his way across that city. He was a man of ambition, intellect, arrogance, and drive – in short, a man of his age … He walked west, in the direction of St. Paul's Cathedral, which then, as now, dominated the skyline … The streets through which he walked were narrow, shadowy, claustrophobic, sloping toward the central sewer ditches.[2]

Once we teach students the Magical Camera, they can do it as well! Here is one student's Magical Camera introduction from a research paper on Race in American Ballet. Notice the sentence that transitions the introduction from the Magical Camera "hook" to the larger topic and then to the thesis:

It is 1955 and a young girl in a tutu stares at her reflection in a mirror. She smooths out the wrinkles in her white costume and greases back the fly-away hairs from her bun. Tears begin to well in her eyes as she takes one final glance at the one reflection with which she is familiar. She holds her breath and she picks up the sponge and powder sitting on her dresser. Layer by layer, she presses and plasters her skin with the color of snow. She becomes itchy and uncomfortable but knows that she must stand still in order for the powder settle on her dark skin. She looks in the mirror at the ghost standing before her. Blinking away the tears, she waits for her cue.

From Jackie Robinson to Barack Obama, America has witnessed the historical rise of exceptional African Americans who have achieved success in their respective fields, but the contributions and efforts of African Americans who have made strides in American dance, like the Ballerina above, are often not recognized. Because our society values entertainment in various forms, it is important for us to recognize how history has shaped these art forms. Equally critical, we must acknowledge the hardships that black dancers experienced and still confront today as they struggle to take the stage alongside predominantly white dancers and largely white audiences. Although several influential figures such as Alvin Ailey promoted equality in dance through the creation of opportunities that embraced traditional African dance, other art forms such as ballet have been "resistant to evolve beyond its roots as an elite, rigidly European art form" (Woodard). Despite the fact that the number of black dancers in American dance companies is slowly increasing, many forms of dance – ballet in particular – are far from being accepting and inclusive of African Americans.

Here is another example of the Magical Camera from a former student's paper on World War I trench warfare:

Powerful rain showers continue to flood trenches along the Western Front. The bare feet of soldiers are rooted to the swampy ground below, making any movement an elusive task. Explosions are heard coming from all directions, as the screams from wounded soldiers continue to intensify. While rats swim between soldiers legs, the powerful smell of rotting human flesh cause many to collapse. This description highlights only a small piece of what trenches were like during World War I. Beginning in 1914, an army's infantry spent most of their time inside of these confined spaces. While there was variety to the trenches, all of them managed to share one common element: A nightmarish lifestyle. Although many outsiders claimed that the trenches were wonderfully built structures, elaborate enough to protect the soldiers within, little did they know of the many horrors that soldiers endured within their habitation. Although trenches were strategically structured, and provided limited safety during battle, life within them was essentially unimaginable; The weather was detrimental, vermin seized the living space, and powerful explosions gave soldiers shell-shock. A soldier who spent merely one month in the trenches inevitably went home changed forever; both their mind and body completely deteriorated. What aspects of trench life could have possibly caused so much physical and mental damage? The combination of miserable weather, intruding rodents, and the bombardment of weaponry, worked together to cause depression, disease, shell-shock, and death. These horrific effects on the soldiers' well-being ultimately made life unbearable during WWI.

Writing Introductions: The Switcheroo

The Switcheroo is a bit more complicated to execute than the Magical Camera but it comes from the same family. I tell my students that the Switcheroo is like the Magical Camera's cousin … probably the cool, older, slightly brooding cousin who listens to indie music.

With the Switcheroo, the writer also uses the Magical Camera to describe a scene or person in detail. The reader thinks that she understands the topic being discussed. Suddenly, the writer reveals a surprise switch that the description was really about something else the whole time. This is why the Switcheroo is a bit harder, since it requires identifying a parallel between two people or situations, tricking the reader into thinking the piece is about one of them, and then weaving in the great reveal.

For example, an author may begin a piece by describing a terrible World War II epidemic of starvation and cruelty, in which parents tragically watch their children die in front of them. After five or six sentences, the reader naturally believes the narrative is about the Holocaust. In a twist, the writer reveals that the depiction is really about the Bengal Famine.

In a similar vein, some of my students wrote introductions about a racist leader during World War II who said terrible things about people who were of a different race. The reader, of course, assumes that the subject is Adolf Hitler. When the curtain is lifted, we find out the person is Winston Churchill, talking pejoratively about Indians. In this student's Switcheroo, you can see how she builds up assumptions that the introduction is depicting segregation in the United States, only to pull out the surprise:

> *A man pushes open the door to a restaurant. The impact of the smell of the food hit those outside, hard. A man with darker skin, starving, melts with hunger after just a single breath in. Temptation building up, he almost pushes the door open himself, just as the man before him did mere seconds ago. Almost. But instead, he didn't. He couldn't. The sign above the door, taunting and cruel, forbade him. Stomach empty already and heart growing emptier by the day, he left his spot on the street and continued walking. While the segregation depicted in this scene can apply to that of the deep South, the intent was to portray what it was like for Indians under the British rule. In the British's attempts to keep the Indians below them, they were segregated and discriminated against harshly. Such treatment was present all throughout the time of Britain's colonization of India. Efforts to make a difference, lead by civil disobedience leader Mohandas Gandhi ultimately resulted in India achieving independence and freeing themselves from the British.*

Assuming you've memorized every word of this book, you will recall the introduction. If not, flip back to the first page. When I discussed my favorite history source, you were meant to believe I was talking about a book. However, I was really using the Switcheroo. The favorite source was actually a painting and the "author" was Pablo Picasso.

Many nimble writers use the Switcheroo. Here is the introduction to a *New York Times* article called "The Only Answer is Less Internet" by Ross Douthat:

> In our age of digital connection and constantly online life, you might say that two political regimes are evolving, one Chinese and one Western, which offer two kinds of relationships between the privacy of ordinary citizens and the newfound power of central authorities to track, to supervise, to expose and to surveil.
>
> The first regime is one in which your every transaction can be fed into a system of ratings and rankings, in which what seem like merely personal mistakes can cost you your livelihood and reputation, even your ability to hail a car or book a reservation. It's one in which notionally private companies cooperate with the government to track dissidents and radicals and censor speech; one in which your fellow citizens act as enforcers of the ideological consensus, making an example of you for comments you intended only for your friends; one in which even the wealth and power of your overlords can't buy privacy.
>
> The second regime is the one they're building in the People's Republic of China.[3]

You can see here how Douthat leads the reader to believe that the first regime he is discussing is China. He expertly weaves in notions of surveillance and ideological uniformity, which we normally associate with China. His Switcheroo, at the end, let's us know that he was really depicting the United States and Western Europe. This should make us think. And worry.

One of the beautiful aspects of learning the Magical Camera and the Switcheroo is that they are transferable strategies; they work not only for social studies papers but also for English essays, personal statements for college, and even how we might produce digital history like films and documentaries.

Writing Introductions: Club Over the Head and Other Strategies

The Magical Camera and the Switcheroo are my go-to introduction techniques that I teach to my students and my hope is that they can leave my course with a mastery of the Magical Camera. They are particularly useful because with a bit of thought and preparation, writers can always use them to start off their pieces with a vivid, gripping hook. There are, of course, other techniques as well for hooking the reader and I share these with my students also.

The "Club Over the Head" is a move in which the writer smacks the reader over the head with a blunt, direct, short, and often folksy statement. Most of the examples below are from journalists, particularly from the *New York Times*, but that is probably because journalists are often great writers.

> From Ross Douthat: "Fair warning: This will be an entire column about a single paragraph."

> From Paul Krugman: "O.K., they weren't supposed to start the trade war until I got back from vacation."

> From Charles M. Blow: "Saturday night I went to the opera."

> From David Brooks' book *The Second Mountain*[4]: "Every once in a while, I meet a person who radiates joy."

> And here's one of mine, from my own college essay: "I guess I talk kind of slow. Or maybe it's the way I pronounce my words."

I find it a bit dangerous for students to start off pieces with quotations, which is sometimes a standard hook strategy. Often they choose quotations that are cliché or ahistorical. Nonetheless, a powerful or absurd quotation can do much to start a written piece off with a bang.

> From Paul Krugman: "'I love the poorly educated.' So declared Donald Trump …"

> From Nicholas Kristoff: "'I hereby sentence you to death.' The words of Judge Clifford B. Shepard filled the courtroom in Jacksonville, Fla., on October 27, 1976."

Writing Introductions: The Thesis

Most teachers agree on the consensus that a thesis statement ought to be concise, specific, and arguable. Where there is a bit of interesting debate is whether or not a thesis needs to appear as the last line in the introduction paragraph. For some, urging students to place their thesis in the expected place ensures that it will be easier for the reader to identify the assertion and then to follow the larger thread of the argument.

I generally encourage my students to place their thesis there if only so they don't get in trouble later on with other teachers. That being said, I also let them know that I am more flexible and have no problem with finding a thesis elsewhere. In authentic writing that is longer than five paragraphs, such as journal articles and books, the thesis by no means comes at the end of the first paragraph. For example, a bold thesis can also function well as the hook of a piece of writing, finding its place in the first sentence.

I also love writing that presents a question in the introduction and leaves the answer hanging. In this format, the writer winds through the evidence over the course of the paper and then finally reveals the ultimate answer, the thesis, in the conclusion.

Writing Body Paragraphs: Tying Students into the TIED Format

The crux of most work in writing instruction is on the body paragraphs. Teachers and researchers have developed a spectrum of practices for supporting students in writing historical body paragraphs. These range from crossing our fingers and hoping for the best, which was my first strategy, to very specific scaffolds for gathering evidence and structuring paragraphs. Naturally, my experience has shown that teachers who work with struggling writers tend toward more scaffolding and those who work with stronger writers tend toward a more hands-off approach. The goal in high school is also to provide more organizational support in 9th and 10th grade before subsequently weaning students off those scaffolds in the upper grades.

It is important to recognize that we often stifle high-needs students by not giving them choice and agency, by not teaching transferable skills like the Magical Camera, and by limiting their voice. When we begin with the presumption that the students can't do the real thing, and then we create too many artificial hoops for them to jump through, by the end they are often so lost and exhausted that there is little reason or chance for them to produce anything that is genuine.

The challenge for teachers is to find the right balance and the right scaffolds for their students. Some of us work with students who won't put pen to paper without intense support. Others have students who will write beautiful ten-page papers with almost no guidance whatsoever. I've had both those types of students. The trick is to realize that we often have some version of both of those students in our classes and sometimes both those versions in the same student. We have students for whom writing is a joy and those for whom it is as torturous as folding a fitted sheet.

Writing scaffolds are wonderful tools but each additional scaffold boxes the author in, sometimes literally, and prevents them from developing the kind of natural, fluid writing process that is actually authentic. That's the rub: when do we give the scaffolds? To whom? How much? What type?

This is when a term like "individualized education" really means something. We need to know what each student requires in order to provide the writing support that will allow each to flourish. Sometimes, the amount of pre-writing scaffolding can get so exhausting and overwhelming that it is no wonder that by the time the student has finished the preparation, he has no more interest or energy to do the actual writing.

I am not familiar with every effective writing scaffold and do not pretend to offer a definitive account. The one that I have used consistently, which I learned at the Facing History School, is called TIED writing. The name is catchy and easy to memorize. It is relatively simple and does indeed follow the generic structure of a basic historical paragraph. It is also easily adaptable for a particular teacher's practice. For example, I changed the meaning of the letter "I" to fit what I believed was necessary in student writing and to provide a bit more clarity.

I don't know where TIED originally came from and so I, unfortunately, don't know who deserves the credit. I spoke to Emily Haines, and asked her where TIED came from. According to her, she learned TIED from an Engligh teacher at the Beacon School and then brought it over to FHS. Here is the basic structure of the paragraph:

T – Topic
I – Important background information
E – Evidence (quotation or specific information to support topic)
D – Discuss the evidence and connect back to topic

This is a strong, foundational paragraph structure. It works. There are many different ways to teach students how to do it. You can model the writing of a paragraph on a topic of interest, such as: who is the best basketball player in the world? You can use models of student paragraphs. Dissect them as a class to identify the different parts. You can also provide other organizational scaffolds before the writing, especially to help students gather the evidence. Below is the basic TIED document that I created to give to students, those who actually write their first draft within the scaffolding boxes. I no longer use these scaffolds because I've evolved toward a more flexible approach to writing, but for those who are searching for paragraph scaffolding these may be helpful. Note that I provide some sentence starters below to help students learn how to integrate their evidence fluidly by providing source information.

Topic	_____ _____ _____ _____ _____ _____ _____
Important background information – Background on topic/ evidence	_____ _____ _____ _____ _____ _____ _____ _____ _____ _____
Evidence – Quote or specific information – Use quote set-up sentence starters	_____ _____ _____ _____ _____ _____ (_____).
Discuss Evidence – Use sentence starter – Show how your evidence supports the topic	_____ _____ _____ _____ _____ _____ _____ _____ _____

Sentence Starters as Quote Set-up

According to Hiram Bingham, "…" (Bingham 21).

In Jared Diamond's view "…" (Diamond 37).

Bernal Diaz de Castillo writes that "…" (Diaz de Castillo 24).

Henry Louis Gates Jr. explains that "…" (Marchese).

Barack Obama argues that "…" (Waldham).

The clothing historian Robert Ross maintains that "…" (Ross 18).

The book *Long Walk to Freedom* states "…" (Mandela).

Once students become better at using TIED, I try to break them out of the repetitive format. First, some students can just write without any scaffolding. But for those who still need some, one way to do so is by providing an "Anyorder TIED document," which lets them know that writers actually play around with the order in which they place key components in a paragraph. Great writers don't utilize a single structure, repetitively, for each paragraph. Here's what that document looks like:

TIED/EDIT/DIET Paragraph Writing

You can actually write a paragraph with these steps in any order!

Important background information - Background on topic/evidence	Evidence - Quote or specific information - Use quote set-up sentence starters from cover page
Topic	Discuss Evidence - Show how your evidence supports the topic

Sentence Starters as Quote Set-up

According to Hiram Bingham, A Yale University Archaeologist, "…" (Bingham 21).

Jared Diamond is a world famous historian. In his view "…" (Diamond 37).

Bernal Diaz de Castillo, a Spanish conquistador and author of *Discovery*, writes that "…" (Diaz de Castillo 24).

Henry Louis Gates Jr., a Harvard professor, explains that "…" (Marchese).

Plutarch, a 2nd century Roman historian, argues that "…" (Waldham).

The clothing historian Robert Ross maintains that "…" (Ross 18).

Writing Body Paragraphs: Quotations vs. Paraphrasing

I have always encouraged students to use quotations because I see them as an authentic part of historical writing. In order to select quotations, students are forced to return to their sources and sift through them, thereby engaging in real historical work. The interplay between quotation (as evidence) and analysis becomes an interesting juggle in the final task of writing.

I recently had a conversation with a few colleagues, however, that challenged my viewpoint. They argued that paraphrasing is more authentic to the field, especially when working with secondary sources, and that paraphrasing allows students to better use their voice and present their own understanding. At first I disagreed, although after more reflection I've found myself staking out a new position. While I'm not sure I agree that paraphrasing is more authentic than quoting, there does seem to be a value in getting students to differentiate between their use of primary and secondary sources by more frequently quoting the former and paraphrasing the latter.

More importantly, I'm a bit stuck once the argument goes in the direction of student voice. Now I'm in a dilemma between the authenticity of selecting and using quotations and the crucial act of providing conditions for student voice, both of which I value. This is one of those times where we, as teachers, need to weigh competing values.

Ultimately, I believe I need to shift my practice toward getting students to more explicitly paraphrase secondary sources and I think the point about student voice is undeniable.

Writing Body Paragraphs: Concessions

The ultimate prize of nuance in writing is getting students to acknowledge another viewpoint. When I learned to write, my teachers told us to take up an argument and defend it wholly. Now, we ask students to explain another point of view. At the Facing History School, we called it an "opposing argument." At Harvest, it was the "counterclaim" or "multiple perspectives." In Scarsdale High School, it is called a concession. The term matters less, but the idea has tremendous importance.

There is an important distinction between a paper that makes a case and denies an alternate viewpoint and one that acknowledges there is another side. The latter adds complexity, nuance, and empathy to the discussion. The act of asking students to recognize the other's point of view forces them to think deeply and empathetically. In this sense, it is not merely a writing convention but also training to be a citizen and a person who can hear another point of view.

The concession can happen at a number of points in the writing. It may become part of the thesis, thereby creating an argument that is, itself, nuanced and incorporative of multiple perspectives. It can occur as a first body paragraph, setting up the opposing point of view before delving into the assertion. It may occur throughout the essay, perhaps as the first sentence of various body paragraphs. Or, the writer might place a counterclaim as a final body paragraph. Sometimes the concession is used as a counterweight ultimately to sharpen the actual thesis; other times the writer might actually give some ground to the opposing perspective.

Writing Conclusions: The RICE Bowl

What makes for a strong conclusion in historical writing? For many years, I struggled with this question in the same way that I did with introductions. And I hemmed and I hawed when students asked for guidance.

After many conversations with educators about this problem, and after reading historical works with an eye on figuring out what real writers were actually doing, I developed four main elements that lead toward a healthy conclusion, which I call a RICE bowl. It is not necessary or even advantageous for a writer to attempt all four elements in one conclusion. It is most likely better to do one or two of them more thoughtfully. I also believe it is perfectly fine for students to write in the first person in the conclusion since so many published authors do so. Here are the steps:

R – Restate the main argument and foundational reasons why you support the argument.

I – Importance … why is this topic important and significant? Why was it important to the people at the time? Why is it important for understanding our world today? Why is it important morally? Why is important within the larger historical conversation?

C – Connections … how does this topic and argument connect to other stories from the past? How does it connect to the world today? How does it connect to the author?

E – Expanding … what else do you want to know? What questions are left for you to answer? Where would you go if you had more time to research and write?

Below, I have an example of a piece of my own writing from that same essay about the British anti-slavery movement and Caribbean slave rebellions. Try to identify the four grains of RICE in the conclusion.

Abolition was a victory won by both white abolitionists and black slaves. The relationship for various groups across the sea was complex and cyclical. The process revealed an Atlantic system in which news and ideas travelled across the sea alongside goods. The zeniths and nadirs of the abolition and antislavery movements clearly influenced blacks' ambitions toward liberty – the successes stoked desires and the failures stoked frustrations. Moreover, slaves influenced each other with their choices, as each rebellion provided other groups with information and examples to inform their choices. Conversely, the choice to rebel had a spectrum of effects on the abolition movement. The initial massacres of the St. Domingue insurrection impaired the efforts of Clarkson and his allies. The later rebellions, though, served to highlight the injustices of the system without overloading white fears. As Hillary Beckles maintains, "By rebelling, Africans in the West Indies made their contribution to the long drawn out international debate on the abolition of slavery." In the end, over the fifty year struggle, it would take the cooperation of two vastly different groups, separated by an ocean, skin-color, and social class, to overcome the obstacles and defeat slavery. While most of them never met in person, they met the challenge together.

In my view, I only really include two grains: restate and importance. As I mentioned earlier, however, using only a couple of grains is fine. As long as you have one type of grain, if it is cooked well, you can still have a good RICE bowl. Here I really tried to emphasize the importance of the two movements, the British protests and the slave rebellions, and how the juxtaposition of those two forces really allowed for incredible change in human history.

In his wonderful book *Range*, David Epstein nicely shows how to use the conclusion to restate and establish importance. He begins by mentioning that people who he spoke to during his research asked for advice on specialization vs. range. This establishes importance. Midway through his conclusion, he writes:

> *The question I set out to explore was how to capture and cultivate the power of breadth, diverse experience, and interdisciplinary exploration, within systems that increasingly demand hyperspecialization, and would have you decide what you should be before first figuring out who you are ... So, about that one sentence of advice: Don't feel behind ... approach your own personal voyage and projects like Michaelangelo approached a block of marble, willing to learn and adjust as you go, and even to abandon a previous goal and change directions entirely should the need arise.[5]*

Epstein is a beautiful writer, and he takes us along on his journey – where he started, where he ended up, and what his advice could be. He doesn't just restate, he retells and reframes and he serves up the "importance" by providing advice. By talking about his own journey in writing this book, he is also making a connection – connecting the topic to himself and connecting us, as the readers, to him as a person.

The final paragraph of Edwin Burrows' conclusion in *Forgotten Patriots* is another wonderful example of how to extract and emphasize the importance of the topic before letting go of your reader. Burrows writes:

> *We hear much nowadays about the wisdom and virtue of the 'founding fathers,' but the story of those dreadful places obliges us to keep in mind that the success of the Revolution depended on the unheralded spirit, selflessness, and humanity of thousands of people not so very different from ourselves.[6]*

Ultimately, he is making the assertion that there needs to be a correction in Revolutionary War historiography, to move away from hagiography of the founders and look more toward the impact of ordinary men and women. This is what he attempted to do in the book and that is why his topic, and the role of those regular people, was important.

Russell Shorto's conclusion of *The Island at the Center of the World* similarly weaves together restating, importance, and connections. He spends most of the conclusion connecting Dutch New York to the more well-known Puritan founding story and to make various connections between the story of the

Dutch colony and the later cultural traits, such as pluralism, evident in New York City. Then he reminds us that it is fine to be direct to make sure the reader gets the point.

> *That's why the story of the original Manhattan colony matters. Its impact is so diffuse that it would be perilous to declare and define it too concretely, so here is a modest attempt: it helped set the whole thing in motion ... The legacy of the people who settled Manhattan Island rides below the level of myth and politics.[7]*

His whole book is an attempt to resurrect the story of New Amsterdam and why it was significant. Thus, by highlighting the importance, Shorto is also simultaneously restating the thesis.

Students can do this too! Here is one student's RICE bowl conclusion about her paper on Jewish athletes during the Holocaust. Her voice comes through vividly as she makes connections between the topic, herself, and contemporary politics. She grapples with current antisemitism as well as the moral complexities athletes must face during times of crisis. Ultimately, by doing so she also identifies the importance of the issue for her own life and for the larger Holocaust histogriography.

> *After researching all these different athletes, I conclude that the Holocaust did impact the lives of many Jewish athletes. For athletes at the Olympic level, sports is more than just an activity to keep busy and maintain a healthy lifestyle. For these athletes, sports becomes their passion and consumes their entire life. They train their entire lives in order to compete at the top level around the world. When we think of the Holocaust, the stories of these athletes are never mentioned. Most of their stories are untold which is sad because many of these athletes dedicated their entire lives to excelling in their sport and reaching the Olympics. These athletes then made the difficult decision to give up their dreams, based on their beliefs for what was right at the time. Today, anti-semitism is still going on all around the world including right here in the United States. People are getting killed in houses of worship while praying just because they are Jewish. Just last week in San Diego, California, a woman was killed in her local synagogue on Passover. This topic relates to me because I am a Jewish athlete training to one day compete internationally and represent my country. I think about what I would have done if I was in that situation during the 1936 Olympics, and if I would have boycotted or competed. If I put myself in the shoes of these Jewish athletes that did compete in 1936 Games, I would give them the benefit of the doubt that they did not know the full extent of*

the Holocaust and the terrible events that were taking place. Knowing now how horrific the Holocaust was, I would never do anything to support the Nazis and would not have competed. This boycott of the Olympics would hopefully send a message to the Nazis that what they were doing was terrible and that one is willing to sacrifice their dreams to demonstrate what is right. Anti-semitism and discrimination should have no place in our society today and I hope that, in time, people will no longer be judged and hated for who they are and what they believe in.

Authentic Assessment: Formal Essay

Task: Write an essay that answers the historical question of your choice about the topic.

Skeleton of the essay:
- ★ Introduction with gripping hook, topic, and thesis/argument
- ★ Body paragraphs (three to five) exploring support for your thesis as well as other perspectives or counterclaims
- ★ Conclusion
- ★ Works Cited page

Make sure to use your readings from class *and* from homework as evidence to support your claim.

Guidelines: In your writing, be sure to …

- ◆ Develop a thesis that provides your position on the topic.
- ◆ Provide supporting reasons for your argument.
- ◆ Make sure your argument considers other possibilities or thesis.
- ◆ Use relevant evidence from multiple sources from this unit and your knowledge to support your argument.
- ◆ Provide analysis of how each piece of evidence supports, extends, or challenges your thesis and reasons.
- ◆ Write three to six pages typed, double spaced, MLA 8 format.
- ◆ Cite where necessary and include a Works Cited page.

For writing tips and examples, visit davidsherrin.net and look at "historical skills."

Formal Essay and Research Paper Rubric*

Learning Goal	Jedi	Samurai	Apprentice
Introduction	– Gripping, vivid hook – Clear specific topic and subtopics – Establishes and develops a compelling, elegant, specific and/or very original question/thesis and its significance	– Standard direct opening to essay – Clear topic – Establishes and develops knowledgeable thesis	– No thesis is present or includes a vague thesis – No clear topic
Selection of Evidence	– Supplies a wide variety of the most relevant, specific, accurate, verifiable, and highly convincing evidence for claim(s) & counterclaim – Expertly paraphrases and quotes where appropriate depending on the type of source and wording – Uses a variety of strong sources including books, journal article, and primary sources – Develops counterclaims or complexities fairly and thoroughly; responds to counterclaims in ways that sharpen the claim	– Supplies some relevant evidence that supports claim(s) – Mostly paraphrases and quotes where appropriate although relies a bit heavily on one – Relies on a few basic secondary and tertiary sources – Develops main points of counterclaims or identifies some complexities or multiples viewpoints	– Supplies reasoning for claims & counterclaim, but no evidence (or) – Overly relies on quotations – Evidence presented does not seem to support claims & counterclaim – Does not acknowledge alternate claims

(continued)

Learning Goal	Jedi	Samurai	Apprentice
Use of Evidence and Argument	– Clearly and thoroughly explains and analyzes how evidence presented supports, extends, or challenges each claim and reasons – Overall evidence, reasons, and analysis strongly supports a coherent and complex argument	– Explains how the evidence presented supports, extends, or challenges each claim and reasons – Overall evidence, reasons, and analysis supports the argument	– There is a basic explanation of how the evidence presented supports each claims – Overall evidence, reasons, and analysis tells a story without a strong argument thread
Historical Context and Accuracy	– Arguments, ideas, and voice reflect a highly informed awareness of how claims fit and relate to the larger context – Correct and specific factual accuracy and chronology that demonstrates a deep understanding of the complexity of the historical content. – Discussion of most important topics and events related to the argument	– Arguments, ideas, and voice reflect general awareness of how claims fit and relate to the larger context – Mostly factual accuracy that demonstrates an understanding of the historical content – Discussion of some of the important topics and events related to argument	– Arguments, ideas, and voice reflect flawed awareness of larger context – No factual information – Errors in major understandings and.or historical details
Organization	– Organization efficiently sequences and synthesizes claims, counterclaims, and evidence to fluidly support argument	– Solid organizational structure with slight disorganization in ideas, chronology, or argument	– Essay is unorganized or lacks clear structure

Sourcing	– Provides deep evaluation of perspective/bias and credibility of sources	– Identifies authorship of sources	– Does not identify correct authorship of sources
Mechanics and Voice	– Sharp, relevant, creative title – Integrates evidence naturally and fluidly – Maintains a vivid, powerful tone, achieving precision in language, and crafting succinct, elegant prose – Perfect standardized English grammar – Includes correct citations for a variety of quality sources – Includes comprehensive bibliography with perfect formatting	– Title that describes core focus of essay – Integrates evidence with lead-in – Maintains an appropriate style by attending to the norms of the discipline – Approaching precision in language with a few slight difficulties in capitalization, punctuation – Nearly perfect standardized English grammar throughout – Includes citations for a variety of sources – Includes bibliography with mostly correct formatting	– No title – Awkwardly integrates evidence into a larger sentence – Plagiarizes – Style is inappropriate (too informal, incorrect genre, etc) – Language lacks clarity in word choice – Does not use citations for quoted or paraphrased evidence
Conclusion	– Expertly uses the conclusion to summarize, raise new questions, make connections, and/or explain the topic's importance	– Uses the conclusion to summarize, and make a few basic points to raise new questions, make connections, and/or explain the topic's importance	– Uses the conclusion to summarize – Does not develop the conclusion

* I created the first versions of this rubric along with my social studies colleagues who helped found Harvest Collegiate: Faye Colon, Steve Lazar, and Andy Snyder. When doing so, we pored over writing standards produced by the C3 Framework, the New York Performance Standards Consortium, and the Common Core. While I have made modifications along the way much of the credit for language and learning standards goes to them.

Notes

1 Burrows, E. G. (2010). *Forgotten patriots: the untold story of american prisoners during the revolutionary war*. New York: Basic Books.
2 Shorto, R. (2005). *The island at the center of the world*. New York: Vintage Books.
3 Douthat, R. (2019, April 13). The only answer is less internet. Retrieved October 7, 2019, from www.nytimes.com/2019/04/13/opinion/china-internet-privacy.html.
4 Brooks, D. (2019). *The second mountain*. London: Allen Lane.
5 Epstein, D. (2019). *Range: why generalists triumph in a specialized world*. New York: Riverhead Books.
6 Burrows, E. G. (2010). *Forgotten patriots: the untold story of american prisoners during the revolutionary war*. New York: Basic Books.
7 Shorto, R. (2005). *The island at the center of the world*. New York: Vintage Books.

3

Research Papers

A research paper is the Holy Grail of social studies authentic assessment. (Research writing is possibly the most difficult task we ask students to perform, but that is also because it most authentically mirrors how most historians have traditionally produced their work) searching out answers to their own questions and producing their results in formal writing. Just like the Holy Grail, however, the authentic research paper is not so easy to uncover in the high school classroom. Too often, we hear the wise voice whispering "you chose poorly …" as our hard work and hopes seem to crumble to dust before us.* In this chapter, I hope to help you choose wisely so as to find that Holy Grail.

After reading the chapter, use the following chart as a plan to "keep the learning real"

How will students determine their research topics and questions for your class?
What will be the source requirements for the students?
To what extent and how will you use outlines, peer-editing, and teacher feedback in the process?

---

* If you don't recognize the reference, please take the time to watch *Indiana Jones and the Last Crusade*. I'm totally fine if you put aside the book to do so.

True research takes considerable classroom and homework time away from content and basic skill-building. When students struggle with foundational skills, it is reasonably hard to muster the nerve to move them onto the more complex task. This is why we so often find research turning into a shell of the real task, and students submitting research papers that are no more than glorified versions of the traditional five-paragraph unit essay.

I'm not blaming teachers here. Any failure that I mention in this book always connects to a way in which I have failed in the past or continue to do so in the present.(In the case of research papers, the problem emerges when we value the quality of the final product far more than the process, and by doing so we overly scaffold the experience in order to obtain a suitable outcome.)As the saying goes, more or less, too often we prepare the road for the student rather than the student for the road.

With research papers we tend to observe the same three camps as in regular essay writing:((1) all students answer the exact same question on the same topic; (2) students have limited choice or differ only in the particular case that fills in the blank of a shared question; (3) students have complete or nearly complete freedom to pursue independent inquiry and historical research.)

Over the course of my career, I have traveled all of these avenues to get students to complete their research papers, but you ought to surmise that I now find myself squarely in camp #3. All of the approaches are authentic, but it is the third path that really meets the criteria of JADE assessments.

Interestingly, even in very progressive educational settings, we might often find many teachers who work with struggling students taking path #1 and providing uniform research tasks; similarly, in progressive settings with high-skilled students we observe the same dynamic, especially to allow for uniform grading practices. When I taught in New York Consortium schools, such as the Facing History School, the social studies research paper, or PBAT, served as the graduation requirement instead of the Regents exam. This liberation from high-stakes testing was thrilling, but it was not liberation from high-stakes assessment. The research paper became the high-stakes assessment. Thus the quality of the final product, more than the authenticity of the process itself, turned into the pot of gold.

Consequently, I heavily scaffolded my students' work and backwards designed courses around one argumentative research question. One year, my American History students all did a research paper on the Civil Rights Movement, something along the lines of whether the movement helped America finally live up to its founding values. Another year, everyone answered a question about the Progressive Era: was the period a time of progress for Americans?

In these heavily directed research assignments, much of the work happened in class and involved sharing resources. The students then each added in a paragraph or two based on their own individual research to answer the question and mix in their personal touch. They mostly completed the work and passed the high-stakes assessment, but I doubt the experience was very meaningful for anyone involved.

When I moved on to Harvest Collegiate (Steve Lazar) heavily influenced my views on student research. Steve is the strongest proponent of student inquiry I have met and he holds extremely passionate views. He argues, convincingly and persistently, that all students can and should do real research regardless of their skill levels. He maintains that if the really hard part for them is the writing, then we could have them do real research and then, especially in the 9th and 10th grades, find a different form of producing their work, such as oral presentations. As in every good social studies department, not everyone at Harvest agreed with Steve's fervent advocacy for student inquiry. Some maintained that the quality of student work suffered when they had too much flexibility. Steve generally countered that the problem with the output was not the open format but rather the support students received within that framework, arguing that student interest and motivation, stemming from their authentic inquiry, generally would produce better work.

At Harvest I taught some of the widest range of students imaginable and I generally opted for an open inquiry framework within the context of the semester course's theme. For example, in my course "Genocide and Justice" the students could choose to write about any genocide and/or choose a compelling lens to dig deeper into the history. I read wonderful papers about women in the Rwandan genocide, the use of clothing as a symbol in genocides, and the issue of justice in the Armenian genocide. And I read some not-so-wonderful papers. Similarly, in my course on "Sports, Fashion, and Politics," I was amazed to see work on soccer and social class and the use of clothing in resistance movements.

My experience has shown, however, that if I had chosen the particular question and required all students to write under my direct supervision, I probably would have a similar spread in quality. The difference here is that with true inquiry the students gained the experience of doing authentic historical research, they did work that interested them, and I got to read unique papers that really told me something about the students and what they cared about.

When I began teaching at Scarsdale High School, one commonality in the department is that all 10th and 11th grade classes do research papers, although there is some variance in terms of how teachers engage their students in that process. Our students are generally quite high-skilled and motivated, which in my view is a perfect recipe for camp #3: the open inquiry research. When working with students who will comply with the research checkpoints and who have a drive to do well in school, it seems to me that one of our primary roles ought to be to take the lid off of the box, to allow them to pursue answers to their own questions, and to perform authentic work in the discipline. No one tells a historian what question to answer: she needs to figure out the right question to ask, which is another form of rigor.

(Allowing for independent inquiry also means that students get to pursue something of personal relevance, which might not be the case otherwise.) Students who love fashion can do a project on the history of clothes in protest movements, looking at Gandhi, Kwame Nkrumah, and the Nadar women of India. Students who love music might look at 1980s British pop and the questioning of gender identity. Gay students might choose to begin their studies of LGBTQ history by understanding the evolution of Gay culture from Weimar to Nazi Germany. Jewish students can dig deeper into Jewish history and look at resistance movements in the Holocaust. (A student might develop a question based around an interview of a grandparent.) Or students who love sports might do a paper on soccer, cricket, and British colonialism.

(Those topics, by the way, are all fascinating areas of research that my students have pursued on their own initiative and turned into superb papers that taught me something valuable about the past.)

The Research Process

(There is no single "correct" way for students to conduct research in your classroom.) I don't think it is necessary for me to elaborate on path #1 (the teacher-directed strategy of research) since such a format is highly dependent on the individual curricular choices around which you might frame your question. Path #1, moreover, would more closely mirror whatever writing process you have developed for unit-length essays.

If you want to do student-directed inquiry and a more open-ended research process, the following ten steps ought to be helpful. As always, you might need to provide more detailed scaffolding within each step for your students depending on their skill level and their prior experience with research. Think of what follows as the bare-bones approach to student research projects, and don't be afraid to add more meat onto it as needed.

I normally spend about one class period per step with my students. I give a brief tutorial and then provide time for them, right away, to get to work putting that research step into action and to meet with me for guidance.

Step 1: Choosing the Topic

Students' topics should be of personal and intellectual interest to them. It may be something they have heard about in class or in life that sparked an interest. It may be related to hobbies like soccer or art, something important to their identity (religion, gender, sexual orientation, etc.), or something the class touched on briefly that they'd like to explore further. Below are some ways students can go about choosing a topic.

These suggested lenses, when combined with many historical events or periods, help to sharpen the focus toward a strong question:

1 Fashion
2 Music
3 Leadership
4 Art and/or dance
5 Women or gender
6 Gay (LGBTQ) studies
7 Sports
8 Propaganda
9 Education
10 Religion
11 Film
12 Justice
13 Social Class
14 Race

One of my students created an online code that allowed us to mix and match lenses with historical events. He called it the "Sherrinator."[1] Essentially, students hit enter and the website then makes the combinations, such as "Fashion in Nazi Germany" or "Women in the Soviet Union" or "Sports in the Cold War" or "Education in Communist China." The simple connection between lenses and time/place makes for great topics.

Step 2: Finding Tertiary Sources

Tertiary sources are descriptions of people and events that are encyclopedic in nature. Database overviews and general website sources like history.com are usually tertiary sources. Tertiary sources rarely make an argument; they are just telling us the "what" and the "when." We usually begin our research with tertiary sources to gain context for the topic, basic comprehension, and to understand what sub-topics we need to further investigate.

If your school or public library provides access to databases, they are usually the best places to start. For example, at Scarsdale, I begin student research by pointing them to "World History in Context" and "Biography in Context."

Students with a public library card can often access databases on the library website. One of the useful functions of databases is that they provide automatic citations for the students and can email them the full text of any article along with the citation.

A second option for tertiary sources is a basic Google search. Here are my tips:

- Keep it simple. Describe what you want in as few terms as possible.
- Use descriptive and specific words.
- Make sure the website looks professional and authoritative. Check the "about" link to see if there is any important bias that needs to be considered. Check with me if you have doubts.

The third option is to go straight to general internet sources that we know provide reliable historical information. A few of my favorites are below. Additionally, students who are researching a topic like the Holocaust can go directly to a comprehensive tertiary source on that topic, such as the United States Holocaust Memorial Museum's Holocaust Encyclopedia.

- PBS.com
- historychannel.com
- biography.com

Step 3: Determining the Research Question

Spending some time with students, after they have read background sources, to talk about their research questions is essential, especially if you are cultivating true inquiry. I create a spreadsheet for my class, using Google Drive, which allows us all to see each other's topics and questions. This also permits me to keep track, to stay on top of changes in topics and questions (which should happen for some students), and to address any concerns about vague or superficial questions. Here are the three tips I provide students, although sometimes it is hard for them to really answer them and they need a peer conference or a check-in with me to be sure about their question.

- Is the question engaging and interesting?
- Is this a real question that experts or thoughtful adults struggle with?
- Are there at least two possible answers to this question? Is it debatable?

Step 4: Finding Books

I insist that students use two books as sources for their research. They may not read the entire book, but the ambiance of the classroom becomes more meaningful, weighty, and authentic when they dig into a book. This is especially the case, nowadays, since so much intellectual work happens (or pretends to happen) through the internet.

I point students toward three locations to find books: (1) the high school library; (2) the local public library; (3) Amazon. I remind them that the books may be very specifically related to their question or the books may be used to help establish context about the larger topic. For instance, in a paper on women in the Rwandan genocide, it is preferable if students get a book with testimonies of women who survived the genocide; however, they could also use a book that serves as an overview of the genocide, thereby contributing to their background information.

A crucial point: although I point students to Amazon, I never expect or encourage students to buy a book for the project. Instead, Amazon has a great search engine for finding books that may not immediately appear in the library's database search engine. Thus, once they've found a suitable book on Amazon, they can subsequently return to the search for that specific title in the library, as it may not have appeared in their library catalogue "subject" search but now it does show up in a "title" search.

Here's some information to look for about the books:

◆ Read the description. Books should be highly reviewed, have four to five stars in the reviews, be at an accessible reading level, and cover the topic.
◆ Number of pages (shoot for 150–400).
◆ Age level (Grade 9 and up).
◆ Publisher (look for a popular press rather than a university press for a high school research paper).
◆ Author's qualifications.

Step 5: Finding Journal Articles

Journal articles are academic texts written for an academic audience. I require students to find and use two journal articles, recognizing that they will often be difficult reads for the students. To find journal articles, my students use JSTOR, but it is important for them to recognize that JSTOR is not the actual journal when they cite the article, but rather the database that finds the journal.

This is probably the most "optional" step in this research process. I'm not sure I would have had all students in all my schools use journal articles, but it is certainly a worthwhile intellectual endeavor for many learners. Many students will simply pick out one to two sentences for their paper. Once in a while, a journal article can become a crucial source for a student.

Step 6: Reading or Raiding

Once students have books and journal articles in their hands, they need to decide whether to ("read" or to "raid" them. Reading a book means going from cover to cover, and taking it all in. "Raiding a book" is a strategy that I learned from Michael Rawson, who was my professor in graduate school and was the runner-up for the Pulitzer Prize in History for his book *Eden on the Charles: The Making of Boston* (By raiding, he means selectively looking for what might help you in your own writing.)

Here are Some Clues About Whether to Read or Raid a Book:

- ◆ The book is relatively short, accessible, and directly related to the question = READ.
- ◆ The book is a memoir, a story, something that isn't linear in its storytelling = READ.
- ◆ The book is extremely long = RAID.
- ◆ The book is extremely hard and has difficult academic wording = RAID.
- ◆ The book only somewhat relates to the question and topic = RAID.

The Basic Process of Raiding a Book Is the Following:

- ◆ Look at the Table of Contents and choose one or a few chapters that seem relevant.
- ◆ Always read the introduction and focus on the author's argument.
- ◆ Read the key chapters. If necessary, read only the first paragraph of the chapter and first sentences in the rest of the chapter. Read more fully a part that seems important.
- ◆ Read the conclusion.
- ◆ Look in the index and search for an important keyword. Locate those pages and read them.

Step 7: Finding Primary Sources

While the use of primary sources, of course, is integral to a strong research paper, it is not a simple task for any high school student and many times in my career I have, regrettably, skipped over this step. That being said, pushing students to locate and use primary sources is crucial because it improves the quality of their research process and their final paper, as well as increasing their own sense of what they have accomplished.

Don't forget: interviews count as primary sources and the experience of interviewing someone involved in the historical event you are researching is unforgettable. We should get students to interview more often, especially their family members. Some of my best pieces of student work have emerged from interviews with grandparents.

To Locate Primary Sources, Try the Following:

- Google the topic + "primary sources." For example, here is a possible search term: 1980 US Soviet Olympic hockey primary sources.
- Google the topic + a specific form of primary source. Examples: (1) 1980 US Soviet Olympic hockey newspaper; or (2) 1980 US Soviet Olympic hockey interview.

Step 8: Outlining and Writing the Paper

Outlining is not my strength as a writer or a teacher. I come more from the "just sit down and let it flow; write and put something messy on the paper" camp. I'm not sure if there is a more official name for that camp. Nonetheless, it is certain that many students do better with an outline. If you need outline templates for students, I'm a proponent of letting them choose a format that works for them. TemplateLab provides a great selection of essay-length organizational structures.

I let students know, before writing, that a research paper should be about 20–50% story and about 50–80% argument. Some teachers maintain that papers are all argument, but I don't agree. There are times when the writer just needs to tell a bit of the story to provide the background context for the argument. Additionally, sometimes the story and argument meld into one, essentially, as telling the story is what helps make the argument. If a topic is very well-known (i.e. the Holocaust), the writer then needs less background context than if it is about something obscure like the Winter War.

Here are two possible structures for research papers that I propose to students, while letting them know that they are by no means the only possibilities:

Option 1	Option 2
• Introduction • Historiography paragraph • Historical Background • Historical Background • Argument • Argument • Conclusion • Works Cited	• Introduction • Historiography paragraph • History/argument • History/argument • History/argument • History/argument • Conclusion • Works Cited

Step 9: Works Cited and Citations

The best online guide for making sure that students are citing correctly is Purdue University's Online Writing Lab, or OWL.[2] I want to emphasize here that students are working on a plethora of new skills with a research paper. I try not to go overboard with my requirements for the specific formatting of citations, especially for non-traditional digital sources.

It is also reasonable for students to use online works cited creators, such as Easybib[3] and Citation Machine.[4]

Step 10: Re-read, Revise, and Repeat

I've never excelled at getting students to meaningfully self or peer edit prior to submitting their work to me. Some students edit their work nicely on their own, but I've never developed a great class-wide system. Other teachers have done so, and it can be a very worthwhile process. I will succeed next year. And, while I'm at it, I will also go to the gym every night after 9:00 p.m.

That being said, I do insist on students revising their papers based on my feedback. If what we are doing is all about learning, then they do need to take into account our suggestions and put it into action.

I count the first draft of a research paper as 50% of the grade, the second draft as 30%, and the presentation as 20%. I weigh the first draft more because I want them to submit their best product and because it is when most of their real intellectual work happens. When I return the papers to them, each student must come speak with me after class, individually. I hand back the paper and first tell them, orally, what I liked most about their essay and then a few specific things to work on. I make sure, in addition to the rubric, to write down two to three things they did well and two to three things to work on.

When students submit their revisions, all changes or additions must be done in red ink or red font and they must resubmit their first draft with the rubric. This way, I don't need to re-read the entire paper. By looking at my comments on their rubric, I remind myself of the two to three constructive pieces of feedback I had provided and then I look at their red-ink additions to see if they made substantive changes.

If they truly edited the paper according to my feedback, I bump their final draft grade up half a letter. If they made a few basic changes, but nothing substantial, I keep their final draft the same grade as their first draft. If they made only superficial grammatical changes and only added in one sentence or so to respond to my major feedback, then their final draft grade will be a half-letter lower than their first draft.

Notes

1 http://tinyurl.com/sherrinator.
2 https://owl.purdue.edu/owl/research_and_citation/resources.html.
3 www.easybib.com/.
4 www.citationmachine.net/mla/cite-a-website.

4

Creative Writing

In this chapter, we look at creative writing formats that allow students to produce authentic writing in social studies beyond the traditional essay. Sections of the chapter cover the following genres in order of typical length of the student's final product: poetry, speeches, perspective pieces, letters to historical characters, film reviews, newspaper articles, and historical fiction. While most of these formats function best as individual projects, films reviews and newspaper articles can easily turn into group projects. So, if you are interested in group creative writing, I would begin with those.

After reading the chapter, use the following chart as a plan to "keep the learning real"

In which unit(s) of your course could you integrate creative writing?
Would your students work individually, in groups, or as a full class?
Which format of creative writing would your class pursue? Or, would you provide choice?

Poetry

Real-World Context

Long before humans recorded their history in academic journal articles, they used lyrical form to share their most important stories and religious ideals. Indeed, poetry may be the oldest medium for written history. Civilizations across the world applied the beauty and soaring metaphors of poetry to describe the ineffable and to remember the heroic deeds of their ancestors.

The poetry of Homer's *The Iliad* retells the mythical account of Achilles and Hector. Depictions of the battle scenes tell us much about ancient Greek society: religious beliefs, codes of honor, ideas of masculinity, military unity, battle tactics, and more.[1] Poetry also served as the medium to spread key teachings in ancient religious texts ranging from the Torah to the *Tao Te Ching*. In the latter, for example, the poetic form is crucial for unraveling the mysteries, conundrums, and ironies of the Tao. It is through poetry that we can best envision the juxtapositions of good and bad, difficult and easy, high and low, and names and nameless.[2]

It is no wonder that humans wield poetry to depict the sacred; the stiffness of prose can seem hopeless to the task of describing the mysteries of the universe and the experience of awe.

More recently, however, poets have also used their craft to participate in the writing of history. Like with painting, the purpose of historical poetry is not to teach the facts, but rather to convey a perspective on the meaning of the past. Maya Angelou was one of the great historical poets, lyrically weaving tapestries of the African-American experience. Her piece "Our Grandmothers" reminds us of the fear and courage of escaped slaves as they avoided the slave-hunters. She poignantly makes an argument about resistance as she describes women laying in the dirt under leaves to hide from baying hounds and stomping hunters who crackle through the branches in the woods.[3]

In my class, I teach some of the works of Senegalese poet and prime minister Léopold Sénghor, one of the leading figures of the Négritude movement. His poem "Prayer to Masks" demonstrates the pride that Négritude artists took in their black heritage, especially as independence movements were rising in Africa. The colorful masks, in their role as conduits to the spirit world, connect us to the past and the strength of his "panther headed ancestor." His poem thus becomes an assertion of cultural pride.[4]

Langston Hughes' "Freedom's Plow" makes an argument about the origin of America's identity and prosperity that differs little from what you might find in an academic text. He starts by reminding us who the founders of this new world really were in their tremendous diversity, including not only the devout pilgrims and the adventurous merchants, but also the slave men and slave masters. Echoing the seminal claim made by Trinidadian historian and prime minister Eric Williams in *Capitalism and Slavery*, he poetically argues that America's wealth originates from the sweat of the slave who turns the soil, plows, plants, and harvests all the food and cotton that nourishes and clothes the people of the land. It is with the axes and labor of the slaves, he argues, that the homes and roofs of America were built.[5]

Bringing Poetry to the Classroom

Poetry is a genre that caters to all topics, although it works best when there is a human, emotional, or empathetic element to the story. Students might gravitate to poetry when it can help them depict suffering, heroism, bravery, or sacrifice. I have seen students produce gripping poems about the Ghanaian independence movement, Jewish resistance in the Holocaust, the rise of feminism, and other topics that involve human drama.

My first connection to poetry in the classroom involved an identity poem project at the Facing History School. I collaborated with a wonderful young poet named Fabian who came to the classroom to regale students with some spoken-word performances and inspired them to share who they were through poetry. An identity poem project works beautifully in a unit or course focusing on identity, such as the Civil Rights movement or immigration.

Below, you will find an excerpt of one poem a student penned about the Ghanaian independence movement. Amidst the rhyme and imagery, a subtle argument emerges: a number of factors and strategies contributed to Ghanaian independence, including boycotts, nationalism, liberalism, the role of leaders like Kwame Nkrumah, and Négritude. The student weaves in an ode to Kwame Nkrumah in Swahili, representing the leader's principal role in pan-Africanism and the idea that Ghanaian independence had meaning outside of the country's border, serving as a spark plug for other movements throughout Africa. Interestingly, this student later told me it was the first poem she had ever written.

> We boycotted in Akosombo
> We striked in Wa
>   We gathered in Elmina
>
> We fought in Bolgatanga
> We must sing in Ashanti
> Dance in Ewe
>   Eat in Fante
>   Live in our Ghana
>
> Our Ghana has now become a republic
> For it is now open to all the public
>   We have adopted our own constitution
>
> to create compromisable solutions.

Oh Kwame Nkrumah
Kiongozi wetu
Mwanzilishi wetu
    Mkuu wa harakati za uhuru wa Afrika
Tunayo deni kwako, ushindi wetu, utukufu wetu, haki yetu ya uhuru.

My experience has shown that students need some support in understanding the concise form of poetry and the general structure, layout, and use of line breaks; my main stylistic suggestions tend to push them to pare down excess words, especially prepositions, in an attempt to make the narration tighter. Students sometimes gravitate toward rhyme, so it is helpful to remind them that they do not need to do that all the time. What really counts is the meaning and the claim, not the way that lines always end up the same.

Keeping the Learning Real: Tips

Apprentice	All students write a poem about their identity
Samurai	All or some students write a poem about a historical event, such as the Civil Rights movement
Jedi	Students create a poetry booklet or magazine to showcase the class' poetry

Authentic Assessment: Poetry

Background: Poetry has always been used as a medium to express historical and political arguments. Some excellent historical poems include Maya Angelou's "Our Grandmothers," Léopold Sénghor's "Prayer to Masks," and Langston Hughes' "Freedom's Plow." Each of these poems uses lyrical form to make an argument about the past.

Deliverable: Write an original poem. Use your piece to develop an argument that answers your compelling question, exploring the key content and ideas that support your claim.

Requirements:

◆ The poem must use the visual formatting of a poem, including short lines and divisions into stanzas.
◆ The poem must be single-spaced with a line break between stanzas. The length of the poem should be about one page.

- ◆ Consider how your word choice, meter, rhythm, symbolism, imagery, repetition, consonance, and other literary devices function to advance the meaning of the poem and to support your historical argument.
- ◆ Use concise language and careful word choice. Avoid excess words, especially unnecessary prepositions.

Considerations

- ◆ Who or what is the poem about? Who is narrating the poem?
- ◆ Does anything change throughout the poem or is the argument and narration consistent?

Artist Statement

Include a one-page artist statement, written in the first person. You should describe:

- ◆ Why you chose to create this piece.
- ◆ What is your historical question and argument.
- ◆ What historical choices you made in creating it.
- ◆ What artistic choices you made and what symbolism you included.
- ◆ What the piece represents about the event.

Historical Speeches

Real-World Context

Historians don't tend to write or give famous speeches, but historical figures certainly do. The skilled use of rhetoric often becomes intimately tied to our memory of important leaders.

The eternal prose of the Gettysburg Address and the Emancipation Proclamation surround Abraham Lincoln's stoic memorial in Washington D.C., connecting the threads of American history from independence to Civil War through the statement: "Four score and seven years ago our fathers brought forth on this continent, a new nation, conceived in liberty, and dedicated to the proposition that all men are created equal."

Martin Luther King Jr.'s legacy is forever tied, somewhat unfortunately, in its simplification of his work to his moving "I Have a Dream" speech at the March on Washington. Franklin Roosevelt cemented himself into the national psyche with, among other words, his First Inaugural Address and his declaration that "the only thing we need to fear is fear itself." Pretty much anything Winston Churchill ever said in public (except his extremely racist comments about Indians) is worth re-reading for the powerful juxtaposition of ideas, passion, and imagery.

A few other speeches have worked their way into my history curriculum. My first assignment ever, as a teacher, involved students rewriting some variation of Pericles' ancient "Funeral Oration." My 11th grade research paper as a student, long ago, was about Chief Joseph so I have always returned to the poetic repetition of his surrender speech:

> *I am tired of fighting. Our Chiefs are killed; Looking Glass is dead, Ta Hool Hool Shute is dead. The old men are all dead. Hear me, my Chiefs! I am tired; my heart is sick and sad. From where the sun now stands I will fight no more forever.*

I particularly love Sojourner Truth's speech "Ain't I a Woman?" for its vivid portrayal of the struggles of being a black woman and the joint diseases of racism and sexism. Sojourner Truth was talking about intersectionality long before the concept became mainstream when she declared:

> *Nobody ever helps me into carriages, or over mud-puddles, or gives me any best place! And ain't I a woman? Look at me! Look at my arm! I have ploughed and planted, and gathered into barns, and no man could head me! And ain't I a woman?*

When I was more energetic, prior to my second child, I used to do a very dramatic reading of Patrick Henry's revolutionary war oration, shaking my fists and shouting the line: "Forbid it, Almighty God! I know not what course others may take; but as for me, give me liberty, or give me death!"

More recent speeches allow us to show students video of the event, such as Ronald Reagan's forceful demands in Berlin: "General Secretary Gorbachev, if you seek peace, if you seek prosperity for the Soviet Union and Eastern Europe, if you seek liberalization, come here to this gate. Mr. Gorbachev, open this gate. Mr. Gorbachev, tear down this wall!"

Bringing Speeches into the Classroom

Our history is filled with remarkable speeches. But, think of all the possible game-changing speeches that were never actually written or given. If reality really includes multiple universes in which every possible outcome happens, then we can imagine an endless array of stirring orations that came into being elsewhere but not in our world.

Historical speech-writing is really a form of role-playing, which I discuss a bit in *The Classes They Remember*. Similar to perspective pieces, speeches are public incarnations in which we take on the experiences and perspectives of historical characters. The writer just needs to pen and deliver the monumental speech that never took place.

In fact, speech-writing is one of the main formats of assessment in the spectacularly successful college role-playing curriculum called Reacting to the Past (RTTP), which began at Barnard College and has extended throughout the country. RTTP holds annual conferences where educators can participate as students, role-playing, to get a real sense of how it works. Professors who use RTTP sometimes develop entire college courses around role-playing. I had the opportunity to sit in on one RTTP class at Pace University. During the class, students delivered a number of speeches, as their characters, which expressed their goals, reasoning, and understanding of key primary sources.

(In my own role-plays, students give speeches to open our Critical Decision Debates. For example, in my role-play on the French Revolution, there is a crucial debate about what to do with King Louis XVI and another one about the proper course for the revolution as violence begins to erupt throughout Paris. In these debates, students begin with speeches and then move on to more free-form discussion.)

Think about the important speeches students could write and deliver, whether as part of role-play units or not. Such speeches can get us behind the scenes to better understand the nuances of important events and movements. I would love to hear a speech from Walter Sisulu at an early ANC Youth League meeting, from a leading German rabbi in 1933, from a Warsaw Ghetto rebel, from an unknown Haitian revolutionary, from Mercy Otis Warren during the Revolutionary War, from Montezuma to his people after the arrival of the Spanish soldiers, or from a female Soviet fighter pilot speaking to her comrades during World War II.

Keeping the Learning Real: Tips

Apprentice	Students write speeches from the perspective of historical characters
Samurai	Students write and perform speeches at the end of a unit
Jedi	Students write and perform speeches throughout a unit as part of ongoing role-play debates

Authentic Assessment: Speeches

Background: A speech makes an argument from the perspective of a particular character. Strong speeches not only look good on paper but must sound good as well. They are meant to be public and persuasive. Some famous speeches include Lincoln's Gettysburg Address, Martin Luther King Jr.'s "I Have a Dream," and Sojourner Truth's "Ain't I a Woman?"

> **Deliverable:** Use your speech to develop an argument that answers your compelling question, exploring the key content and ideas that support your claim.

Requirements:

- Two to four minutes.
- Attempt to adopt the character's perspective, personality, and linguistic particularities but in general avoid adopting fake accents.

To consider:

- Be specific on details.
- Consider your word choice and tone for communicating with your audience.
- Practice the speech. Speak slowly, loudly, and pause where relevant.

Perspective Pieces (Diaries and Letters)

Real-World Context

Perspective pieces tell about the past from the point of view of one or more characters, speaking in the first person. Most perspective pieces that students write take the form of letters or diary entries. In that sense, while they are similar to speeches, they differ in the intended audience. A speech is meant to be public and composed as such. A diary or letter is meant to be private or personal, and thus the tone and language may be strikingly different.

We have access to countless letters and diaries from history, ranging from *The Diary of Anne Frank* to the *Diary of Samuel Pepys*; from the journals of Lewis and Clark to the collection of letters written between John and Abigail Adams. Letters serve as crucial historical resources, especially for the study of the early modern world.

In terms of perspective pieces as historical fiction, Margaret George, author of books like *Helen of Troy* and *Elizabeth I*, excels at the genre, especially in the way that she gives voice to females who were silenced in the past. One example is her book *The Memoirs of Cleopatra* that tells the story of the famous Egyptian monarch from her own point of view. The opening words reveal the beauty of this historical and literary form:

> *Warmth. Wind. Dancing blue waters, and the sound of waves. I see, hear, feel them all still. I even taste the sting of the salt against my lips, where the fine, misty spray coats them. And closer even than that, the lulling, drowsy smell of my mother's skin by my nose ... And then ... the memory is torn apart, upended, overturned, as the boat must have been. My mother gone ...*[6]

Most of what we know about Cleopatra comes from outside sources, especially from Roman texts written by men. This is problematic since the Romans despised her and despised powerful women in general, thus leading many of the earliest sources we have about Cleopatra to be so negative in nature. The ways in which powerful Romans attacked her for her sexuality has a message that echoes down until today and allows students and readers to make interesting connections about women, sexuality, and power. Consequently, Margaret George's *The Memoirs of Cleopatra* is not just fun reading; it is an attempt to enter into the historical conversation and correct the (likely) inaccuracies of the original sources and most of the subsequent historical interpretations based on those sources.

Similarly, Philippa Gregory wrote a fantastic first-person historical fiction account called *The Other Boleyn Girl* about Henry VIII's sibling mistresses. The highly respected intellectual and writer Gore Vidal penned a historical novel called *Burr*, written in imaginary first person narration by Aaron Burr's contemporary Charles Schuyler.

If the Land of Oz were a real place (and I'm pretty sure it really was a twister and not a dream), then *Wicked* would have been one of the great historical perspective pieces of all time.

Through perspective pieces we get a better sense of the emotions, doubts, and choices experienced by individuals in history. We better understand the complexities of the past and the ways in which important events influence the lives of ordinary or extraordinary people.

Bringing Perspective Pieces into the Classroom

Perspective pieces are some of the most popular assessment options for my students, especially those students who enjoy creative writing and find the traditional essay format a bit staid. When I offer menu options, sometimes around one-third of my students choose to write diaries or letters.

My use of perspective pieces began long ago at the Facing History School when I first developed my Weimar Republic and Spanish-Aztec role-plays. As I mentioned above, speeches and perspective pieces click perfectly with a role-play unit. Role-plays asked students to take on the point of view of individuals from the past and to carry those perspectives throughout events and historical changes. Students dig deep into the lenses of their characters to try to understand the past from one person's changing point of view.

In that sense, perspective pieces function as the most inherently authentic assessment for role-play units. For example, a student who takes on the character of an Aztec farmer and experiences that character's life from before Cortes' arrival until after the fall of Tenochtitlan, a few years later, can write about that journey and his insights in a perspective piece. This format was not only the most engaging but also the most relevant assessment to provide in this case. Perspective pieces often became the required assessment for role-play units since they capture, more than an academic essay, what we had actually been learning during that unit: historical perspective.

When I moved on to Harvest Collegiate, I develop some Humanities classes, including "Love and Power," a gendered history course in which we looked at relationships in history and used case studies such as Cleopatra and *Les Misérables* to try to understand both the larger historical context of those time periods and the social history of gender and marriage. I became more interested in developing students' skills in sourcing, which asks the reader and the writer to think about the context, credibility, and bias of the source. Not all sources are created equally and the role of the historian is to not only figure out what the sources say but also how and why they say what they do. We discussed sourcing quite often in our department meetings at Harvest Collegiate and when I developed a unit on Cleopatra sourcing became a primary focus.

Since much of the unit focused on the ways that Romans wrote and since we needed to dig around and behind those sources to understand who she really was, a Cleopatra unit worked perfectly for a perspective piece. I asked students to write about Cleopatra from the perspective of Cleopatra, Marc Antony, Julius Caesar or perhaps even one of her servants. One of the first truly powerful perspective pieces that I read as a teacher was from a student who wrote in such a gripping manner, from Cleopatra's perspective, about how she could be so misunderstood by the world and by the powerful men around her.

Perspective pieces however can also be one option in a larger menu project. In this case we need to think about how to frame a perspective piece for any historical unit of study. Perspective pieces work best to make an argument when they look at change over time from two differing perspectives on the same event. Thus, I asked students to write about two events from the perspective of the same character and consider how the character's perspective changed; for example, does a peasant's perspective change at all during the French Revolution? A slave's during the Haitian Revolution? A Muslim merchant's during Indian independence?

Or, I ask students to look at the same event from the perspectives of two different characters; they might delve into the Salt March or the Boston Massacre and try to understand how Indian, British, or American individuals viewed those same events differently. In that case, the question is not about what happened in the event but the meaning of the event for the people involved.

One other key to strong perspective pieces is to get students to begin with a moment. If they've already practiced the Magical Camera, they can transfer that tool to this medium. The best perspective pieces start with a vivid scene, zoom out to connect to larger issues and themes, and then sometimes zoom back in to the scene at the end to bring us back to the original moment.

Here is an example of part of a student's perspective piece.

Caesar? Never Heard of him

Written by Ptolemy XIII, transcribed by Roxy

It was her. Cleopatra.

Why had she come back!? Wasn't it clear that I was the one who was more fit to run the country!? After all, I had overpowered her, I was the one who chased HER out not the other way around. She must think that she can still bully me around like she used to before. Well not any longer! No way that she can make me just her little brother again! I won't let it happen!

I was about to order my guards to arrest her, when I saw another person walking right by her side. He was an older man, maybe in his fifties. He was pale, and was wearing some sort of armor on him. I couldn't recognize its origin, I couldn't recognize his face. He looked vaguely familiar, much like Cleopatra's guards had. It felt like I had met him once or twice. Surely this wasn't the leader of wherever the heck she went, she would never actually *talk* to them. No way. Never.

Still slightly in awe of the fact that she was here in this room with me and not actually missing forever like she was supposed to be, I asked her who he was. But it wasn't her who responded, it was the mystery man. He was Julius Caesar of the Roman Empire. I knew of the Roman Empire, but I had no clue who this fool was, walking into my court in my country with his soldiers. Who did he think he was?

Cleopatra finally spoke up, telling me that he was on her side. I was baffled, Cleopatra had made allies while she was away. Why did she always have to be so good at everything!? It just makes me frustrated because she has all the good ideas and it's just not fair. Why couldn't she just let me have the country to myself? She always gets what she wants so now I finally got what I wanted and she just wants to take it away from me. She's just a big mean bully!

I screamed out in protest, telling them that this was my country and they were to leave immediately or suffer the consequences. Neither of them were looking too intimidated by me, but it was always worth a shot to try and convince them to go away without me having to hurt them.

But then, the unthinkable happened.

Caesar walked up the hall. The look on his face was indistinguishable. He looked angry, but he also looked calm and collected. He had a weird sort of smirk on his face that made it seem like he took pleasure in watching us attempt to get them to leave. I was terrified of what was to come next, every step he took felt like I was one step closer to my own demise. He had a deathly aura about him. But it was not me who he approached, it was Pothinus.

Caesar stabbed him right in the heart. Right there in front of me.

My world shattered. I wanted to cry out so badly, but I couldn't let him know that he got to me. Pothinus, the only person I had ever felt a strong emotional connection with, was now dead. I had loved Pothinus more than anyone, he was always there for me through thick and thin. He advised me in my political affairs, and he had comforted me at night. He had always known what was best for me and he tried to lead me in the right direction so I could become a great Pharaoh one day. He was more of a father to me than my birth father, more familial and kind to me than my own sister – and I just witnessed him get killed.

I was done playing games, I kicked Caesar out of my court, and I officially declared war on Rome. If he was going to hurt my family and my country, then so be it, but he had to do it in an honorable way – not like some coward doing his dirty affairs in private. No, he would have to fight me and my entire army in the fields of battle. I would avenge Pothinus, even if it meant having to lose my own life as well.

In this second example of a perspective piece, it is evident how the student builds his argument about female pilots in the Soviet Union. While they took on a groundbreaking role, it was not without persecution and difficulties. Additionally, the story allows him to weave in the larger changes in gender norms in the Soviet Union as well as the ultimate limitations of those transformations.

I ached for sleep and for warmth, the most recent tears that had slid away like traitors from the prison of my eyes had frozen on my cheeks. My ill-fitting clothes itched and bunch; I was a large woman, but the male pilot whose hand-me-downs I wore must have been a true Soviet bear of a man. I had even torn up my previously threadbare blanket to have enough rags to fill up my massive boots. They were shoes I would never be able to fill on my own. Even with the extra padding, my feet had long ago turned numb and I hoped I would not lose another toe to frostbite. The rest of my body felt as cold as fallen snow lying undifferentiated against a background of freezing, stifling sameness. A truly Soviet experience.

General Winter was a harsh commander, without him we never would have driven the Germans from the Motherland, but if we did not safeguard our warmth, he would cut us down just as easily.

With a jolt, I realized I had landed at our small, barren airfield. I was unsure how much time I had spent in the sky, dawn was cresting over the horizon.

I exited my Kukuruznik, and was instantly assailed by a loud, strange mechanic.

"Did you notice anything wrong with your plane's wings in the air? Is the engine good enough to fly again? How soon can you take off?" he asked, his barrage of questions cracking my crystalline exterior.

"Who are you? Where is Boris? He usually handles my plane," I responded with my own set of questions. And Boris is much less abrasive, I added silently.

"Wait, are you a woman?" The weird mechanic asked, sounding shocked.

"Of course, this is the 587th's airfield," I huffed.

"No, it isn't, I think you have managed to land at the wrong airfield," he snorted, "Exactly why we should not let women go above their station."

"Excuse me, comrade, but I fear you have been led astray. Our Great Comrade Stalin himself commanded the creation of our regiments. And Comrade Lenin recognized the equality of women during the Revolution, have you been misled by the mistruths of the Nazi pigs? Do you require a commissar to educate you properly?" I said, putting only a thin veneer of false sincerity on top of my threats.

It was good to feel the hot flame of indignation spark up in my chest. Despite what the Party proclaimed about gender equality from distant Moscow, the reality was little had changed in the way of men's attitudes since my grandmother's day under the Tsar. But, I had little chance of swaying a commissar to my side of the debate over a man. The young, naive mechanic, however, did not need to know that.

Keeping the Learning Real: Tips

Apprentice	Each student writes an individual perspective piece for a role-play unit
Samurai	Students write perspective pieces for historical characters in a unit without role-play
Jedi	Students choose different historical characters during a unit and write letters back-and-forth to each other throughout the unit

Authentic Assessment: Perspective Piece

Background: A perspective piece tells a historical story and makes an argument through first person narration. Some famous perspective pieces include *The Memoirs of Cleopatra* by Margaret George and *The Other Boleyn Girl* by Philippa Gregory. Perspective pieces make use of vivid language, action, dialogue, and thoughts. The goal is to weave in very specific historical detail in a way that seems authentic to the narration.

Deliverable: Use your perspective piece to develop an argument that answers your compelling question, exploring the key content and ideas that support your claim.

Requirements:

◆ You must write two entries, each of which is about two pages. These two entries must involve different time periods and events from the perspective of one character OR it may take place at one time being told from the perspective of two different characters.

- ◆ Double-spaced.
- ◆ You may choose to be a famous leader or an ordinary person. Make sure the character's personality, experience, identity, and viewpoints get fleshed out in the pieces.

To consider:

- ◆ Be specific on details on the event.
- ◆ Set your story within one specific day, one moment, one event. What does your character experience? What is his/her point of view on this event?
- ◆ Who does your character admire? Fear? Love? Hate?

Tips:

- ◆ Include some new fun and creative personal info and surprises about your character.
- ◆ Include dialogue.
- ◆ Use detail and specifics (within reason) to discuss the events and your character's life. Look for ways to creatively include actual quotations from primary sources.

Letters to Historical Characters

Real-World Context

One mini-genre in literature is the epistolary novel, which involves stories told entirely through documents, most often letters. In this case, the letters are often written between characters. This can create a type of multiperspectivity when the letters deal with the same events from the point of view of different characters. Letters serve a particular function in literature, allowing an increased sense of informality and characterization through the first-person narration. They permit us, the readers, to feel like we are a part of a conversation. And who doesn't like to eavesdrop a bit?

A number of authors have utilized the exchange of letters as the backbone of historical fiction. One of the most celebrated is Alice Walker's *The Color Purple*, which begins with a letter to God:

G-o-d,

Two of his sister come to visit. They dress all up. Celie, they say. One thing is for sure. You keep a clean house. It not nice to speak ill of the dead ...[7]

Another wonderful epistolary historical novel is Karen Hesse's *Letters from Rifka*, a story about a young Russian Jewish immigrant who recounts her travails in America in her letters to her cousin Tovah. The novel begins:

> September 2, 1919
> Russia
>
> My Dear Cousin Tovah,
>   We made it! If it had not been for your father, though, I think my family would all be dead now: Mama, Papa, Nathan, Saul, and me. At the very best we would be in that filthy prison in Berdichev ...[8]

One of the must-read books on race in America in the past decade is Ta-Nehisi Coates' *Between the World and Me*, composed as a letter from the author to his adolescent son. As Coates explains in an interview with Jason Diamond, he was conscious that he was following a convention begun by James Baldwin, whose essay "The Fire Next Time" took the form of a letter to his nephew. Coates starts his powerful book with the type of blunt statement that I identify as a great hook in my section on introductions:

> Son,
> Last Sunday the host of a popular news show asked me what it meant to lose my body.[9]

Bringing Letters into the Classroom

One of the most important organizations to shape social studies education in the United States over the past decades has been Facing History and Ourselves. The organization began with curriculum on Holocaust education and has since expanded its offerings. My first public school, the Facing History School, was affiliated with Facing History and Ourselves, receiving frequent curricular guidance and training. While teaching there, I had the opportunity to become very familiar with Facing History's philosophy.

At its core, the organization seeks to develop connections between students and the historical content. The organization's mission is for students to move away from viewing history as something that happened to someone else in another time, and move toward seeing it as something that happens to all people, at all times, including to ourselves. Consequently, when we learn history, we face the history and then must face ourselves; we need to make that crucial connection to our own experiences to understand the material and make meaning out of it.

Facing History's methodology asks students to learn about Nazi propaganda and then to think about bullying and name-calling in school; to consider bystanders who did nothing to help Jews during the early years of Nazi rule and to simultaneously consider times they stood by and did nothing while something unjust was taking place, however small it might be in comparison. Students learn about upstanders who rescued Jews, hiding them in their homes, and they reflect upon a time they may have helped a stranger.

In my view, writing a letter to a historical character fits into the epistolary tradition as well as Facing History and Ourselves' curricular philosophy. The act of writing a letter to Cleopatra, Marie Antoinette, Nelson Mandela, Winston Churchill, or lesser known figures in history like Helen Suzman, Abina Mansah, or our own great-grandparents who immigrated to America is an act of connection; it brings us into the history and it brings the history into our own lives. It is, directly, an act of participating in the historical conversation and making meaning by linking ourselves to that story.

Letter writing allows us to transcend time, to talk to the past, to ask questions, and to tell those who lived before us how the world is similar or different today. Letters are powerful, but they are not a format that students are necessarily familiar with. They most likely need to see a few examples and/or get an actual model of a letter format. This creates a nice transfer skill, as practice doing this in the correct format can lead to more familiarity with formal letters they will need later on, such as cover letters.

When I taught a major unit on Cleopatra and her relationships, students wrote a letter to her, thereby erasing millennia of chronological distance and connecting themselves to the past. Here were the basic guidelines:

Topic of the letter: Love and relationships! Write to Cleopatra and tell her the following:

- ★ The most important things you learned about love and relationships/marriage in her time.
- ★ Your opinion of her relationship and her choices.
- ★ Ways in which love/relationships are similar or different between her time period and our own.
- ★ How your view of her compares to the views of other historians.
- ★ Your hopes and dreams for your future love life and relationship(s).

Similarly, after reading *Abina and the Important Men*, a graphic history that I describe more fully in Chapter 6, students gain a real sense of empathy for a formally forgotten person in history. Abina, a 19th century West African woman, would have had no idea that 150 years later students are learning about part of her life. I want students to talk to her and let her know that she mattered. I imagine she would be awed by that knowledge. So here's what I ask them to do:

> **Write a letter to Abina:** For this option, you need to tell her what you know/understand about her, why her story is important, and why she should be remembered. After you revise your letter based on my feedback, you need to then find a beautiful place outdoors, video yourself reading your letter to her, and then send the video to me.

There's something beautiful about students sitting in a forest reading a letter to a woman who lived long ago about what they have learned from her.

Keeping the Learning Real: Tips

Apprentice	Students write letters to the main historical character of a unit
Samurai	Students choose different individuals to write letters to within a larger period or event
Jedi	Students write a letter to a historical figure and write the character's imaginary response as well

Authentic Assessment: Writing to a Historical Figure

Background: A letter allows you to communicate privately and personally with someone. For centuries, letters were a crucial form of communication. Write a letter to a historical figure from our unit and share what you have learned and what it has meant.

> **Deliverable:** Use your letter to develop an argument that answers your compelling question, exploring the key content and ideas that support your claim.

Requirements:

- ◆ Write in the first person.
- ◆ Be candid, open, and detailed.
- ◆ Single-spaced.

To consider:

- ◆ Be specific on details of that person's life.
- ◆ Focus on specific days, moments, and actions. What is your point of view about those events?

Tips:

- ◆ Include some new fun and creative personal info.
- ◆ Include dialogue, thoughts, emotions.
- ◆ Use detail and specifics (within reason) to discuss your life and the character's life.

Film and Book Reviews

Real-World Context

To me, "film review" is synonymous with "Siskel & Ebert." Those who review are also called "critics," but the criticism can be positive or negative. The important point in such a piece is to look at the film not simply as an object of entertainment, but also as a cultural and historical artifact. Film reviews are mostly about weighing the artistic value of the movie. While reviews of historical films like *Long Walk to Freedom*, *Lincoln*, and *Hidden Figures* focus on the acting, plot, and flow, they also tend to add in discussions of the film's historical accuracy and argument.

For example, Abbie Bernstein's review of *Long Walk to Freedom* emphasizes Idris Elba's capacity to portray the power and presence of Nelson Mandela, but also the inadequacies of attempting to fit a life of that magnitude, and the corresponding heft of the Anti-Apartheid Movement, into two-and-a-half hours. She writes thoughtfully about the crucial historical problem of the film:

> *because so much is going on, we get very little of the causes, only the results —*
> *we not only don't know how Mandela rose to leadership of his fellow activists,*
> *we barely know who the other people are. Do they have any influence on him*

or each other? Are there turning points for Mandela, or is he the same man simply surviving crushing circumstances to eventually triumph?[10]

This is more than a claim about style; it is digging into the historical conversation.

Similarly, A. O. Scott's review of *Lincoln* in the *New York Times* highlights Daniel Day Lewis, who plays the protagonist and "eases into a role of epic difficulty as if it were a coat he had been wearing for years." Still, the review also participates in the historical conversation, recognizing that the film's connection to history requires an analysis that goes beyond praise of the acting. Scott writes:

The question facing Lincoln is stark: Should he abolish slavery, once and for all, even if it means prolonging the war? The full weight and scale of this dilemma are the central lesson 'Lincoln' asks us to grasp. The film places slavery at the center of the story, emphatically countering the revisionist tendency to see some other, more abstract thing – states' rights, Southern culture, industrial capitalism – as the real cause of the Civil War.[11]

Here, the reviewer is making an argument about the film's claim and how it connects to a larger historical discussion about the cause of the Civil War, a discussion involving some of the most prominent American historians.

Scott's review of *Hidden Figures* also combines a critique of the style with one of the historical substance. He writes that the movie's storytelling structure, "is content to stay within established conventions. The story may be new to most viewers, but the manner in which it's told will be familiar to all but the youngest." In the same piece, he also tries to weed out how the movie deals with the complexity of the historical narrative, explaining that

"Hidden Figures" effectively conveys the poisonous normalcy of white supremacy, and the main characters' determination to pursue their ambitions in spite of it and to live normal lives in its shadow. The racism they face does not depend on the viciousness or virtue of individual white people, and for the most part the white characters are not treated as heroes for deciding, at long last, to behave decently.[12]

The message the movie attempts to share about the complex, invidious, and sometimes subtle nature of racism is crucial, and Scott effectively highlights it in his review.

Reviews extend beyond films, of course, and one of the roles of historians is to participate in the tradition of peer book reviews. Book reviews are wonderful resources for the classroom, as they tend to offer a concise summary of the author's argument and how the work fits into the larger historiography on a particular topic. Book reviews, whether in academic journals or mainstream newspapers like the *Washington Post*, are windows that allow the general public to witness the conversation between experts.

For instance, Elizabeth R. Varon, a professor of American history at the University of Virginia, provides a glowing review of Eric Foner's recent book *Gateway to Freedom: The Hidden History of the Underground Railroad* in the *Washington Post*. In her review, Professor Varon argues that Foner adds a crucial element to our understanding of the abolition movement:

> *In his carefully argued new book, Eric Foner aims to set the record straight. Drawing on his deep expertise in the history of abolitionism, Foner demonstrates that one cannot understand the origins of the American Civil War without taking into account the resistance and activism of fugitive slaves and their antislavery allies*[13]

and that "Foner dispels the lingering aura of myth surrounding the Underground Railroad by documenting scores of stirring escapes." One of the key roles of the academic, in fact, is to publish reviews such as this one to ensure high standards of scholarship.

Sometimes, reviews are far more critical and can lead to a fascinating back-and-forth between scholars. William H. McNeill, a former professor at the University of Chicago, wrote a balanced review praising and critiquing Jared Diamond's *Guns, Germs, and Steel* in a 1997 edition of *The New York Review of Books*. He begins with a humorous and perceptive barb about the title:

> *The book is oddly titled, for Diamond has little to say about guns and steel, though he devotes a chapter to the role of germs in human history. A better title would be History Upside Down: A Biological View of the Human Past.*[14]

Jared Diamond then responded to McNeill in a lengthy letter to *The New York Review of Books*, which then led to a subsequent reply from McNeill. This is one of the best examples of how history is really a conversation, and the use of reviews and letters helps us all benefit from it.

Bringing Reviews into the Classroom

Reviews tend to function better as "click" assignments than as a "menu" option. I've never offered reviews as one option among others; it seems to fall in a different category than creating a painting or song, possibly because the latter are about originality and reviews are about critiquing someone else's creation.

A review is a great assessment when the class has used an array of sources to understand a particular topic and then had the chance to burrow deeply into one particular source. For example, a class may study the Indian independence movement using multiple sources and then critique the famous film *Gandhi* for its historical accuracy and the relevance of its claim about Gandhi's role. A class could study the abolition movement and then review *Lincoln*; the Holocaust and then review *Schindler's List* or *The Pianist*; the Anti-Apartheid Movement and then review *Long Walk to Freedom*.

Of course, students can also review books if they've really had the chance to read an entire one. My class reads the entire graphic history *Abina and the Important Men*, which provides an excellent opportunity for a book review, particularly if they post the review on Amazon.

One possibility, which I have often used in the past with students, is to give a film review assignment to the entire class on a specific topic and allow each student to choose the movie from a list. I have done this type of task for units on the Cold War, genocide, and the Civil Rights movement. This level of choice obviously requires a topic with a large catalogue of potential films.

One other wonderful aspect of this genre is that students can produce the traditional written review or it could become a digital video review, in which students speak into the camera about the film in the same way they do for a testimonial. They can do this individually, or as a group panel conversation. For an example of what this looks like, check out Kenneth Turan's video review of *Lincoln* on the *Los Angeles Times* website.

Keeping the Learning Real: Tips

Apprentice	The entire class reviews one film, such as *Long Walk to Freedom*
Samurai	Students study about a particular topic and then choose a film from a menu to review
Jedi	Students review a few films and then have an "Oscar" deliberation about which film gets the award

Authentic Assessment: Film Review

Background: For the past 60 years, filmmakers have used movies to try to help the public better understand genocides. In what ways can we use film as a source to comprehend genocide? Watch one of the following films about a genocide and then write a two-page film review that assesses the film's success in sharing key knowledge and understanding of the genocide.

Film Choices:

1 *The Pianist* – the true story of a Polish piano player who hides in the Warsaw ghetto.
2 *Schindler's List* – the most acclaimed Holocaust movie of all time, about a German businessman who attempts to save Jews.
3 *Life is Beautiful* – The story of a father and son together in a concentration camp.
4 *The Boy in the Striped Pajamas* – A fictional account of a young boy in a concentration camp.
5 *Defiance* – An account, based on a true story, of Jewish rebels who fight back in the forests of Belorussia.
6 *Lark Farm* – A family's experience during the Armenian Genocide.
7 *The Killing Fields* – The Genocide in Cambodia.
8 *Sometimes in April* – Rwandan Genocide.
9 *Beyond the Gates* – Rwandan Genocide.

Supporting Questions:

- What did you find most interesting? What scenes stuck with you and why?
- Do the characters face any difficult moral crisis where they have a tough decision of "right or wrong" to make? What choice do they make? Do you agree with that choice? Why or why not?
- Why do you think the filmmakers wanted to make this movie? What did they think it would add to our understanding of the genocide?
- Is this a film based on a true story or is it a fictional account? Does that affect your sense of its meaning, purpose, or importance?

Authentic Assessment: Film Critique

Directions: In groups of three to four students, conduct a six to ten minute panel movie review of *Long Walk to Freedom*, using the accompanying documents to help flesh out your review.

Central Question: Out of five stars, how do you rate the film in capturing the story of the Anti-Apartheid Movement? Why?

Supporting Questions:

- What is the most important lesson of the Anti-Apartheid Movement that the film should try to capture?
- To what extent does the film capture the emotional and empathetic connections that a viewer should make? How does it achieve or not achieve that goal?
- What does the film include or not include historically? Does it achieve historical accuracy or does it leave out key aspects of the story?
- If you could change two aspects of the film, what would they be? Why?

Newspaper Articles

Real-World Context

In Chapter 7, I discuss the connection between journalism and history in the section on newscasts. Certainly, print journalism serves the same function as television broadcasts in creating our first draft of the news.

Looking back at newspapers on the day following a major event, we can see how journalists initially tried to understand and deal with the magnitude of becoming part of history. On August 9, 1945, the *International Herald Tribune* posted the following headline: "Atomic Bomb Revolutionizes War; Hits Japan Like 20,000 Tons of TNT." A few paragraphs into the piece, the article depicts the triumphant nature of the American government's response,

> *"We've spent $2,000,000,000 on the greatest scientific gamble in history —*
> *and won," President Truman said. "We are now prepared to obliterate more*
> *rapidly and completely every productive enterprise the Japanese have above*
> *ground in any city. We shall completely destroy Japan's power to make war."*[15]

In a sense, the newspaper article was already entering into a debate that would later become a mainstay of American social studies classes: was the United States justified in dropping the atomic bomb?

Whereas the front page on the day after Hiroshima mentioned a few *other* topics related to the war, on September 12, 2001 the *New York Times*, naturally, covered only one story on its cover. The frontpage headline screams out in full caps: "U.S. ATTACKED; HIJACKED JETS DESTROY TWIN TOWERS AND HIT PENTAGON IN DAY OF TERROR."[16] Below, in slightly smaller font that includes normal capitalization, we see headlines such as "President Vows to Exact Punishment for 'Evil'" and "A Creeping Horror."

On that day, following one of the most traumatic surprises in history, much of the newspaper covered the terrorist attacks. The editorial headline was "War Against America: An Unfathomable Attack," and it begins poetically: "Remember the ordinary, if you can. Remember how normal New York City seemed at sunrise yesterday, as beautiful a morning as ever dawns in early September."[17] Every op-ed piece sought to grapple with the monumental nature of what had occurred. The following were the op-ed headlines:

- "New Day of Infamy" – William Safire.
- "A Different World" – Anthony Lewis.
- "A Grave Silence" – Maureen Dowd.
- "America's Emergency Line 9/11" – Bill Keller.

When we move past the international section and arrive at Business News, we find the main headline: "The Financial World is Left Reeling by Attack." Even the sports section and the baseball diamonds were not places of refuge on that day: "Selig, in a Sense of Mourning, Cancels Baseball Games."

Clearly, the newspaper was doing more than telling the news. It was opening a conversation about history.

Bringing Newspapers into the Classroom
One of the interesting characteristics of print journalism, which makes it such a stellar medium for social studies students to share their knowledge, is that it allows the writer to tell the story from so many angles. When the *New York Times* told the first history of the September 11 terrorist attacks, it did not just relate what happened. It revealed what took place at the towers, what ordinary people saw, how firefighters and police officers responded, the emotions of observers, the response of government leaders, potential global consequences, how intellectuals were reacting, the effects on business, and probably least important, the effects on the baseball schedule.

This is a tremendous template for students' demonstration of understanding. The newspaper format allows them to show a wide-range of perspectives and angles on a particular topic or event. Writing one article gets the student to one point, probably displaying comprehension of historical facts. Putting together a few articles from different sections of the paper allows the student to provide, in one place, almost a wide-range historiography of the event.

Newspapers allow us to turn one assignment into a political, cultural, social, and economic history. Adding in real or imaginary quotations from interviews with ordinary people leads the student(s) to produce a more contemporary subaltern history. Including an op-ed section with competing perspectives and arguments permits the student to highlight the complexity of the event.

Everything we study in class was once news and is therefore worthy of significant coverage in the local daily. That being said, I'm more apt to include a newspaper option in a modern history course so that it more authentically reflects a format of communication that existed at the time. I've had students put together great spreads with four to six different short articles, including opinion pieces, about topics like the Fall of the Bastille and the 1933 German election.

Nowadays, the available programs for creating newspaper designs are far superior than even a decade ago. Students with Macs often go straight to the program "Pages," which offers superb templates. Otherwise, students can take advantage of free online newspaper-makers like Flipsnack or news-paperclub.com.

Writing newspapers is slightly different stylistically than writing formal essays. Students may need help writing headlines, ledes, and organizing the information so that the most important ideas come out first. Additionally, they might need to see some actual newspapers to get ideas for the different sections, what op-ed pieces look like, and how to format the final piece.

Keeping the Learning Real: Tips

Apprentice	A student produces one newspaper article about an event
Samurai	Students individually or in groups put together a larger newspaper spread about an event, including articles in the national, international, culture, financial, and op-ed sections
Jedi	Students as a class create newspapers from different countries (or ideologies) about the same event, thereby revealing complex historical perspectives. For example, a class could create newspapers about the French Revolution written by Jacobins, royalists, a British press, an American press, etc.

Authentic Assessment: Newspaper

Background: Journalism is sometimes considered "the first rough draft of history." We can look back at newspapers to understand what happened in the past and how people reacted to and grasped events from their time. Newspapers attempt to cover the recent past from a variety of angles and include interviews. Some great newspaper coverage from the past includes the *International Herald Tribune* after the dropping of the atomic bomb and the *New York Times* on September 12, 2001.

> **Deliverable:** Use your newspaper article(s) to develop an argument that answers your compelling question, exploring the key content and ideas that support your claim.

Requirements:

- ◆ A careful attention to detail and historical accuracy.
- ◆ Consideration of perspectives, arguments, and complexity.
- ◆ A thoughtful attention to layout, formatting, and headlines.

Tips:

- ◆ Make your historical question and argument/thesis clear.
- ◆ Ensure that the identities of people you "interview" are clear.
- ◆ Plan out how your articles might combine information, dialogue, and analysis.

Artist Statement

Include a one-page artist statement, written in the first person. You should describe:

- ◆ Why you chose to create this newspaper.
- ◆ What is your historical question and argument.
- ◆ What historical choices you made in creating it.
- ◆ What choices you made in the layout.
- ◆ What the piece represents about the event.

Historical Fiction

Real-World Context

Many of the greatest novels of all time are works of historical fiction and novelists have been writing history for generations. Part of history is knowing what happened but part of history is about really understanding how people experienced the past, and for this second goal historical fiction works wonders to help the reader *feel* the past. The *American Historical Review* now reviews historical fiction as authentic history, such as in its December 2016 issue that looks at Amitov Ghosh's *Ibis Trilogy*.

Charles Dickens wrote historical fiction, and one of the most famous lines in literature comes from an 1859 book about the 1789 French Revolution: "It was the best of times, it was the worst of times" begins *A Tale of Two Cities*. Much of Tolstoy's *War and Peace*, of course, depicts Napoleon's invasion of Russia and its consequences on Russian society and the lives of nobility such as Countess Natasha Rostova and Count Pierre Bezukhov. My favorite book to teach when I had the chance to create interdisciplinary Humanities courses at Harvest Collegiate was also 19th century historical fiction: Victor Hugo's gripping masterpiece *Les Misérables*, which portrays the social injustice and revolution in 19th century Paris as experienced by Jean Valjean, Javert, Cosette, and Marius.

Much historical fiction nowadays is quite a bit more readable, with gripping plots and quick paces. Some of them, however, still require more than a month to finish. As a fan of 17th century Dutch history, a compact book *Girl with a Pearl Earring* by Tracy Chevalier helped to whisper life into Dutch Renaissance culture and the era of Rembrandt. One of my favorite novels of all time, *The Pillars of the Earth* by Ken Follett, somehow made me fly through 983 pages about medieval cathedral architecture, masonry, and church politics. My first major historical fiction read, which I adored in high school, was James Clavell's 1152 page masterpiece on feudal Japan, *Shogun*. I read it the summer before learning about samurai and the Tokugawa shogunate in world history, and what I learned through that historical fiction gave me the sense that I really grasped the history. I've come back in the past few years to try to read it again, but either a shorter attention span or the duties of parenthood have kept me from finishing it a second time.

As I write this chapter of the book, only one week ago America lost one of its greatest literary masters: Toni Morrison. A considerable number of Morrison's treasures could be considered historical fiction, including the one I read and loved in 11th grade English class: the Pulitzer Prize winning *Beloved*. Written in 1987, *Beloved* follows the life of a former slave, *Sethe*, in post-Civil War Ohio. Similarly, Alice Walker's *The Color Purple* is a National Book Award winner that takes as its subject the lives of black women in 1930s Georgia. Even Harper Lee's *To Kill a Mockingbird*, written in 1960, is essentially a historical fiction account of the summer of 1936 and the fictional Maycomb County trial of Tom Robinson. Long before I read those books, a young adult historical fiction novel about segregation in 1930s Mississippi, *Roll of Thunder, Hear my Cry* by Mildred D. Taylor, served as my first real source, as a nine or ten year-old, to help understand African-American history.

It is evident, to anyone who has ever read historical fiction, that the authors pursue a similar level of research and attention to historical detail as do the historians who produce journal articles. The process necessitates true historical dedication; it is only the outcome that is a different genre. When I first began teaching at the Facing History School, I realized that many of the historical sources that I used in class did little to convey the grandeur, emotion, and reality of the past; students learned the facts without grasping the story. I recalled my own love of *Shogun* and *The Pillars of the Earth*, but realized, unfortunately, that there was no way to integrate 1,000 page tomes into a packed curriculum.

At that point, I sat down to write my own historical fiction book called *The Blade's Path*; it was about a jeweled sword that travelled through the various ancient civilizations that we learned about in class: Mesopotamia, Egypt, China, Greece, and Rome. Each chapter was, essentially, a short story set in one of those civilizations. I can attest to the incredible amount of historical research, including time spent in the archives of the New York Public Library, it took to provide the right background context and rich historical details. I used the book in class for a couple of years and students loved it. Unfortunately, I didn't have the time or bandwidth as a young teacher to really pursue publication of *The Blade's Path* and I set it aside for over a decade. Now that we enjoy access to user-friendly self-publishing tools, I ought to practice what I preach to my students and finally publish the book.

Bringing Historical Fiction to the Classroom

The possibilities for historical fiction is endless; all historical topics are suitable. Authors have written incredible historical fiction about such a wide range of historical periods and events already, so there should be no reticence in encouraging students to dig into their interests.

We can also think about pushing students to produce metaphorical or allegorical historical (or political) fiction. George Orwell's *1984* is essentially political science fiction, or historical futurism. It functions, though, as an allegory of the totalitarianism of Orwell's contemporary reality. Students can create allegories about the past or present; doing so requires them to make arguments and to think symbolically.

Historical fiction assignments click well with units that use fiction to teach history. For example, when I've taught about ancient Greece, I normally have my students read *Oedipus* to learn about Greek culture and notions of fate and the role of the gods. Afterwards, students write creative pieces that demonstrate their understanding of key ideas in the book. Below are two creative writing options I provided to them:

Oedipus Historical Fiction

Option 1: Write a creative story using the characters from the story of *Oedipus*. What happens if Oedipus' parents do NOT give him up as a little baby? You may set the story at any time in his life and tell it as a story or as a play.

Option 2: Write a creative story about a character who tries to escape fate. You may set the character in ancient Greece or in NYC today.

When I taught a course on "Genocide and Human Rights" at Harvest Collegiate, I wanted students to demonstrate their understanding of the content and themes by creating allegorical historical fiction. The act of thinking symbolically to that level was perhaps a higher-level task than simply writing an essay, and fiction allowed for students to consider empathy and characters' experiences, which is crucial to this type of historical topic.

Final Project: A Fictional World's Human Rights/Genocide Story

Artistic Mission: Create a fictional world and a fictional story (it could be based loosely on another fictional universe or even a real place) *of at least ten pages* where a human rights abuse or genocide happens. This fictional text should serve as an allegory for what has happened in our own world. Your story MUST also include some type of resistance.

Your story must consist of at least five parts:

1   Beginning and gradual worsening of crisis
2   Description of the worst events of the crisis
3   The use of propaganda or justification from the perpetrators
4   Some type of resistance
5   Some type of resolution

You must also include:

1   Name of place/society
2   Names of groups
3   At least four key individuals with different character traits
4   Description of the world (geography of place, foods, art, languages, religions, etc.)

Here is an example of the beginning of one student's genocide and human rights allegory:

Dath

On the surface, the water in the Flores Sea seems calm. Underneath however, lies the buzzing world of Atlantica. Everyday, the Dath people drive through the currents of the sea rushing to get to work. The children play among the coral reefs and the multicolored fish. In Atlantica, a whirlwind of rainbows makes up the population. Throughout Atlantica, four counties are what hold the community of the Dath people. In Ula County, those with red skin make up the majority of the population in that region. The color of fury and strength constantly dart around the area, making the county a strong one. In the Hyacin County, those with skin as blue as a whale live together. In Ira county, the Dath people who have yellow skin live together and produce the energy of Atlantica. These three counties are full of rich life and wonder, but in the fourth, there lives a small population of those whose skin color is of orange, green, and purple. They live in Mau, a county that is neglected, to say the least. With dirty water and little resources, the rest of the Dath community in the three other counties disregards the intercolor people. With such a colorful and lively world, everything seems beautiful. But uncover the colorful surface and all you get is the remainder of evil.

"Agnes, come over here!", said Rodney, the young green boy. On the television screen flashed the election results.

Breaking News

Landorus, representative of Hyacin County in Parliament has won the election and is now our new minister.

Agnes, not being the most caring person about the election reluctantly comes out of her room to view the results. "Damn, that sucks," she says.

"'Damn'? That's it?", replies Rodney, shocked at the fact that Agnes doesn't have an opinion.

"So what? What's gonna change Rodney? Every intercolor person is gonna be discriminated against? Like we haven't been since our existence. I'm used to it and I'm honestly surprised at the fact that you're shocked. Everyone knows Atlantica is colorist, Landorus winning just supports it." Too upset to say anything, Rodney turns away and the fiery girl walks back to her room.

Keeping the Learning Real: Tips

Apprentice	Students write historical fiction about real people they have studied
Samurai	Students write counterfactual historical fiction stories
Jedi	Students create an allegorical story using a fantasy or science fiction realm to depict key themes and ideas of the course or unit

Authentic Assessment: Historical Fiction

Background: Historical fiction sets an imaginary story within the context of true historical events or periods. Historical fiction novels offer detailed and accurate descriptions of the past and require a strong understanding of history. Some famous works of historical fiction include *A Tale of Two Cities*, *Beloved*, *To Kill a Mockingbird*, and *Shogun*. Historical fiction requires the use of vivid language, characterization, plot, action, and dialogue. The goal is to weave in very specific historical detail in a way that seems authentic to the narration.

> **Deliverable:** Use your piece of historical fiction to develop an argument that answers your compelling question, exploring the key content and ideas that support your claim.

Requirements:

- Four to ten pages.
- You may write one continuous piece or include parts of two separate chapters of the book.
- Double-spaced.
- Create one or more characters. You may choose to write about a true famous leader or an imaginary ordinary person. Make sure the character's personality, experience, identity, and viewpoints get fleshed out in the work.

Tips:

- Include some new fun and creative personal information and plot twists.
- Include dialogue.
- Use detail and specifics (within reason) to discuss the events and your characters' lives. Consider creatively weaving in quotations from actual primary sources.

Creative Writing Rubric

Learning Goal	Jedi	Samurai	Apprentice
Claim & Reasons	– Establishes and develops a compelling, elegant, or very knowledgeable claim *about the narrator's viewpoint* and its significance – Provides coherent, complex, sophisticated supporting reasons for character's choices	– Establishes and develops precise, knowledgeable claim *about the narrator's viewpoint* – Provides coherent, sometimes complex supporting reasons for character's choices	– Establishes vague claim *about the narrator's viewpoint* – Provides basic reasons to support claim
Complexities	– Develops complexities and doubts fairly and thoroughly – Establishes complex contrasting perspective or notions of change	– Develops complexities and doubts fairly – Establishes some complex contrasting perspective or notions of change	– Describes one viewpoint – Does not develop notions of change or multiple perspectives
Context	– Arguments, ideas, and voice reflect a highly informed awareness of the larger historical context	– Arguments, ideas, and voice reflect general awareness of the larger historical context	– The paper shows some awareness of the context, but not how the claims relate to it
Significance	– Answers the question "So what?" for the narrator and his/her choices and viewpoint	– Provides a basic answer to the question "So what?" for the narrator and his/her choices and viewpoint	– Only vaguely alludes to larger meaning of the story

Voice	– Completely captures the character's voice – Achieves precision in language, and crafts succinct, elegant style, and word choice – Expertly captures emotions, symbolism, dialogue, actions, and thoughts through senses and metaphors – Expertly describes an experience for the narrator and how it relates to the larger context	– Mostly captures the character's voice – Approaching precision in language – Captures emotions, dialogue, actions, and thoughts – Describes an experience for the narrator and how it relates to the larger context	– Somewhat captures the character's voice – Sometimes maintains an appropriate style by attending to most norms of the discipline – Captures some emotions, dialogue, actions, and thoughts – Describes the narrator's perspective and how it relates to the larger context
Accuracy	– Correct and highly specific factual accuracy about the background historical context – Expertly integrates details from primary or secondary sources as part of the story	– Correct and specific factual accuracy about the background historical context – Integrates details from primary or secondary sources as part of the story	– Generally correct factual accuracy about the background historical context – Integrates some details from primary or secondary sources as part of the story

Notes

1 Johnston, I. (Trans.). (2010). *Iliad*. Retrieved October 7, 2019, from http://johnstoniatexts.x10host.com/homer/iliad_title.html.

2 Tzu, L. (2012). *Tao te ching: annotated & explained*. (D. Lin, Trans.). Woodstock, VT: SkyLight Paths Publishing.

3 Angelou, M. (2015, July 14). Our Grandmothers. Retrieved from www.poemhunter.com/poem/our-grandmothers/.

4 Sénghor, L. (n.d.). Prayer to Masks. Retrieved October 7, 2019, from https://allpoetry.com/Prayer-To-Masks.

5 Hughes, L. (1943). Freedom's Plow. Retrieved October 7, 2019, from https://allpoetry.com/Freedom's-Plow.

6 George, M. (2015). *The memoirs of Cleopatra: a novel*. New York: St. Martins Griffin.

7 Walker, A. (2003). *The color purple*. Orlando, FL: Harcourt.

8 Hesse, K. (2009). *Letters from Rifka*. New York: Square Fish.

9 Coates, T.-N. (2016). *Between the world and me*. Toronto: CNIB.

10 Bernstein, A. (2013, December 1). Movie Review: MANDELA: LONG WALK TO FREEDOM. Retrieved October 9, 2019, from www.assignmentx.com/2013/movie-review-mandela-long-walk-to-freedom/.

11 Scott, A. O. (2012, November 8). A president engaged in a great civil war. Retrieved October 9, 2019, from www.nytimes.com/2012/11/09/movies/lincoln-by-steven-spielberg-stars-daniel-day-lewis.html.

12 Scott, A. O. (2016, December 22). Review: "Hidden Figures" Honors 3 black women who helped NASA soar. Retrieved October 9, 2019, from www.nytimes.com/2016/12/22/movies/hidden-figures-review.html.

13 Varon, E. R. (2015, January 23). Book review: 'Gateway to Freedom,' by Eric Foner. Retrieved from www.washingtonpost.com/opinions/book-review-gateway-to-freedom-by-eric-foner/2015/01/23/adf8f06a-7fed-11e4-8882-03cf08410beb_story.html.

14 McNeill, W. H. (1997, May 15). History upside down. *The New York Review of Books*. Retrieved October 2019, from www.nybooks.com/articles/1997/05/15/history-upside-down/.

15 *International Herald Tribune* (2015, August 5). 1945: Hiroshima hit by atomic bomb. Retrieved from https://iht-retrospective.blogs.nytimes.com/2015/08/05/1945-hiroshima-hit-by-atomic-bomb/.

16 Kleinfield, N. R. (2001, September 12). U.S. ATTACKED; HIJACKED JETS DESTROY TWIN TOWERS AND HIT PENTAGON IN DAY OF TERROR. Retrieved from www.nytimes.com/2001/09/12/us/us-attacked-hijacked-jets-destroy-twin-towers-and-hit-pentagon-in-day-of-terror.html.

17 The war against America; an unfathomable attack. (2001, September 12). Retrieved from www.nytimes.com/2001/09/1/opinion/the-war-against-america-an-unfathomable-attack.html.

Part 3

Creative and Artistic Assessments

5

Oral Communication

This chapter delves into a plethora of ways to assess students' knowledge through oral communication beyond the traditional full-class presentation. The ability to communicate verbally is just as important as being able to do so in writing. Moreover, many students who struggle at writing can communicate their knowledge far better orally. The chapter will provide guidance and examples for assessing students through: podcasts, panel, roundtable, or fishbowl discussions, debate, oral history interviews, gallery walks and museums, and student-led lessons. This order of assessments generally proceeds in terms of level of complexity for the student and for the teacher. Podcasts are easy for individual students to produce and may require little support from the teacher, depending on the goal, whereas student-led lessons and museum exhibits necessitate far more planning.

After reading the chapter, use the following chart as a plan to "keep the learning real"

In which unit(s) of your course could you integrate oral communication assessments?
Would your students work individually, in groups, or as a full class?
Which form of oral communication projects would your class pursue? Or, would you provide choice?

Podcasts

One of my favorite stories of how someone can take a winding and unique path to arrive at his vocation is about my good friend, Bishop Sand. After college, Bishop entered medical school but found the experience, interestingly, a bit intellectually stultifying. He then decided to become a science teacher and we taught together at the Facing History School, where we commiserated about the challenges of teaching over a weekly lunch at an Indian restaurant in Hell's Kitchen. Like many teachers, he struggled a bit his first year in a really tough environment and then gradually found his groove, his way of engaging students, and his teacher voice, eventually becoming an excellent biology teacher.

Bishop, however, is a bit of a 21st century Renaissance man. He is a talented painter and then he discovered his real passion: audio production. Before podcasts really hit mainstream, he fell in love with the WNYC science podcast "Radiolab" and began to envision a different future. I was disappointed when, after a few years, like many young teachers Bishop decided to leave teaching, although in his case at least he didn't go to law school. Instead, he created his own science podcast called "Sift," in which he interviewed leading thinkers on a variety of fascinating topics from taxonomy to the science of sports. He loved the science *and* audio aspects of podcasting, spending hours fiddling over the background sound effects.

Once I moved to Westchester, podcasts became a staple of my commute. Without the train I have less time for reading. With my commute being my main time for learning, I only had a few options. I tried audiobooks. Other than *Long Walk to Freedom*, I couldn't maintain focus on long stories. One person speaking monotonously is a recipe for daydreaming and distraction. I found it impossible to concentrate on the stories.

There are a number of elements that make podcasts interesting, at least the best ones: great writing, good narration, interesting/engaging interviews, conversations and multiple voices, breaking down difficult concepts to make sense to the audience, music, and if needed, additional sounds and effects. The variation in delivery whether because of juxtaposed voices in interviews, interactivity, and/or sound effects helps the listener stay focused and provides for a more multi-layered experience than audiobooks.

There is a wide-range of production value for podcasts, thereby opening up myriad possibilities for students. Some involve no more production than two guys chatting in a garage in front of an iPhone, while others like "Radiolab" dive deeply into sound effects, storytelling, and sensory experiences. This range provides more flexibility for teachers looking to integrate audio into their classes. There are now more than 800,000 podcasts in Apple podcast, resulting in 14 billion downloads in 2019, with about 144 million

Americans listening to at least one during the year. This is clearly a legitimate way to communicate a story.

Driving every day makes podcasts a lifesaver and one of the main ways that I continue to learn. I listened to Bishop's beautiful "Sift" podcast and then began searching out the history ones. I found a wealth of history podcasts. Some are really driven by the narrative, such as "Revolutions," which looks at a new revolution each season in minute detail. This type of history podcast is more about what happened than about argument.

Other history podcasts gather together leading historians to discuss a particular topic. "Backstory" is a podcast that brings together historians like Brian Balogh of the University of Virginia, Nathan Connolly of Johns Hopkins University, and Joanne Freeman of Yale University. The show's format takes a contemporary issue of importance and traces its "backstory" in the American past, connecting the present to the past. Recent shows tie Labor Day into the story of labor history, the protest at Standing Rock to the history of indigenous resistance, and the term "man up" to the history of masculinity in America.

Some journalists participate in the historical conversation, often trying to uncover a hidden story or reshape our views on the past. Malcolm Gladwell, in a typically charismatic fashion, offers a "Revisionist History" that makes us rethink events that appear to have their place in history set into stone, such as Brown v. Board of Education in his episode "Miss Buchanan's Period of Adjustment." Similarly, *Washington Post* journalist Lillian Cunningham presented a new look at our founding document in "Constitutional" and at our leaders in "Presidential."

And Bishop? I'm thrilled that he finally achieved his dream. He is now the head producer at Lillian Cunningham's new *Washington Post* podcast "Moonrise," which looks at the history of science through the story of the Space Race. Bishop's audio flare pulsates in the background. In episode 1, I love the way that Lillian places her podcast within the larger historiography surrounding the Space Race:

> *It's a perfect story – the moonshot. It starts with a visionary president engaging the country in a noble pursuit against an adversary and it ends with a demonstration of, yes, political might, but also the capacity of the human spirit. But in the 50 years that have passed since the moon landing, presidential documents have been declassified. Once-secret programs have been revealed. So when you ask space historians today, "Why did we go to the moon?," you get very different and interesting answers. Starting with the fact that while it might have been Kennedy's decision to go to the moon, it definitely wasn't Kennedy's idea. I began tracing the story backwards.*[1]

Podcasts are now one of the main ways that I continue to learn more history. It is time that we made them a medium through which our students can produce history.

Bringing Podcasts into the Classroom

The wide variety of podcast formats allow students to play with their product. Some might choose to add in more audio background, others might focus on real or imaginary interviews, and still others might simply speak into an audio recorder. In truth, podcasts are really shows that put out multiple episodes through an RSS feed, so in reality students are more likely to create one episode that is a single audio feature than a full series. Nonetheless, even if producing only one episode it is meaningful to ask students to consider the title of the podcast series, the target audience, the types of sponsors they would pursue, and how they might pitch this podcast to a platform such as NPR. In fact, to add to the authenticity of the project, students can now submit their podcast to NPR's annual "Student Cast Challenge."

Certainly, pretty much any topic can be turned into an episode, ranging from personal narratives about race and gender (following the format of *The Moth*), a discussion of great turning points in history, or multiple students talking about a historical controversy.

There are really two paths that teachers can take in terms of podcast assessments. One is to use the podcast as a vehicle to record (and share) a conversation between students about a particular book, topic, or question. This becomes more like a panel discussion, but the act of recording and sharing (even if only with the teacher) increases the stakes and seriousness of the discussion. The second path is to really ask students to spend more time on the production, to consider story, narrative, target audience, interviews, and sound effects. As the teacher, I would focus more on the story, narrative, and argument rather than the audio quality; nonetheless, we should at least encourage and push the students to learn some of the audio production by including music in the background or a few sound effects.

Keeping the Learning Real: Tips

Apprentice	Students create a one-episode audio feature about a particular topic
Samurai	Students create a one-episode audio feature about a particular topic using sound effects, music, and interviews
Jedi	The class creates a real podcast series with different groups taking on different episodes

Authentic Assessment: Podcast

Background: Throughout the 20th century, radio was a crucial means for communication and learning. For many decades, radio was one of the main forms of entertainment for American households. In the 21st century, podcasts have emerged as important mediums for producing history. Some historical podcasts include "Revolutions," "Backstory," and "Moonrise."

Deliverable: Use your podcast to develop an argument that answers your compelling question, exploring the key content and ideas that support your claim.

Requirements:

- Four to eight minutes.
- A careful attention to detail and historical accuracy.
- A thoughtful attention to volume, sound effects, music, pacing, articulation, outside guests.
- Introduce yourselves, the podcast series title, and the podcast episode.
- Breakdown possibly unknown information for the audience.
- Include real or imaginary interviews where necessary to bring in multiple voices. How and when do you introduce them and their backgrounds?
- How many hosts will there be? One or two? Will there be a conversation?
- If this is a narrative, what is the drama? What is interesting or surprising about this story and how do you incorporate it? How do you make it "visual" by including sensory details?

Artist Statement:
Include a one-page artist statement, written in the first person. You should describe:

- Why you chose to create this podcast.
- What is your historical question and argument.
- What historical choices you made in creating it.
- What artistic choices you made and what symbolism you included (in your sound effects).

(◆ What the podcast represents about the event.
◆ Who is the target audience.
◆ What would you include in your pitch to a publishing platform about why this podcast should get picked up.
◆ What do you want audiences to take away from hearing this?)

Oral History Interviews

Oral history occupies an interesting space in the larger field of history. As the Oral History Association explains on its website, "Oral history is both the oldest type of historical inquiry, predating the written word, and one of the most modern, initiated with tape recorders in the 1940s and now using 21st-century digital technologies."[2] In other words, long before we relied fully on the written word as the authority in history, humans passed down their stories verbally. Now, with new technologies, oral history has again emerged as a valued way to transmit information about our past.

Donald Ritchie, a historian in the United States Senate Historical Office, explains in his book *Doing Oral History: A Practical Guide*, "Oral History collects memories and personal commentaries of historical significance through recorded interviews. An oral history interview generally consists of a well-prepared interviewer questioning an interviewee and recording their exchange in audio or video format."[3] Whereas in the early 20th century oral history lacked the gravitas of written history, much has changed in the field. Columbia University offers a graduate degree in oral history, while many other institutions of higher education provide courses and training in the methodology. Philip Napoli is a beloved professor at Brooklyn College who teaches courses on oral history there; to my later regret, I never took one of them while doing my master's degree in history at that institution.

A number of consequential works of oral history appear online and in transcribed textual format. Sometimes, oral histories appear purely in their primary source form: as interviews. Other times, historians use the interviews as sources and compile them into a larger secondary source oral history.

Svetlana Alexievich, a winner of the Nobel Prize in Literature, recently published an incredible book *Last Witnesses: An Oral History of the Children of World War II*. The book is composed of interviews. Alexievich shares the story of Volodia Parabkovich, who was 12 years old during the war. Volodia describes: "Outside the city they shot at us point-blank. People fell to the ground … In the sand, in the grass … 'Close your eyes, sonny … Don't look,' my father begged."[4]

Many museums, such as the United States Holocaust Memorial Museum, hold oral history collections, which are often available online.[5]

I first conducted an oral history of my grandfather, Joseph Brandman, about his experience during the Holocaust. Nearly two decades later, this interview became part of my larger *Brandman Holocaust Memorial Museum*. More recently, I interviewed my in-laws about their extraordinary lives growing up in northeastern Brazil, hoping that this oral history will become a treasure for the family to pass on.

Bringing Oral Histories to the Classroom

Many people argue that we are suffering, today, from an epidemic of loneliness and isolation. Every chance we give students to have a meaningful conversation with someone else, especially the elderly and/or their family members, brings a spark of connection to the world. Interviews can be stressful on both sides; I actually get really nervous when interviewing other people because I have the sensation that I am invading their privacy. Once underway, however, I realize that most interviewees love the attention and I love the connection.

Simply put, interviews are powerful educational experiences. My colleague from Harvest Collegiate, Andy Snyder, was the teacher who turned me on to interviews. Andy is an exceptional educator and somehow, also, a great juggler, ultimate frisbee player, table-tennis player, chess player, debater, and more. Essentially, he has beaten me in every competition we've ever faced off in. He'd probably even do a better job of raising my kids, although I haven't yet brought up that option to him. Andy taught me that interviews are a way to build meaningful experiences, personal connections, and deeper learning. Sometimes, in conversations with him, it even feels like an interview. He is very present and he asks deep, probing questions that go beyond normal small talk.

His influence led me to push students, more often, to interview family and community members to learn directly from the experiences of others, to include interviews in their research papers, and to document their own family oral histories. Students of mine have collected oral histories for research papers, interviewing grandparents about experiences in the Holocaust, the Cold War, and beyond.

With an oral history, we need to consider how students will share their findings. Simply making a recording is not enough if the oral history is the actual project, rather than serving as a source in a larger piece of research. Below, I've included an adapted version of Steve Lazar's Oral History Project on American immigration.

Keeping the Learning Real: Tips

Apprentice	Students interview a family member about a historical event
Samurai	Students interview a family member about an event and include the evidence as part of a larger research paper
Jedi	The class composes an oral history on a particular event based on compiling each student's oral history interview

Authentic Assessment: Oral History Project

Requirements:

◆ Transcription – The process of transcribing the interview may be one of the most important things that you do in this project. This is the moment in which you are recording history and you need to give the task the utmost care.

◆ Summary Sheet – You must provide a typed Summary Sheet as a cover. It must include the following information:

- Name of Interviewee:
- Date of Birth:
- Main topic discussed:
- Three main ideas from the interview:

◆ Five to seven sentence biography of the interviewee.

◆ Post-Oral History Reflection:

- What are the first five words that come to mind after your interview experience?
- Identify one or two things that the interviewee said that surprised you.
- What did the interviewee say that connects to things we've learned about the topic in class?
- How did the interview go?

Panel, Roundtable, and Fishbowl Discussions

Real-World Context

While a debate is the pursuit of victory, a conversation is the pursuit of knowledge and wisdom. Perhaps the most famous exemplar of a panel discussion is

NBC's *Meet the Press*, the classic Sunday morning news show in which talking heads, including Democratic and Republican politicians, discuss key stories from the week. This show can get combative as the format is geared toward Red and Blue foot soldiers squaring off to win the argument.

Historians engage in similar panel discussions although usually they are more civil and constructive in purpose. The idea of a historical panel is to dig deeply into a topic or question so as to flesh out various perspectives and lenses of understanding. In March, 2016, for example, a group of six esteemed historians of the Civil War and Reconstruction gathered for a panel discussion on the origins and legacies of the Fourteenth Amendment. They sat in front of what appears to be a chalkboard and behind a long wooden desk. Most of them had a bottle of water to hydrate for the long, nearly two-hour discussion. Eric Foner, for example, discussed the weakness of an amendment that was essentially a compromise that failed to achieve all that the radical Republicans had hoped for. Amy Dru Stanley, a professor at the University of Chicago, connected the amendment to the 1875 Civil Rights Act and its support for the universal right to amusement, which she argues is a transformation in our understanding of humanity. Thankfully, we have access to the video of the panel discussion through the website of the Gilder Lehrman Center at Yale University.[6]

Thus, we can learn from them and get the sense of the give-and-take of historical arguments as scholars debate a great question. Similar panels take place at countless universities. The Radcliffe Institute at Harvard, for example, held a discussion between six prominent female historians such as Joyce Antler and Alice Kessler-Harris on the important theme: Why history matters. The discussion specifically focuses on the importance of women's history and the role of Gerda Lerner. It is a conversation about the field of history and the ways that Gerda Lerner pushed the envelope and pressured the discipline to include women's studies as a legitimate sphere within history. One main argument that emerges in the panel is the idea that women's history is not only academic; it is also a social movement.[7]

Bringing Panel, Roundtable, and Fishbowl Discussions to the Classroom

How do we get our students to do the same thing? In my career, two teachers have been most influential in teaching me how to get students to talk and listen to each other: Zoe Roben and Andy Snyder. Running a small group or class-wide discussion is a bit more complex than a podcast, but does not require some of the great leaps I will discuss later on.

Zoe was an English teacher at Harvest Collegiate for a number of years. She is brilliant, kind, and soft-spoken; she listens to others and makes them feel good about themselves, even if the original idea mostly came from her.

I sat in on Zoe's class one day while her students were engaged in a fishbowl conversation about the book *Ender's Game*. I learned more in that class from Zoe about the pedagogy surrounding student discussion than at any other point in my career. During the entire discussion, Zoe basically did not speak.

What was the key? Zoe recognized that teacher intervention is often what prevents students from having an authentic conversation. So, instead she provided the structure and practice to allow the learners to feel comfortable speaking to each other, rather than to the teacher. For that to happen, the teacher must be willing to recede to the background.

Andy also thinks deeply about conversation in the classroom. Before he joined Harvest, I attended a workshop that he led about student discussion. It was memorable because he had us role-play and practice conversation by miming and demonstrating good listening posture. One of the best moments each year, now, in my class is when I have the students practice their listening posture. It was Andy who taught me that we need to push for conversation over debate, for learning over victory, and for consensus over triumph.

I once co-taught a week-long intensive class with Andy, and following the class I wrote him a long note about what I had learned from seeing him teach, part of which involved discussion:

> *Today, I noticed that in our class debrief we didn't just talk about their ideas but the process of their conversation. We started the debrief by you modeling, with me, how questions can push a pair-share further. Then, when we brought it back to the debrief, rather than jump into the content you asked "so what was one thing something did in the conversation to make it a better discussion?"*

Finally, it was both Andy and Zoe that taught me the crucial role of students as discussion coaches in a fishbowl conversation. Students can observe each other, provide feedback, and thus both the "coach" and "trainee" learn how to get better.

Oral communication is as important as written communication in conveying historical knowledge and the advantage of oral communication is that it asks students to make an argument and garner evidence to support it while also listening to each other, asking questions, and answering questions. A conversation is richer than a one-way presentation. It requires students to hear and consider alternative viewpoints, reassess their argument, and incorporate new information. Sometimes, students will change their mind because of what another student has argued. In short, discussion is a multifaceted and difficult learning experience and assessment that combines interpersonal intelligence with analytical argumentation. In a strong conversation, students do not dominate each other and they work actively to bring quieter students into the fold in a gentle and friendly way.

I utilize three formats of discussion – panel, roundtable, and fishbowl – that achieve mostly the same goals and are all related to the real-world examples mentioned above. There are a few important differences. First, panel discussions usually take place behind rectangular tables whereas roundtables happen in schools, bizarrely, when we push four tables together to make a square.

In panel discussions, I break the class into groups of about four students and they go off to different places to have a private discussion, which they film. Afterwards, they send me the video clip and I watch it to evaluate. I use panels as the culmination of individual or group learning; in other words, I have given students a set of sources to make sense of, and then the panel becomes a way to show what they know and to grapple with larger meaning. Panels also work best when there are many documents to work off of in order to address an important overarching question. One of the most important historical questions that any panel can discuss is: why is the event important? We need to make sure students have access to enough information and a complex question so they are not simply repeating themselves in the conversation.

One of my effective panel discussions comes off of my Haitian Revolution unit. Students have already studied the French Revolution and I provide a number of primary, secondary, and tertiary sources that allows them to develop an understanding of the Haitian Revolution. Students have the opportunity, in groups, to determine their own learning calendar over four to five days so that they decide when they will read and discuss each source. At the end, they videotape an eight to 12 minute panel discussion, amongst themselves, about the question they have developed. Students can bring notes and texts to the conversation but they shouldn't read – they should have a conversation. It is fine to plan out a general trajectory for the discussion, as long as they are proceeding without a script.

Roundtable discussions, which are commonplace in Consortium schools, are less about sharing ideas and more about sharing work. Whereas a panel serves as a meeting place to connect around a question, a roundtable functions as a way to see what other students have produced, to learn from them, and then to ask questions and have a conversation about those pieces. Roundtables can function in the same way, to some degree, as a jigsaw activity. Students may learn about different revolutionaries, or revolutions, and then come together to share in small groups what they have learned. Students may share their best work from the year, or a roundtable can serve as a venue to demonstrate what they've learned from their research paper. Students find roundtables to be a more intimate and less stressful form of presentation than the full-class presentation.

The fishbowl format is the best way I've ever found to cultivate a strong and thoughtful discussion among a full class. (Essentially, half of the class is in an inner circle (in the fishbowl) participating in the conversation, while the other half is outside the fishbowl observing) I opt for the fishbowl structure for us to (swim in the deep end of a complex text) For example, my class reads a piece by the anthropologist Bernard Cohn on the complex nature of the cultural diffusion of clothing in colonial India. In the fishbowl, students discuss the question: How are clothes and power intertwined in colonialism? Similarly, during our unit on the Russian Revolution and the USSR, students read excerpts of journal articles about peasant revolts against Stalin's collectivization plans. One of the fishbowl questions about the article is: To what extent did Stalin actually achieve a totalitarian state in the USSR?

The other way I might use a fishbowl is a synthesis overview of an entire unit. So I might take the essential questions of a Holocaust unit as the basis of the discussion. What caused the Holocaust? Or, in an American Revolution unit, students might prepare for their summative assessment through a fishbowl discussion: whose statues should appear at the front of the Museum of the American Revolution? Lastly, we might take up a fishbowl discussion to consider the success or failure of a particular revolution. Was the French Revolution successful? Was the Iranian Revolution successful?

I first fell in love with the fishbowl format when I watched Zoe Roben's class do it at Harvest Collegiate. Zoe's format involves the students in the outside circle pairing up with a student in the middle and observing just that one participant throughout the discussion. The observer provides feedback on the number of times that the student participated, the types of comments that they made, etc.

Andy frames the outside observer as the coach (During the fishbowl discussion, at certain breaks, that coach has the opportunity to provide advice and guidance to the participants in the middle.) It is almost like a boxing match, in which those in the middle participate for about four or five minutes, and then at the buzzer they meet with the coach, who then gives the "boxer" a pep-talk or words of encouragement and even for a new idea of what to discuss. Before our first fishbowl discussion of the year, I play a clip of Rocky's coach talking to him in the corner between rounds. There is a palpable excitement, then, in between rounds of the fishbowl when the coaches get to pretend to do those things coaches do: pour water on them, yell in their faces, and provide tips.

Fishbowl discussions involve students in the conversation more than any other authentic format that I've discovered (Students who will never raise their hand in a full-class discussion often participate actively in the midst of a fishbowl.)

I begin by having partners plan for the first round together, not knowing who will be called into the middle. I ask each partner to choose a role: Dory or Nemo; Woody or Buzz; Moana or Elsa. Once I've given them five minutes or so to prepare, I call all the Nemos or Moanas to the middle to talk and they have about five minutes to address one or two open-ended provocative questions about the text or about an essential question of the unit. When the buzzer goes, the speaker returns to meet back with the coach who provides the pep-talk and words of advice.

Often times, the most talkative students enter and dominate in the first round, but once the quieter students have met with their coaches and gotten a boost of encouragement and a new idea, they come out thoughtfully and proactively in the second round to make sure they get into the conversation. It is inspiring to watch.

When discussions are happening in real-time, and we want to assess them, we need to consider how to do it. Comments and responses are flying by and it is not easy to keep track of what is happening in a way that makes for fair assessment. Here, I want to suggest two approaches.

(First, if you include participation as a grade, then a formal panel, roundtable, or fishbowl discussion is a perfect opportunity to simply assess whether or not each student participates.) In this case, we are really talking about a quantitative judgment. Do they participate once, twice, or a few times? Additionally, are they respectful towards others, allowing their peers to speak and, even better, inviting shy students into the discussion? Since students are most likely to participate in a formal discussion, assessing what happens in these situations tends to be a generous act by focusing on a moment of strength rather than weakness.

Second, it is also possible, although difficult, to grade the content of the comments using a rubric. To do this, it is best to have one sheet for the entire class with a few standards to evaluate for each student. A quick check-mark for comments that meet certain standards is sufficient to keep track.

One of the dilemmas in a formal discussion is that the open format may seem to reward the most aggressive students; since students are facilitating the discussion and I'm not calling on students, it may allow some to dominate the discussion by consistently inserting themselves into it. However, I make it clear to the students ahead of time that I'm looking for a conversation; that is, students should be thoughtful enough to allow others to participate and gracious in a situation in which a few students speak at once. I tally off one check for every time a student participates, but if he proposes a question to another student who has not yet entered into the discussion, then he gets two checks. If two students speak at the same time, and one student continues to make the comment while the other students provides an opening to allow the other to continue, the former student gets one point and the latter earns two.

Keeping the Learning Real: Tips

Apprentice	Students record panel discussions on a topic in small groups
Samurai	Students share their work from the semester in roundtable presentations
Jedi	The whole class engages in an interactive coaching fishbowl discussion

Authentic Assessment: Panel Discussion

Background: Historians use multiple authentic formats to make their arguments, including panel discussions. Historians love to get together to discuss complex questions about the past. The goal of these conversations is not necessarily to arrive at an agreement, but rather to further our thinking about the topic and to dig deeper into its complexity. There are myriad great panel discussions available to watch online.

Deliverable: Use your panel discussion to develop an argument that answers your compelling question, exploring the key content and ideas that support your claim.

Requirements:

You may work with three to five students, one of whom may be the moderator who guides the discussion and moves forward with new questions.

- ◆ The panel must be six to 12 minutes long, videotaped.
- ◆ You should carefully consider your clothing, your location, the scene setup, and the background. Do you want any props on the table?
- ◆ Consider how your group plans to interact. You may have notes, a general guideline for the discussion, and texts to refer to. You should not have a script and should not read. Your goal is to have a conversation.

◆ You may begin with "talking points" for each of you, but that should lead into questions and conversation. Make sure all participate in the discussion. Listening and asking questions is more valuable than dominating others. Refer to comments others have made previously in the discussion when relevant. It is also okay to admit things you don't know and further questions you have.

Begin by introducing each member of the panel. You may want to consider having one person be the "moderator" who introduces everyone and asks the questions. In this case, the moderator should also step in to give insight and answers throughout the presentation.

Debate

Real-World Context
At one time, it would have seemed incomprehensible for an entire class to debate and for the experience to seem authentic. After the 2020 Democratic primaries, however, with 20 candidates lining up over two days, it is starting to appear like a real CNN debate.

Debates have always played an important role in American politics and served as one of the primary means for voters to understand the positions and personality of the candidates.

The most famous of all political debates in American history is probably the series of seven Lincoln–Douglas debates held in 1858 to grapple with the issue of slavery. We would never again use this format, as it began with a 60 minute opener from one candidate, moved on to a 90 minute response from the other, and then a final 30 minute rejoinder from the first speaker.

Other great debates from American history involve the nature of social movements. Malcolm X and James Baldwin debated in 1963 over the proper path for the Civil Rights Movement. James Baldwin expressed interest in a world "in which there are no blacks and there are no whites. It does not matter." Malcolm X responded: "as a black man, and proud of being a black man, I can't conceive of myself as having any desire to lose my identity." Later on, he declared, "as soon as the black man undergoes a reappraisal of himself … he says to himself, why should he wait for the Supreme Court to give him what a white man has when he is born."

A subsequent debate between Baldwin and conservative intellectual William F. Buckley in 1965 also took an unusual format by today's norms. Baldwin spoke for about 20 minutes and then so too did Buckley, with no give-and-take between them. It is particularly poignant to watch Baldwin explain, in front of what is almost completely a white audience, that

In the case of the American Negro, from the moment you are born every stick and stone, every face, is white. Since you have not yet seen a mirror, you suppose you are, too. It comes as a great shock around the age of 5, 6, or 7 to discover that the flag to which you have pledged allegiance, along with everybody else, has not pledged allegiance to you.

This is the type of debate that shoots for a win-lose outcome, as the audience, the Cambridge Union Society, voted 540–160 in favor of the proposition that Baldwin upheld: The American Dream is at the expense of the American Negro.

An organization called "Intelligence Squared" seeks to use debate to "restore critical thinking, facts, reason, and civility to American public discourse." Intelligence Squared hosts debates on a variety of topics, in front of an audience, that usually brings in two experts who are on one side of the issue and two on the other. Some issues relevant to a social studies classroom include the following propositions:

◆ The U.S. Should Let In 100,000 Syrian Refugees.
◆ Negotiations Can Denuclearize North Korea.
◆ Globalization Has Undermined America's Working Class.

Like the Baldwin–Buckley debate, the Intelligence Squared format seeks to establish a winner and loser by comparing people's views on the proposition before the debate with their views after the debate. The side that marks a greater percentage change in those favoring its position "wins" the debate.

Debates on controversial social and political issues are fascinating. Historians also debate, but their forum is not usually "live" in front of an audience; rather, the historical debate is an ongoing process of point/counterpoint about the past. Historiography, essentially, is the part of history that follows this debate. In fact, when we think about what makes a good question in history, one of the primary components is that it is "debatable."

So, historians might participate in a debate over who was the greatest or worst American president. C-SPAN runs a poll of historians who vote on the best president while a History.com "History Faceoff" presents the differing views of two historians on that question, with Joseph Ellis favoring George Washington and Harold Holzer advocating for Abraham Lincoln.

Every great topic in history is a debate, although it rarely takes place in real-time: what caused the fall of the Roman Empire? What caused the Holocaust? Was the United States at fault for military dictatorships in Latin America during the Cold War? Why did the West "diverge" from the rest of the world in the past few centuries? Should the U.S. have entered World War I?

Bringing Debates into the Classroom

I'm actually not a huge fan of debates, but that doesn't take away from the fact that they are authentic and that students *love* them. As mentioned previously, I've been really influenced, albeit reluctantly, by the points made by Andy Snyder. Andy taught me that the problem with debates is their win-lose format, which really serves to keep students from listening to each other and learning from each other. Well, they do listen so as to develop rebuttals, but they don't actually listen to consider the other's view as having some validity.

The point of school, he maintains, is to converse and to learn. Debates aren't a real conversation if those participating aren't really open to having their minds changed or finding some kind of middle ground. So, the format of debating used by Intelligence Squared, for example, is engaging but it also means that the speakers don't concede or identify nuance and there is no attempt to reach consensus or an actual solution.

That being said, classroom debates do electrify the atmosphere, spark student interest, and get learners to go above and beyond. For those students who thrive on the adrenaline of competition, a debate is one of the only academic activities that really provides that sense of win-lose play. Any great historical, social, or political question can lead to a great debate; the issue is really figuring out how to organize the process. Debates can function as summative assessments for any unit, or as practice formative assessments that prepare students for a further assignment, such as an essay.

Unlike the Democratic primaries, we don't want ten speakers at a time. Steve Lazar, my former colleague at Harvest Collegiate, produced a wonderful debate on Golden Age Civilizations at his previous school, Bronx Lab School, together with Rachel Apple and Anissa Harris. The question was: Whose Golden Age was the Greatest? Options included Rome, Song/Tang Dynasty, Golden Age of Islam, Gupta Empire, Hellenistic Greece, Byzantine Empire, Incan Empire, and West African Empires. It broke the students into small teams and essentially narrowed down winners in a bracket over multiple rounds, almost like the NCAA tournament. While Steve now maintains that the question is too contrived and devoid of real context, the tournament format, especially since it was done during March Madness, certainly added pizzazz to the experience.

One of the beauties of debate as an assessment format is its versatility both in terms of content and structure. Here's my preferred debate format, which I developed after modifying one of the formal structures of the Speech and Debate club and which I used for an American History debate that cut across units. Who Shaped America More? Teddy Roosevelt, the suffragettes, Woodrow Wilson, the flappers, FDR, or the Greatest Generation.

Speaker	Time limit (minutes)	Purpose
Side 1	4	Present claim
Side 2	4	Present claim
Open Q&A	3	Alternate asking and answering questions
Rebuttal	3	Refute the opposing side's arguments
Open Q&A	3	Alternate asking and answering questions
Side 1	3	Explain reasons that you won
Side 2	3	Explain reasons that you won

Keeping the Learning Real: Tips

Apprentice	Students debate in small groups
Samurai	A class-wide debate with students on teams
Jedi	An NCAA style knockout debate tournament

Authentic Assessment: A Debate

Background: Debates are commonly used in politics, history, and civic action to allow people to stake opposing claims and defend them. Some great debates in history include the Lincoln–Douglas debates, John F. Kennedy vs. Richard Nixon, James Baldwin vs. William F. Buckley, and contemporary Intelligence Squared debates.

Deliverable: Use your debate to develop an argument that answers our compelling question, exploring the key content and ideas that support your claim.

Requirements:
  A careful attention to detail, purpose, timing, and accuracy.

Tips
  ◆ Make your question and argument/thesis clear.
  ◆ Pay attention to both big ideas and specific detail.
  ◆ Listen to the other side and respond.
  ◆ Speak loudly, clearly, and at a moderate pace

Format

Speaker	Time limit (minutes)	Purpose
Side 1	4	Present claim
Side 2	4	Present claim
Open Q&A	3	Alternate asking and answering questions
Rebuttal	3	Refute the opposing side's arguments
Open Q&A	3	Alternate asking and answering questions
Side 1	3	Explain reasons that you won
Side 2	3	Explain reasons that you won

Gallery Walks and Museums

Museums are vital institutions for the public to learn about crucial topics in our world and for adults to continue in a process of lifelong learning. While we normally think first of art, museums also exist in the disciplines of science, math, technology, and history. Architects, educators, and curators of museums carefully compose the layout, organization, and display of artifacts – visual, auditory, and sensory – so as to cultivate an immersive experience. The December 2019 issue of the *American Historical Review* discussed the historical value of seven museums, including the Namibian Independence Memorial Museum.

The United States Holocaust Memorial Museum is one example of an institution whose function lays in the arena of history and politics. It declares, as its mission, that it exists as "a living memorial to the Holocaust," and that it is meant to inspire "citizens and leaders worldwide to confront hatred, prevent genocide, and promote human dignity."[8] The museum's permanent exhibit takes a chronological approach across three floors of artifacts, guiding the visitor through the Nazi Assault, the Final Solution, and the Last Chapter. I still remember when I visited with my father. I was 18 years old and he told me it would be okay if I got emotional and cried. Fifteen minutes into the museum, I was fine and he was an absolute emotional wreck. The museum had achieved an additional purpose of connecting the visitor, my father, empathetically with the history and ensuring that I, the teenager, was morbidly embarrassed.

The list of history-focused museums is impressive. Here are just a few:

◆ National Museum of American History.
◆ National Museum of African American History and Culture.
◆ National Civil Rights Museum.

It is worth remembering that many museums display art not only to teach the visitor about art, but also about the cultural and historical context in which it was created. Thus, the Metropolitan Museum of Art's incredible Egyptian gallery is an immersive experience in the history of ancient Egypt. The statues of Hatshepsut, one of the female rulers of ancient Egypt, show her wearing the traditional male kingly headcloth and kilt. Yet, in the statue, she still maintains a distinctively female body. This statue teaches us something important about gender, clothing, and power in ancient Egypt. I'm just not sure exactly what it is. Similarly, the National Museum of Ecuador displays pre-Columbian artifacts that connect the visitor to the indigenous history of the region. I have not been to the National Museum of African American History and Culture because I, typically, forgot to pre-order tickets before our trip to Washington DC, but my friend Bishop told me about the experience of beginning in the darkness evoking the slave ship and gradually working your way up toward the light of freedom.

Similarly, other museums serve as venues to teach about the intersection of science and history. The National Air and Space Museum provides powerful lessons on the Cold War and the Space Race. Seeing the original rockets and shuttles that brought humans into space in the 1960s becomes an unforgettable glimpse into history. One of my first great experiences as an educator was volunteering, while in college, at a Star Wars exhibit at the Air and Space Museum. Clearly, I was using my time wisely to increase my social cachet and improve my future job prospects. One of my favorite museums I have ever visited is the Deutsches Museum in Berlin. It is an incredible science museum that lays out the history of radio, computers, boats, airplanes, and more.

The American Historical Association describes the role of the "Historians in Museums" within the larger field. In museums, historians take on jobs as curators, collections managers, and museum educators. To do this type of work, most curators, for example, require a masters or doctoral degree in the field of Public History. Many universities offer advanced degrees in Public History, including American University, George Mason University, New York University, and Howard University.

Simply put, museums are vital venues for disseminating history.

Bringing Museums to the Classroom

I learned about "Gallery Walks" in my first professional development session at the Facing History School. At the time, all FHS teachers attended at least one professional development session run by Facing History and Ourselves. The gallery walk is a favorite methodology of Facing History because it is student-centered and it cultivates a connection or interaction between the student, the artifact(s), and the overall topic(s). The simple act of standing up, walking around the room, and silently viewing artifacts on an issue like slavery, Civil Rights resistance, or Jewish resistance in the Holocaust helps to create a more immersive and empathetic experience. It is what brings the "ourselves" into the "history."

In that context, however, the gallery walk was a teacher-produced activity meant for student learning. Years later, I took a similar structure, but transformed it to be about how students could display their work and communicate their understanding. To some extent, a gallery walk or student-created museum essentially functions like a science fair. Students have something to show, and they need to be alongside that piece to explain it to visitors. By putting all of the student work together, the class has created a museum gallery, especially if we connect the topics thematically, think about the layout of the room(s), and write introductory museum plaques.

Naturally, a museum gallery meshes nicely with an art project, whether painting, sculpture, dance, video or a conglomeration of many forms. I'm including the museum gallery in the Oral Communication chapter because a primary characteristic of the project is that the student is there to speak to visitors, to explain her work, to point out its meaning and argument, and to answer any questions.

My first foray into this type of work took place at Harvest Collegiate when I co-planned a semester course on Revolutions with Andy del-Calvo and my student-teacher, Daniel Marshall. Andy focused his content on Cuba and Haiti, whereas my class dug into France and Iran. One of our learning goals involved students expressing their knowledge and historical arguments through multiple mediums, including art. For their final research project for the course, students not only produced a four to six page paper but also a piece of artwork to teach and express their arguments.

Harvest Collegiate had always cultivated a strong culture of public performance assessment. As a Consortium school, we gained exemption from the Regents exam and, instead, required students to produce a mini-dissertation and to defend it in front of a panel of teachers in order to graduate. As practice, our sophomores presented symposia discussions in front of classes, which involved groups of three students having an eight to ten minute conversation about their research projects and then taking questions from the class. Such a format allowed learners to share their newfound knowledge with a wider audience.

Andy, Daniel, and I wanted to do something even bigger. Given the artistic focus of our classes, and our joint theme, we chose to put on a "Revolutions Museum Night." Each student was asked to produce their final piece of art and then write an artist statement to explain it. The honors students for the course then took the artwork and organized them into galleries of common themes, whether focusing on a particular revolution or ideas like "women in revolutions." We hosted the event after school so that we could invite parents and move more freely between galleries. The whole school was invited and the student-presenters were given times that they needed to be in front of their artwork to explain it and answer questions, and other times that they could wander through the galleries as visitors. In other words, we staggered each student's experience between being a presenter and a visitor.

Since it was an assessment, we asked visitors speaking with the student-artists to fill out rubrics about the artwork and presentations after conversing with each presenter. It was a pass-fail project, which made the grading easier as the students had already put in enough work to get their art ready for the Museum Night. At one point, we gathered in the main commons to watch a performance; two of Andy's students, who were sisters and top-notch dancers, had choreographed an interpretive dance about the Cuban Revolution, certainly a highlight of the evening.

Since then, my students have put on smaller galleries for each other: on colonial resistance and as a format for them to share their research projects. In the latter case, rather than the student presenting his findings in front of the whole class in a traditional presentation, students create artwork or a poster board to share their work, set it up in the room, and present as visitors and their classmates come by to look at the products and ask questions.

My 9th grade colleagues at Scarsdale High School (Carlos Bedoya, Patrick Healy, Brendan Lee, and Kate Krahl) took the museum concept to another level. They collaboratively designed a brilliant end-of-year culminating project in which students, in groups, designed an entire museum experience about topics within the Age of Exploration. Each group designed their own museum or wing about the era, which allowed them to delve into the complexities, problems, and consequences that came with exploration. Many of those exhibits became incredibly immersive and used the multisensory approaches typical of actual museums, including things the visitors could touch or hear. Additionally, some groups developed various paths the visitor could take as he or she made choices, creating a type of choose-your-own-adventure experience that allowed the visitor to understand the difficult choices ordinary people had to make in complex situations.

Student-led Lessons

Real-World Context

One of the main things historians do is teach. They don't always do it well; sometimes they stand in front of a room and lecture aimlessly for 60 minutes. To be fair, I used that strategy last year to teach about Napoleon and post-revolutionary France. Nonetheless, it is a well-established tradition that historians speak publicly about the past in order to teach a classroom full of students. In fact, historians probably spend more time directly teaching about the past than writing about it. This seems pretty straightforward, so I'm going to move on to discuss how to make it happen.

Bringing Student-led Lessons to the Classroom

Andy del-Calvo was the one who really introduced me to the power of students *teaching*, rather than students presenting. "They can do what we do," he suggested to me one day, "if we just train them to do it." So, that's what he set out to do.

ADC took our honors 10th graders and taught them some basic lesson planning and pedagogical moves. Their honors requirement was to teach a lesson about the role of women in revolutions. Each group, within the honors cohort, took on a different aspect of the theme "Women and Revolutions." They prepared for a few months, meeting once a week. Finally, we took one week of the semester and they taught the class. They had a warm-up, an activity, a text, guiding questions, a closing, etc. It was far from a presentation; it was an engaging lesson.

I took ADC's innovative groundwork and brought it to Scarsdale. There, I tried it out in a project about mid-19th century American history: westward expansion, slavery, etc. I realized that since I was not an expert in this era, this was a great opportunity for students to research and teach the content; this also provided them with a practice research experience before the actual research paper. We took a week for students to read, discuss, and plan their lessons. Then, I scheduled each group for one day to teach. They had to prepare an assigned homework for the night before with guiding questions. For the lesson, each group prepared a warm-up, texts to discuss, an activity, and prepared questions. The result was magic: students taught for about six days and the result was far more engaging than endless presentation lectures.

Since then, I've incorporated student-led lessons in many of my classes. Of the oral communication assessments in this chapter, student-led lessons are the most difficult to prepare since essentially you need to teach them some discussion protocols and strategies. I explicitly model a handful of discussion strategies early in the year to give students options for how to stimulate a real conversation. I also point them to my JADE learning site as a resource for discussion protocols.[9] In my Race and Ethnicity elective, students lead weekly book talk lessons about a chapter from our books as well as separate lessons on Race and the Media. In my City 2.0 class, students lead lessons on current events in New York City. When students lead, once I have taught them to ask a few good questions, utilize a strong discussion protocol, and step back to allow the class to have a deep discussion, the results are often as good or at times better than if I had done it myself. Thus, once the preparation is done, the fruits are quite sweet as they lead to strong learning experiences and a bit of a breather for you when students are really leading a lesson.

Students can teach about any topic in social studies. It is up to you to figure out which one makes sense for you. A good starting point is: which topic do you not want to teach?

Keeping the Learning Real: Tips

Apprentice	Students lead a current events lesson
Samurai	Students lead a weekly book (or chapter) talk discussion
Jedi	Students lead a lesson on a historical or political topic

Authentic Assessment: Leading a Lesson on a Book Chapter or Article

You are going to be in charge of understanding and teaching one chapter in one of our books. You need to TEACH it to the class. This is not a mere presentation; you must develop a lesson around the chapter or article.

Part 1: The Lesson Requirements

1   Your lesson should be 30–40 minutes long. Organize your lesson for yourself and the students with a Google presentation. You must send me your lesson three days before the presentation date.
2   Ask a warm-up question. What is a big question raised in the chapter? (7 minutes).
3   Ask for student responses on the reading. You may consider asking one of the following:

    1   What questions did it raise?
    2   What surprised you?
    3   What did you disagree with?
    4   What did you learn?

4   Activity: Choose an activity or discussion protocol to dig deeper into the reading. You may use one of the suggested protocols from the JADE learning website.
5   Introduce an additional source to add a new idea or to make a comparison. The source may be another text, article, video, song, or other piece of media. Ask two to three targeted questions about the new source or use one of the discussion protocols.
6   Include a closing question that connects the chapter in some way to another person or idea we have discussed, to our school, or to our town.

Part 2: Your videotalk (50 points) – due three days after your lesson presentation

1   Send me a video of yourself, talking for no more than 6 minutes about the chapter, what you learned, and what you found interesting and important.
2   Discuss what you did well in the lesson and what you could have done better/differently.

Discussion and Oral Communication Rubric

	Jedi	Samurai	Apprentice
Argument	– Establishes and develops a compelling, elegant, or very original claim and message – Overall discussion, evidence and analysis strongly supports a coherent and complex argument	– Establishes and develops precise, knowledgeable claim and message – Overall discussion, evidence and analysis supports a coherent argument	– Establishes basic claim and/or message – Overall discussion, evidence and analysis somewhat supports a coherent argument
Historical Context and Content	– The discussion successfully captures and teaches complex facts and ideas about the historical content and makes the viewer understand AND want to learn more	– The discussion captures and teaches some complex facts and ideas about the historical content	– The discussion captures and teaches some general facts and ideas about the historical content
Accuracy	– Correct and specific factual accuracy that demonstrates a deep understanding of the complexity of the historical content	– Correct and specific factual accuracy that demonstrates an understanding of the historical content	– Mostly correct factual accuracy, demonstrating a general understanding of the historical content
Selection of Evidence	– Supplies a wide variety of the most relevant, specific, accurate, verifiable, and highly convincing evidence for claim(s) & counterclaim – Uses a variety of strong primary and secondary sources – Develops counterclaims or complexities fairly and thoroughly; responds to counterclaims in ways that sharpen the claim	– Supplies considerable relevant, accurate, verifiable, and mostly convincing evidence for claim(s) – Relies on a few strong sources – Develops complexities fairly – Develops main points of counterclaims	– Supplies some basic evidence that supports claim(s) – Relies on one to two basic sources – Does not acknowledges multiple viewpoints

Analysis	– Clearly and thoroughly explains and analyzes how evidence presented supports, extends, or challenges each claim and reasons	– Clearly explains how the evidence presented supports, extends, or challenges each claim and reasons	– There is some general explanation of how the evidence presented supports, extends, or challenges each claim
Communication	– Speaks in an articulate, clear, fluid, and confident manner – The work expertly captures the tone, style, and format of the genre/medium – Student speaks without reading	– Speaks clearly and at appropriate volume – The work captures the tone, style, and format of the genre/medium – Student often relies on notes	– Speaks at appropriate volume but struggles a bit to articulate ideas – The work somewhat captures the tone, style, and format of the genre/medium – Student reads a prepared script
Interpersonal	– Participant speaks respectfully and kindly to other students, acknowledges their contributions – Participant looks at other students – Participant asks and answers questions to make it a conversation – Participant kindly and respectfully includes quieter members in the discussion	– Participant speaks respectfully to other students – Participant responds to other students – Participant makes comments and statement when appropriate – Participant includes quieter members in the discussion	– Participant speaks – Participant makes individual comments when appropriate – Participant ignores the need to include quieter members

Notes

1 Cunningham, L. (2019, August 13). "The tale of the blue light". Retrieved from www.washingtonpost.com/graphics/2019/national/podcasts/moonrise-the-origins-of-apollo-11-mission/.

2 Oral History: Defined (n.d.). Retrieved from www.oralhistory.org/about/do-oral-history/.

3 Ritchie, D. A. (2003). Doing oral history: a practical guide. Oxford: Oxford University Press.

4 Alexievich, S. (2019). *Last witnesses: an oral history of the children of World War II*. (R. Pevear & L. Volokhonsky, Trans.). New York: Random House.

5 www.ushmm.org/collections/the-museums-collections/about/oral-history.

6 "Equal protection: origins and legacies of the fourteenth amendment" (n.d.) Retrieved October 9, 2019, from https://glc.yale.edu/lectures/evening-lectures/20152016/equal-protection-origins-and-legacies-fourteenth-amendment/video.

7 "Why history matters" (2014, January 24). Retrieved October 9, 2019, from www.radcliffe.harvard.edu/video/why-history-matters-panel-discussion

8 Mission and History (n.d.) Retrieved from www.ushmm.org/information/about-the-museum/mission-and-history

9 https://davidsherrin.wixsite.com/jadelearning/historical-skills.

6

Art

History, politics, and art have always been intertwined. From the days of Mesopotamian craftsmen carving stela that depicted the victories of their monarch, artists have used their talents and skills to tell their version of the past. Both visual and performing arts serve as joyful and creative forms for students to make their historical and political arguments.

Of any assessment, art is perhaps the one that best encapsulates the notion of choice and voice. Art allows us to choose how to represent our ideas and the medium leads to a vivid articulation of each student's particular voice. Art helps everyone see each student more fully as not just a student, but a person.

This chapter will explain why we should have our students express historical arguments through art and how to make it happen, beginning with visual arts and then moving onto genres that combine image and text and finally focusing on performing arts. The topics in this chapter are as follows: painting and illustration, fashion design, monuments and memorials, picture books, graphic histories, dance, and music.

After reading the chapter, use the following chart as a plan to "keep the learning real"

In which unit(s) of your course could you integrate art as an assessment?
Would your students work individually, in groups, or as a full class?

Which genre of art would your class pursue? Or, would you provide choice?

Painting and Illustration

Real-World Context

In the Baker Library at Dartmouth College, the great Mexican painter José Clemente Orozco bequeathed to humanity an astounding work of history called *The Epic of American Civilization*. The mural consists of 24 panels that cover all four walls; one of my favorites, and one that I have often looked at with my class, is called "Cortez and the Cross."

In the panel, Cortez stands in full battle armor, long sword pointed to the ground as he rests in triumph. A priest kneels behind him, clutching a large cross. They are all in gray, almost like ghostly spirits. On the right, nude forms lie on the ground, seemingly in agony, faces hidden, forms distorted. Off to the left, behind the mechanical gray of warfare, the viewer can perceive a blood-red sea holding aloft the Spanish caravels.

This is not a historical argument about the role of smallpox or the influence of Cortez' indigenous allies, the Tlaxcalans. This is not a nuanced portrait of negotiation, hostage taking, military victories and defeats on each side. This painting is a powerful denunciation of barbarity, a cry against colonialism, a reminder that the 20th-century Mexico that Clemente Orozco knew came out of the brutal destruction of native cultures and the death of real people. It is a reminder of what greed, ambition, and religious fervor can do when unleashed.

José Clemente Orozco was by no means the first nor the last visual artist to paint a version of history or to make strong political statements. Well before him, the great Renaissance painters retold the stories of the Bible and the ancient Greek myths. The renowned street artist Keith Haring made his name in the 1980s with chalk outlines and murals on provocative topics meant to spur dialogue about gay rights and AIDS. He also composed art to protest apartheid in South Africa. His 1984 painting *Free South Africa* has two panels drawn in his typical bubble style; the top features a large black figure in a noose being beaten by a smaller white figure holding a club. There is a red X on the white figure's chest. The bottom panel shows the black figure stomping victoriously upon his oppressor. Both the relative size of the figures and the juxtaposition of the two panels help the viewer understand Haring's desperate plea for justice.

The contemporary artist, Titus Kaphar, produced a painting called *Behind the Myth of Benevolence* in 2014, which was born out of a conversation he had about history with a former schoolteacher who remarked that Thomas Jefferson was fascinating and that "there was slavery, but he was a benevolent slave owner." Kaphar's artistic response to that historical argument is a remarkably three-dimensional piece that shows half of Thomas Jefferson's face on the right side of an unfolding curtain. On the left side, we see the face and shoulder of a black woman. The viewer might imagine that the woman is Sally Hemmings, Jefferson's slave mistress. To some extent, she is. But as Kaphar explains on his website, she is also meant to represent all of the black women "whose liberty was taken from them, and whose tragic 'relationships' have been shrouded by historically inaccurate narratives of deified men in positions of power."[1]

Recently, I took my Race and Ethnicity class on a field trip to the Brooklyn Museum to view Kaphar's piece *Shifting the Gaze*, in which he recreates Frans Hals' *Family Group in a Landscape* before using white paint to cover the white figures and obscure them from view, thereby highlighting the image of a black boy who otherwise would have been overlooked. You can actually see Kaphar spread the white paint over the figures by watching his TED talk.[2] By doing so, Kaphar is participating in the historical conversation about who matters in history and in art. The museum plaque explains that

> this work points to the dominance of a European bias through which histories, including art history have been written ... Kaphar drew attention to an individual whose race and class historically would have placed him at the margins of seventeenth-century European society.

In other words, his art is a work of subaltern history.

Kaphar is not only an example of a brilliant artist and thinker who uses history as the muse for much of his work; he is also an example of someone whose intelligence was overlooked by traditional academic settings. In a conversation with Krista Tippett, on the podcast *On Being*, he remarks, "I struggled academically in school. I was that kid that got kicked out all the time. I got kicked out of kindergarten, literally. My GPA in high school was .65."[3] Did he fail school or did school fail him? In the end, he tells the listener, he only had the chance to make his first painting when he was 27 years old.

Contemporary artists break through barriers, opening up a wide array of possibilities for students. Their works, and social critiques, often bridge fine art, pop culture, and the political, providing a sense of the fluid nature of the contemporary artist and the multi-genre nature of much art today. Black artists like Kehinde Wiley are prominent in the art scene today, and they often add in the additional element of references to hip-hop, black history, and critiques on race, class, and gender. Wiley, who achieved popular fame through his official portrait of Barack Obama at the National Portrait Gallery, often engages in "street casting" in which he collaborates with black strangers who he meets on the street. In a painting like "Shantavia Beale II," he works with the subject to choose a famous painting from the European canon and the subject then re-enacts the pose.

As the Brooklyn Museum's exhibit on his work explains, Wiley makes a "riff on specific paintings by Old Masters, replacing the European aristocrats depicted in those paintings with contemporary black subjects, drawing attention to the absence of African Americans from historical and cultural narratives."[4] He places black men wearing hoodies and jeans gallantly, like Napoleon, atop horses or lying on the ground as if in a Rembrandt. In his own introduction, he describes how his work is a "new way of seeing black and brown bodies" and a picture of "how young people adorn themselves and celebrate and fall in love."

Painting and illustration serve as key outlets for integrating art into authentic assessment in social studies. Visual arts tell a story and exist at the symbolic level; they allow for a wide-range of possibilities and they urge the artist to use symbolism to make an argument about the past or the present, whether in one genre or more.

Bringing Painting into the Classroom

Any historical topic can be the subject of a wonderful drawing, painting, or even a collage. Moreover, students can choose from a spectrum of styles, whether realism, impressionism, surrealism, etc. It requires no great magic on our end to incorporate painting or illustration as an assessment. Just let the kids go. The beauty of a collage is that it allows students to communicate on an abstract visual level even if they don't have the illustration skills to make their vision come alive through drawing.

Below you can see how one student, clearly a tremendous artist, uses art to develop an argument about the Soviet Union's policy of collectivization, which led to peasant resistance. The artwork shows soldiers, bread, and the imposing figure of Stalin who attempted to gain total power over the country. He demonstrates how Stalin's economic policies forced Ukrainians to give up their bread to the rest of the USSR and Soviet peasants to give up their grain and cattle, thereby leading to starvation. Even with Stalin's apparent totalitarian rule, however, there was still peasant resistance. The peasant holds up a fist with red light radiating outward, showing that the real strength in Soviet communism lay in the peasants and workers rather than in the totalitarian leaders.

One of the best ways to get students to produce high-quality historical art is to take the time to show them some of the aforementioned examples of how painters build argument into their works. Caution students against a basic

Figure 6.1 Example: A student's visual art project.

piece of historical art, which tells a story without making an argument. It just shows us what happened. Instead, a stronger piece evokes an emotional reaction from the story, it exudes hope or despair, it makes us consider something new, it connects two ideas, it reveals monumental effects. José Clemente Orozco, Keith Haring, Kehinde Wiley, and Titus Kaphar all achieved those goals with their art. Now it is time for our students to do the same.

Here, we can admire how one student integrates a plethora of symbols to make her argument about the Algerian War of Independence. Algerians, being swept up by the wave of French colonialism, are struggling to hold onto their flag. Meanwhile, on the foreground, we can see Algerians trying to cut the chains of French imperialism. Her argument, from the painting, appears to be that it required tremendous effort for Algerians to resist the multifaceted and powerful onslaught of French colonialism.

Figure 6.2 Example: A student's visual art project.

Keeping the Learning Real: Tips

Apprentice	Individual students create paintings or drawings about a particular historical topic
Samurai	The class creates artwork and shares their work with each other through an in-class gallery walk
Jedi	The entire class organizes their artwork into different galleries and opens the exhibition for other classes, parents, and members of the community to view

Authentic Assessment: Painting

Background: Visual art has often been a medium through which artists have acted as historians. Art should intrinsically makes an argument about the subject matter through its aesthetic. It doesn't simply tell us what happened, it tells us something meaningful about the event. Some wonderful artists, from the past and present, who have made art into historical texts include Diego Rivera, Frida Kahlo, and Henry Taylor.

Deliverable: Use your painting or illustration to develop an argument that answers your compelling question, exploring the key content and ideas that support your claim.

Requirements:

◆ Careful attention to detail and historical accuracy (even if the art form is not realism).
◆ Thoughtful attention to subject matter, symbolism, tone, mood, placement, form, color, and texture. Use these visual elements to tell your story and to make your argument.

Artist Statement

Include a one-page artist statement, written in the first person. You should describe:

◆ Why you chose to create this artwork.
◆ Your historical question and argument.
◆ The historical choices you made in creating the piece.
◆ The artistic choices you made and what they mean.
◆ The symbolism you included and the meaning of the symbolism. How does the symbolism advance the argument?
◆ What the piece represents about the event.

Fashion Design

Real-World Context

Throughout history, clothing has played a crucial role in human society, culture, religion, and politics. I would not argue that historians generally create fashion, but rather that fashion has been a legitimate medium to discuss politics and social issues. Our great world religions all apply symbolic meaning to certain clothing, thereby identifying believers and separating out clergy with holy vestments.

Sartorial distinctions, in fact, have also differentiated social classes. Many societies, in the past, had regulations about who could wear certain types of clothing, which were called sumptuary laws. In France's Old Regime, for instance, sumptuary laws separated members of the three estates and made sure that the wealthy bourgeoisie could not outdress their 2nd Estate superiors, the nobility. So, when the three estates gathered for the Estates General in 1789, only the 2nd Estate could wear gold embroidery and the most prestigious puffs and sashes.

Sumptuary laws were particularly strict in feudal Japan, ensuring that every social class wore particular forms of clothing and that the rich merchants could not outdress the poorer samurai. I wish I could pretend my own lack of style were due to a sumptuary law.

Clothing has also played a role in most revolutions. The *sans-culottes* radicals in France, during the violent uprisings in the mid-1790s, literally earned their name for their choice to don pants rather than breeches. Communist Revolutions in Russia and China led to particularly drab and utilitarian styles that de-emphasized gender and wealth in favor of Marxist uniformity. Similarly, the Iranian Revolution resulted in an increase in the use of traditional Islamic clothing, especially due to the mandatory veil for women in public.

Fashion also played a central role in the cultural diffusion, or hegemony, of colonialism. The British colonial policy in India sought to prevent Indians from using British clothing in order to maintain the cultural hierarchy and segregation. Many urban Indians, however, especially those from minority communities, attempted to gain access to British fashion as a gateway to more power and prestige. Similarly, lower caste people, such as the Nadar women, tried to co-opt British power through their clothing, so as to increase their status. As such, many Indians developed syncretic fashion styles, adopting British suits with indigenous headgear or British pants along with native shirts.

Likewise, fashion proved crucial for colonial resistance. The Indian flag, today, proudly displays the spinning wheel, which is a reference to Gandhi's movement for economic and cultural self-reliance through the re-adoption of homespun cloth. Cloth boycotts and the return to simple, traditional Indian clothing served as a catalyst for much of the great satyagraha campaigns. Similarly, Kwame Nkrumah's preference for kente cloth spurred Ghanaian nationalism and helped spark the first independence movement in Africa. Gandhi and Nkrumah both understood well that fashion is culture, and culture is political.

Bringing Fashion Design into the Classroom

I first became interested in teaching about the history of fashion, or better said, the interaction of clothing and history, at Harvest Collegiate. There, I created semester courses with student interests in mind; and it was clear to me that students were extremely interested in what they and others were wearing. I developed the course "Sports, Fashion, and Politics" to look at the ways in which sports and clothing have influenced our political history as well as the ways that historical events transformed people's clothing.

The major eras and events we examined were colonialism and the Cold War and much of the coursework involved an exploration of many of the historical trends I explained above.

The culminating "click" project of our colonialism unit asked students to design a piece of clothing for an imaginary 1946 colonial resistance fashion show. The novice designers needed to consider symbols, colors, and cultural artifacts of their particular location, whether India, Ghana, Nigeria, or Vietnam. I brought a local fashion designer into the class for three to four days to teach students the basics of the fashion design process and to give them feedback on their work. We even took a trip to some fabric stores in the garment district to find inspiration. Here was my original assignment from years ago:

Colonial Fashion Show

The year is 1946. In your group, choose one or two countries (suggestions: Ghana, India, Nigeria, Kenya). As a group, you will put together a "colonial protest fashion show." You will design the clothing of three or more women or men as a form of protesting the colonial rule and create a final group portfolio. These could be "ordinary people" protesting or even a future president. Questions to think about:

- What elements would make something "anti-colonial fashion?"
- What colors, images, patterns, symbols, and words would you like to incorporate into the clothing?
- What are you hoping to achieve?

Schedule:

Day 1: Research, sketch ideas
Day 2: Create mood boards
Day 3: Begin drawing
Day 4: Getting swatches
Day 5: Edits and color

*On Day 6 the fashion pieces are due, and you need to submit a one-page written artist statement where you describe the choices you made, why you made them, and how they show a protest.

The final performance was a fashion show. Students didn't need to actually make their clothing on fabric, but they did walk the red carpet runway holding an image of their design. I had taken pictures of each design, so as I called the student's name and he or she walked the runway through our cafeteria, music pumping, I projected an image of the design on the wall.

The fashion show was one of my great successes in the course and, in truth, in my career. It was a far more successful than when I took that same class to sit-in on an NYU class called "History of Soccer" only to realize that I had shown up on the wrong date and there was no class that day.

Excerpt from a student's fashion design artist statement:

My first design consists of churidaar kurta with red churidaar trousers underneath a patterned kurta. The red of the churidaar symbolizes the blood shed for Indian independence, particularly of non-violent protesters, such as was seen at Jallianwala Bagh massacre. The pattern of the kurta represents the cycle of power. No government is eternal, and the eventual overthrow of British rule in India is inevitable.

There are more possibilities for integrating fashion design into our history classes than we might imagine. My student-teacher, Bassem Elbendary, developed a wonderful project while we were teaching colonialism and resistance in Egypt. Since the focus was on cotton, we had all students bring in a white cotton shirt and actually draw their argument about the importance of cotton in Egyptian colonial history on the t-shirt.

You certainly do not need to be teaching a course on clothing and politics to bring fashion design into the curriculum. Students could create uniforms and logos for major revolutionary movements, whether for the Bolsheviks, the 1776 patriots, or the Jacobins.

Fashion makes for a wonderful option within a menu approach, since young people who love fashion tend to really be passionate; my anecdotal experience, although a bit of a generalization, is that young fashionistas tend to be rather put off by traditional school. When they get a rare chance to bring this passion into their schoolwork they respond with their heart and soul.

Keeping the Learning Real: Tips

Apprentice	Students illustrate and color their fashion designs on paper or using a graphic design program
Samurai	Students make the actual clothing using fabric
Jedi	The entire class puts on a historical fashion design show, proudly displaying their clothes on the runway

Authentic Assessment: Fashion Design

Background: Fashion design has often been a medium through which artists have engaged in politics and politicians have engaged in art. Fashion makes a statement; therefore, fashion is intrinsically an argument. Some examples of the intersection between fashion and politics include Gandhi's use of home-spun cloth and Kwame Nkrumah's adoption of kente cloth in their colonial resistance movements.

> **Deliverable:** Use your fashion design to develop an argument that answers your compelling question, exploring the key content and ideas that support your claim.

Requirements:

- Careful attention to detail and historical and cultural accuracy.
- Thoughtful attention to subject matter, colors, symbolism, tone, style, image and word placement, form, color, and texture/material. Use these visual elements to make your statement and to make your argument.

Considerations

- Who will wear the clothing? Leaders? Ordinary people?
- Is the clothing gender-specific? If so, why did you choose that gender?
- What style do you want to use for the clothing?
- How would you actually make the clothing?

Artist Statement

Include a one-page artist statement, written in the first person. You should describe:

- Why you chose to create this fashion design.
- Your historical question and argument.
- The historical and cultural choices you made in creating the design.
- The artistic choices you made and what they mean.
- The symbolism you included and the meaning of the symbolism. How does the symbolism advance the argument?
- What the piece represents about the event.

Sculptures, Monuments, and Memorials

Real-World Context

Monuments and memorials are public art and public history. Their primary goal, in many ways, is to use their size, placement, and magnitude to shape public opinion about a person or an event.

We know many famous memorials but sometimes we don't recognize them as works of history. Mount Rushmore, with its four majestic presidents staring down at us in benevolence and wisdom, is making an argument about history. As the National Park Service website maintains, the monument is meant to be about more than the four men; instead, it is meant to "tell the story of the birth, growth, development and preservation of this country."[5] Indeed, the monument itself falls within a school of American history, with its emphasis on the Great Men and their impact on our country.

In Washington, DC we can visit some of the most famous ones: The Washington Monument reaching to the sky, the Lincoln Memorial's depiction of the president sitting stoically as he is surrounded by his own beautiful words, and the Jefferson Memorial with the third president standing and serenely gazing into the distance, also surrounded by his poetic language.

This summer, I visited the FDR and MLK memorials for the first time. At the former, I was struck by the contrast with Lincoln's memorial, in which the grandeur and size make a profound statement about the man. The FDR memorial is humbler yet it achieves an impact in a different way. It is not about one moment with greatness, but rather a path through his story. Remarkably, it begins with Roosevelt sitting humbly in a wheelchair, and as you progress down the path, through his presidency, you meet other statues: men with hunched shoulders waiting outside a government office, worn-out farmers looking for hope, and then, finally, his wife Eleanor. The memorial ends with a larger statue of Roosevelt, hinting that he grew stronger during his time in office; simultaneously, the experience connects FDR with his period, the events of his time, and the people he tried to help.

The newest addition to the National Mall, the Martin Luther King Jr. Memorial, reveals the extent to which this format of art is inextricably tied to history. Every decision made becomes part of the historical and political conversation. Since its inauguration, workers have had to erase a botched inscription. There have also been critiques about the realism of the depiction of MLK, the type of stone used, and the background of the sculptor. A reading of Edward Rothstein's review of the memorial in the *New York Times*, "A Mirror of Greatness, Blurred" shows how a review of the art turns into a

Figure 6.3 *The Breadline* located in the Franklin Delano Roosevelt Memorial, Washington, DC. Photograph taken by author.

discussion of history and a disagreement about King's intentions when he declared "Out of the mountain of despair a stone of hope" and the use of that quotation as the framework for the monument.[6] What did occur to me, when I was there, was that the placement of King's memorial alongside those of Lincoln, FDR, Washington, and Jefferson is profound and makes a crucial historical argument: a non-presidential citizen, like MLK, can have as much of an impact on our country as a president. Martin Luther King Jr. earned a place in the pantheon.

Of course, not all memorials are about famous leaders. We move on to the war memorials: the forgotten soldiers of the Korean War trudging persistently through the grass, draped in somber parkas and holding their guns; the seemingly endless names of casualties on the Vietnam Veterans Memorial; the newer and more abstract World War II Memorial with its 56 pillars, fountain, and triumphal arches.

Monuments and memorials are scattered throughout the United States and throughout our world. They tell stories big and small; they tell of leaders and unknown heroes. Ed Dwight was a highly respected air force pilot and

Figure 6.4 *The Stone of Hope* located in the Martin Luther King Jr. Memorial, Washington, DC. Photograph taken by author.

nearly became NASA's first black astronaut. When racism, most likely, prevented him from moving forward, he became a successful entrepreneur and a stellar artist. His monuments to African-American history remind us of crucial stories from Texas to Memphis to Atlanta. His Medgar Evers Memorial in Mississippi recalls the Civil Rights activist's work and tragic assassination; his Underground Railroad Memorial in Detroit, along the river, shows a group of runaway slaves gazing into Canada as they prepare to enter the land of true freedom. They stand tall, exuding hope and dignity, as the conductor points the way. The work's argument reminds us of the communal resistance movement, the dignity of the slave, the unquenchable desire for freedom, and that even in the north no former slave was truly free until he or she had crossed the border.

Bringing Monuments and Memorials into the Classroom

Monuments and memorials are so powerful for student authentic assessment because they function as public history, influencing the memory of our communities. Any monument is, inherently, making an argument about what we should remember and how we should remember it. Monuments are claims of historical importance. What and who deserves to be remembered?

Such memories are meant to be timeless, but we saw from 2015 to 2017 how the public's memory and understanding of the past can change. After the Charleston church shooting, there was a great outcry for the removal of Confederate memorials, which led to the extrication of monuments across the country, including 31 in Texas alone. Political leaders, journalists, and activists weighed in publicly on the question over whether towns should remove or repurpose statues highlighting the lives (and actions) of Confederate heroes.

In addition to the contemporary political weight of the issue, what was really taking place was a conversation about public historical memory. Statues in public places are works of history – they make an argument about who and what deserves to be remembered, about what we care about in our past, and about what we value in our narratives. The debate was about how we choose to tell our towns' and country's history.

It is incredibly powerful for students to participate in this conversation, since history is really a conversation about our past and what it means. Few mechanisms, in fact, are more authentic to history than the debate over what we honor. There is a wonderful episode of the podcast "Presidential" that addresses this very question: why is John Adams the only major founding father without a memorial in the nation's capital? As Lillian Cunningham explains, "A John Adams memorial is nowhere to be found in DC.[7]" David McCullough, one of his most important recent biographers, explains that part of the reason is that his political party, the Federalist Party, is now defunct and thus there is no major constituency to push for an Adams memorial.

Monuments and memorials make for a great student project because it asks them to consider not only the subject matter but also the placement. Monuments can be about the famous or the unknown, they can be at a historic site or a symbolic location, they can include one person, a group, abstract imagery, stillness, or action. Monument projects are, indeed, monumental because they ask students to think on multiple levels and to enter into historical and political discussions about our memory. When artists bid to make a monument, they are literally making a claim for why their vision represents the truth.

One of my best monument projects asked students to propose a monument to be placed at the center of the Museum of the American Revolution.

Students had to describe the subject matter of the monument, which ranged from petitions for George Washington to Native American soldiers to Mercy Otis Warren. As it was a new museum, participating in the conversation around a potential monument to be placed front and center seemed particularly authentic, especially since they wrote to the director of the museum with their proposals (and they received responses). That dialogue between them and the museum was game-changing for how they saw social studies and the possibilities of what they could do in class and beyond.

Another successful monument project asked students to think symbolically and personally about the Bill of Rights and to create a monument celebrating one amendment's importance to the community. This allowed students to connect with the Bill of Rights by thinking about each amendment's significance to them and to the school, and to ultimately have the voice and choice to make an artistic argument about one of them.

Bill of Rights Monument

Carefully read all the amendments to the Constitution. Decide on one amendment that is particularly important to the successful functioning of a school like our own for all of our students. Think deeply about that amendment and why we should honor its message and values. Create a 3D monument design to celebrate the amendment and its importance. Then, write a one-page letter to your principal, proposing that the school commission an artist to create the actual monument. In the letter, be clear about where the monument should be placed. In your proposal, make sure to explain why this amendment and/or right is so important to our community and why we should honor it.

Since memorials are about public historical memory, they can be particularly powerful projects when they are meant to challenge traditional historiography. My teaching of ancient Egypt and Rome has often focused on Cleopatra and understanding why negative portrayals of her throughout history have really been about gender; that is, the writers' negative reactions to her as a strong female leader who had relationships outside of marriage. Consequently, my students created memorials of Cleopatra answering the question: how does this memorial contribute to our memory of Cleopatra and how does it compare to the views of other historians of Cleopatra?

Monuments and memorials can involve any subject in history, since the project really asks students to tell a story, choose what or who is important, and symbolize that importance. Events such as Westward Expansion, abolition, suffrage, Japanese internment camps, Gandhi's satyagraha campaigns, and the Anti-Apartheid Movement are all prime topics for this type of project.

Keeping It Real Tips

Apprentice	Students write a letter proposing a particular monument and send the letter, including a draft design
Samurai	Students make a 3D model of the monument or memorial
Jedi	The entire class works collaboratively to create an immersive monument experience

Authentic Assessment: American Revolution Museum Memorial

Background: A new museum opened this year in Philadelphia: the American Revolution Museum. Unfortunately, it has no statue or monument about the American Revolution at its entrance.

Deliverable: Choose a subject for the monument. You may choose a person, group, event, or idea.

★ Create a prototype for the monument, either a three-dimensional sculpture or an illustration of one side of the sculpture.

★ Write a letter to the director of the museum explaining your monument's argument about the American Revolution and why it should be placed at the entranceway to the museum.

Requirements:

◆ Careful attention to detail and historical accuracy (even if the art form is not realism).

◆ Thoughtful attention to subject matter, size, symbolism, tone, mood, placement, form, color, and texture. Use these visual elements to tell your story and to make your argument.

Letter

Include a one-page letter, written in the first person, following the structure of a formal letter. Make sure your "ask" is in the first paragraph. You should describe:

- Why you chose to create this monument.
- Why the subject matter of the monument is important for our historical memory and deserves a place at the center of the museum.
- What kinds of controversies might this monument create? Why might some people react negatively and/or argue against its creation?
- The historical choices you made in creating the monument.
- The artistic choices you made and what they represent.
- The symbolism you included and the meaning of the symbolism. How does the symbolism advance the argument about the American Revolution?
- What the piece represents about the Revolution.

Authentic Assessment: Redesigning a Memorial

Background: Many people have argued that the Jefferson Memorial needs a redesign to capture our current evolving understanding of the founder and his role in American history. The Trust for the National Mall is considering redesign options for the Jefferson Memorial that would keep the current statue intact but add additional elements.

> **Deliverable:** Choose at least one change for the monument based on your historical understanding of Thomas Jefferson and his role in American history.
>
> - ★ Create a prototype for the redesigned monument, either a three-dimensional sculpture or an illustration of one side of the sculpture.
> - ★ Write a letter to the director of the Trust for the National Mall explaining your redesign for the Jefferson Memorial and why it should be accepted. What argument is it making about Thomas Jefferson?

Requirements:

- Careful attention to detail and historical accuracy (even if the art form is not realism).
- Thoughtful attention to subject matter, size, symbolism, tone, mood, placement, form, color, and texture. Use these visual elements to tell your story and to make your argument.

Letter

Include a one-page letter, written in the first person, following the structure of a formal letter. Make sure your "ask" is in the first paragraph. You should describe:

- Why you chose to create this redesign.
- Why the subject matter of the memorial is important for our historical memory and why the redesign improves our historical memory.
- What kinds of controversies might these changes lead to? Why might some people react negatively and/or argue against the changes?
- The historical choices you made in creating the memorial redesign.
- The artistic choices you made and what they represent.
- The symbolism you included and the meaning of the symbolism. How does the symbolism advance the argument about Thomas Jefferson?
- What the piece represents about Thomas Jefferson and his legacy

Picture Books

Real-World Context

When I was a child, the picture books that made the greatest impact on me were ones about cats who liked to wear hats and men who took advantage of extremely kind trees. Nowadays, there are picture books about everything: informative scientific ones about crustaceans or volcanoes, pop-up geographies in which the Himalayas emerge from the page as if born from a tectonic collision; books about having two moms or about losing a pet.

Many picture books, additionally, serve as the first history books for kids. Before I had my own litter, I once had dinner at my friends, Adam and Liora (Liora is an excellent cook and I highly recommend having dinner there!), and Adam said, "hey, you're a history teacher, I bet you'd like to read this picture book about George Washington to my daughter." He was certainly right about me being a history teacher. The book was interesting, if a bit long to read aloud, although certainly quicker than reading a biography by Ron Chernow.

At home, my large collection of books about 17th-century Dutch colonial history are now in boxes in our storage room, while our bookshelves proudly display classics like *Knufflebunny*, *Number One Sam*, and *The Snatchabook* (all highly recommended). Two books that I particularly appreciate are *The Soccer Fence: A Story of Friendship, Hope and Apartheid in South Africa* and *Locomotive*, both historical picture books that I now make my unfortunate dinner guests read to my children. Unfortunate, of course, because I don't cook nearly as well as Liora.

My oldest son now knows far more about apartheid and westward expansion than I did at age six. At that age, however, I knew far more about He-Man. *The Soccer Fence* is a beautiful story of a black South African boy, Hector, who loves playing soccer and sees a group of white children playing ball at the home where his mother works. They refuse to allow him to join in. The book intertwines the story of the boy hoping to play soccer with a real ball on green grass with the history of Nelson Mandela being freed from prison and the victory of an integrated South African national soccer team, Bafana Bafana, in the 1996 African Cup of Nations. The book closes with Hector standing, longingly, outside of the soccer fence that separated him from the luscious green turf. The blond boy finally opens the gate. "I stepped through the soccer fence,"[8] Hector narrates, symbolically, to emphasize the end of apartheid.

Picture books are sophisticated forms of communication because the language must be concise and the images really count. There is a wide variety in types of illustrations for picture books, ranging from abstract forms to paper cut-outs to photographs of clay figures to realism. In the case of *The Soccer Fence*, the gorgeous illustrations by Jesse Joshua Watson serve to tell us everything the author, Phil Bildner, can't pack into the limited word count: the dazzling beauty of South African hairstyles, the simplicity of homes in the townships, the joy on Hector's sister's face while playing soccer, the wealth of the white neighborhoods, the pride and excitement on proud black South African faces at the news of Mandela's release, and Hector's despondence at experiencing apartheid through the segregation of sports.

Locomotive, by Brian Floca, tells the story of a trip west on a train in 1869, soon after the completion of the transcontinental railroad. The book, written in lyric form, is rife with information, including facts about the technical workings of the pistons and the meals served at the railroad restaurants (buffalo steak, antelope chops, or chicken stew). Children love that it describes the difficulty of using the toilet on a moving train, which was essentially only a hole in the floor. At the end of the book, the argument emerges when Floca explains that locomotive and the industrious workers brought the four corners of the country together.[9]

This is a claim about Westward Expansion and the role of the trains that is made in American history classrooms each year across the country. The fact that it is made in a picture book as well should make us consider the power of this medium.

Bringing Picture Books into the Classroom

The picture book is another format that has the potential for simplicity in that students might simply tell a story accompanied by illustrations. Thus, when they begin the project, providing some examples of picture books that include political and historical arguments can be a fruitful exercise.

When students take-on the challenge of making picture books, they will engage with a complex task in which they must consider symbolism, story, character development, visual layout and illustration, historical detail, and, of course, argument. The multifaceted nature of this genre actually makes it harder for students to produce than many other forms of art. Moreover, a picture book cannot simply tell the story; like all artful authentic assessments, it must make an argument. The process is not easy and requires the student to work on many levels by considering the overarching message, symbolism and abstraction, and small details of illustration. A picture book is one of the best ways for students to develop disciplinary literacy and really engage in the constructivist work of the historian in intertwining narrative and argument so as to share meaning with a larger audience.

Picture books can work for any unit in social studies; their endless variety and options allow students to use them to teach young people about the lessons of the French Revolution, to illustrate an important concept in social psychology, to serve as a first encounter with the Holocaust, or to tell the story of a lesser known character in history, such as Ruth First or Walter Sisulu. A picture book can also be used to explore a particular document, such as a letter or a court case, in order to explicate it, reveal its background, and make it understandable to a larger audience. For example, I own one picture book in Portuguese that includes beautiful drawings and explanations for each of the rights in the Universal Declaration of Human Rights.

When students are planning out their books, it is helpful to remind them that they can use people, animals, balloons, or even colored pencils as characters in their story to make their point. What can they draw and how can they use that character to develop their larger messages?

In my classes, individual students have produced wonderful picture books on a range of topics when I have given open "menu" choices. I have also had entire classes create picture books when the theme really clicks. In my "Race and Ethnicity" elective, for example, all students make a picture book to explain to elementary school students one important lesson about race. The incredibly authentic aspect of this project, you might guess, is that we can then travel as a class to read these picture books in one of the district's elementary school classes. We did this for the first time this year and it was, simply, magical to see high school students reading their books about race to 4th graders. Similarly, when my psychology elective made picture books about topics like conformity, I then read them to my own children and videotaped their responses to show to the student-authors. My kids enjoyed the books so much they refused to allow me to return them to the students and they took a spot on our bookshelf (until the end of the year).

Keeping It Real Tips

Apprentice	Students create beautiful and thought-provoking picture books by hand
Samurai	Students create their picture books and take them to an elementary school to read to younger learners there
Jedi	Students publish their picture books using an online self-publishing platform

Authentic Assessment: A Picture Book

Background: Historians use multiple authentic formats to make their arguments, including picture books. There are a number of wonderful picture books that share with young children stories of the past. A great picture book, even while concise, makes a historical argument and uses the text and the images to support that argument. Some of my favorite historical picture books include *The Soccer Fence* and *Locomotive*.

Deliverable: Use your picture book to develop an argument that answers your compelling question, exploring the key content and ideas that support your claim.

Requirements:

- ◆ Title page with a creative, relevant title.
- ◆ 12–20 pages.

- Vivid illustrations of any style.
- Consider how your character choices, symbolism, dialogue, thought bubbles, color, tone, and style all function as evidence to support your historical argument.

Considerations

- Who are your characters? What do they do and say? How does that help their characterization?
- What is the story? Is there a conflict in the story?
- What style do you want to use to illustrate the story? What color tones?
- How do you want to depict the characters?
- How do you portray your argument in addition to the story?

Artist Statement

Include a one-page artist statement, written in the first person. You should describe:

- Why you chose to create this picture book.
- What is your historical question and argument.
- What historical choices you made in creating it.
- What artistic choices you made and what symbolism you included.
- What the piece represents about the event.

Graphic Histories

Real-World Context

"We should check out this awesome graphic history of a female slave in West Africa that my girlfriend read in a college history course," Andy del-Calvo mentioned one day in passing. He was my student-teacher at the time and we were collaborating on his first unit: colonialism and colonial resistance in Africa. He was from California and used the word "awesome" pretty frequently about things like pencil sharpeners and kite-flying so I first took his suggestion dubiously. But he was enthusiastic and I had read *Persepolis* and had some idea of the workings of a graphic novel, so I decided to give it a shot. Surprising, despite my love for Star Wars, Dungeons and Dragons, and fantasy books, I never really got into comics. I loved reading but my mind tended to work best in the linear flow of a traditional text rather than the multi-genre and multi-directional flow of comics.

"Sure," I said, wanting to encourage him to pursue a new and innovative path of teaching. The following day, he brought in a copy of the book and we sat down to look through it together. It was immediately clear that *Abina and the Important Men* was by no means a soft "cartoon." It was written by Trevor Getz, Professor of African History and History Department Chair at San Francisco State University, and illustrated by a South African artist, Liz Clarke. It was a serious work of history that had won the American Historical Association's James Harvey Robinson Prize.[10]

Looking at *Abina*, I understood how the field of history had progressed since my last course in college. Here, we had in our hands a beautifully illustrated story of an unknown woman, possibly a slave, who brought her former owner to a British colonial court in the Cape Coast colony to accuse him of illegal slavery. The first part of the book, the graphic history story, brings to light thought-provoking themes of gender, slavery, power, colonialism, agency, and the meaning of history. The second section of the book included fascinating historical text, written by Getz, that describes the discovery of Abina's story in the Ghanaian archive and the process of producing her story by consulting other primary and secondary sources. The book also includes the original trial transcript as well as commentaries by other historians of Africa.

Since Andy brought *Abina* into my course, I have found many other graphic histories produced by eminent historians, including one free online graphic history of the Haitian Revolution called "The Slave Revolution That Gave Birth to Haiti," written by Duke University historian Laurent Dubois. Since *Abina*, Liz Clarke has become a sought-after illustrator of graphic histories, such as *Inhuman Traffick: The International Struggle Against the Transatlantic Slave Trade: A Graphic History* and *The Great Hanoi Rat Hunt: Empire, Disease, and Modernity in French Colonial Vietnam*. The *American Historical Review* took a major step in widening the scope of history in its December 2018 issue by reviewing a number of graphic histories, including John Lewis' *March* and Joe Sacco's *Footnotes in Gaza*.

Bringing Graphic Histories into the Classroom

After ADC and I developed the unit, we co-taught it and immediately recognized how the students connected to the graphic text in a way that I had seen few of them do with traditional histories. As I wrote in an article "Unsilenced: Rescuing a Voice through a Graphic History," which I published on *Medium*:

> *Too often historians only give us the final product. They do all of the work, the thinking, the synthesizing, and the guessing and they leave us out of the process. Reading and teaching* Abina *is different. We can shuffle between the primary source transcript and the secondary source graphic history. We can interject with key historical context.*

Many of my students had learned to read graphic novels more fluently than I had, and the visuals supported struggling readers. I contacted Professor Getz (who prefers to be called "Trev") and we began a correspondence and collaboration in developing curriculum for his book for the high school level.

As we considered the assessment for the unit, I developed two possibilities and gave students the choice: (1) write a letter to Trev to discuss their insights, understandings, and further questions about Abina's story; or (2) create their own graphic history, using his methodology, about another story in African colonialism. With Trev's help, I located original newspapers from the 19th-century *African Times*, and subsequently developed the graphic history project.

Students began with short original stories about the Anglo-Ashanti Wars that were far more comprehensible to 19th-century readers who understood the context than to 21st-century teenagers. The students did background research to flesh out and understand the larger context of the article until the stories started to make sense. Finally, they composed their graphic histories, in groups, using the additional research to expand upon and explain the primary source. I called this type of research "Backwards History" or "Historical Sourcery," since we were beginning with an obscure source and then using research to make sense of the source as if by sorcery. Here, the "click" assignment builds off of the main resource of our unit and allows students to use Abina as a model for understanding how to compose the various parts that make a graphic history work.

From that moment on, graphic histories have become a staple of my assessment repertoire. It is a fantastic genre for conveying perspective (using thought bubbles), emotion (using facial expressions), symbolism, and complex historical arguments. Moreover, those students who love cartoons or graphic novels, and those who love to draw, gleefully gravitate toward the option.

Graphic histories work best when limited in scope since they take considerable time for students to produce. I've used the medium as formative assessments to determine students' understanding of one event and its importance. For example, we read primary sources on the Storming of the Bastille and students produce a small one-page graphic history on the event and its importance. Or, for a larger unit's summative assessment, you could consider asking students to produce two pages of their "graphic history book" on the French or Iranian Revolution. By doing two "pages" they can show separate moments in the revolution, far afield in time, and therefore make an argument about change and/or one character's changing perspective on the revolution. Hence, one page could be about a merchant's glee at the Storming of the Bastille and another at his dismay during the Reign of Terror. This works especially well when students have seen a few models of graphic histories to really understand how the genre functions.

Any historical event with gripping conflicts, competing perspectives, and multiple characters would make for a stellar graphic history. In other words, anything worth studying would also be ripe material for a student graphic history.

Keeping It Real Tips

Apprentice	Individual students create page-length graphic histories as formative assessments to check understanding of a reading
Samurai	Students work individually or in groups to create multi-page graphic histories that present a historical argument
Jedi	Students publish their graphic histories using a self-publishing platform

Authentic Assessment: A Graphic History

Background: Historians use multiple authentic formats to make their arguments, including graphic histories. Graphic histories are similar to graphic novels, but they are historically accurate histories that use a comic-book format. Some great graphic histories include *Abina and the Important Men* and "The Slave Revolution That Gave Birth to Haiti."

Deliverable: Use your graphic history to develop an argument that answers your compelling question, exploring the key content and ideas that support your claim.

Requirements:

◆ Title page with a creative, relevant title.
◆ Three to five pages and/or 20–40 cells.
◆ Vivid illustrations of any style.
◆ Consider how your choice of cell sizes and layout, character choices, symbolism, dialogue, thought bubbles, color, tone, and style all function as evidence to support your historical argument.

Considerations

- Who are your characters? What do they do and say? How does that help their characterization?
- What is the story? Is there a conflict in the story?
- What style do you want to use to illustrate the story? What color tones?
- How do you want to depict the characters?
- How do you portray your argument in addition to the story?

Artist Statement

Include a one-page artist statement, written in the first person. You should describe:

- Why you chose to create this graphic history.
- What is your historical question and argument.
- What historical choices you made in creating it.
- What artistic choices you made and what symbolism you included.
- What the piece represents about the event.

Dance

Real-World Context

Dance brings us into a different realm: performing arts.

Take a look at Alvin Ailey's "A Dance Tribute to Civil Rights."[11] The side-to-side motions, the upright posture, the slow leg kicks, the determined fingers raised, the running in place, hopping to the side as if to avoid a policeman's incoming club, and tired hands raised in joy at well-deserved justice – all of these gestures and steps have meaning to advance a claim about the importance of the Civil Rights Movement and the determination of the foot soldiers who made it happen.

"The Flames of Paris," similarly, is an attempt to utilize dance to disseminate a particular historical and political argument. Choreographed in Russia only about a decade after the Russian Revolution, the work premiered on the eve of the anniversary of the October Revolution. It is meant to portray the glory of the French Revolution, thereby setting the Russian Revolution within a larger pattern of world history and great societal transformations. Here, we see the influence of state-directed art, where the purpose of art is not only to depict history, but also to tell history in a way that benefits the state's own narrative.

"The Flames of Paris" follows the story of Jeanne, beginning with the indignities that her father faced under the Old Regime and culminating in her participation in the Attack on the Tuileries Palace and the joyous celebration after the defeat of the 2nd Estate. At the final celebration, those in the mob twirl and bend their knees deep symbolizing dance steps that clearly originate more from Russian folk dancing than French ballet, cementing the connection between the ballet's story and the triumph of the Russian Revolution. It is also evident, when watching "Flames of Paris," how costume functions in dance to help us discern the identities of the characters, in this case as aristocrats or common members of the 3rd Estate.[12]

Bringing Dance into the Classroom

Dance will attract a different type of student than painting, one who is drawn to kinesthetic expression and performance.

I hold only two grudges against Andy del-Calvo. That's not too bad, since grudges run in my family. After all, my great-grandfather's half-brother (or half-nephew?) was the famous mobster Mickey Cohen.

First, Andy's class defeated my class in a head-to-head Julius Streicher mock trial; and this was a mock trial that I had written and done countless times before. I found this unacceptable. I wanted to win!

Second, Andy's students performed an interpretive dance before any of mine ever did, and he won't let me forget it. For years, even back when he was my student-teacher, I always offered interpretive dance as an assessment option but I never had any student take me up on it. It takes a rare teenager who is willing to perform in front of peers. Then, Andy and I teamed up to put together our first major "Museum Night" of art about historical revolutions. The only true performance art, amidst countless paintings and sculptures, was an interpretive dance about the Cuban Revolution from two sisters in Andy's class, both of whom were excellent dancers. The performance was what most people talked about the next day: the beauty, power, and emotion that radiated from those dancers. I was proud of those two dancers, but not thrilled about losing that round.

Until today, the day I'm doing my final edits, Andy and I were tied in interpretive dance performances, which I believe ought to be the ultimate measure of "highly effective" in the Danielson Framework. Today, a student dance about Ghanaian responses to colonialism put me ahead four performances to three. It is never easy to get kids to throw themselves out there, so vulnerably, in front of their peers. The effect when it happens, though, is unforgettable. Andy and I could each tell you exactly what happened in those interpretive dances. How many essays do we remember like that?

Few artistic productions are viewed with as much suspicion by teachers as the idea of "interpretive dance." It may seem soft, silly, or childish.

Nothing could be further from the truth. Dance requires tremendous time and attention to the choreography, deep thought about the symbolism, practice to execute the moves, as well as consideration of the music, speed, tone, and expressions – all of these factors have meaning and should be understood as evidence about the larger argument.

Students could use dance, with its spectrum of styles, to capture an array of historical events. The ones that I've seen happen in my classroom (or Andy's) have involved historical change, most often focusing on resistance to oppression or on revolutions: African independence movements, Meiji Restoration, and Cuban Revolution. Dance's multifaceted nature combined with the musical background works nicely to illustrate transformations.

Other history options that might serve as the background for a stunning choreography include Indian colonial resistance, the India-Pakistan Partition, 1948 Arab-Israeli War, the Haitian Revolution, the French Revolution, the Chinese Revolution, the British anti-slavery movement, anti-Apartheid resistance, etc. These topics, along with American history ones like the Underground Railroad, the Civil Rights Movement, the Suffrage movement, feminism, and Native American struggles are probably what will lead to powerful and meaningful historical interpretive dances.

Keeping It Real Tips

Apprentice	Students create individual dance performances
Samurai	Student groups create and perform multi-act choreographies
Jedi	The entire class puts on a dance show

Authentic Assessment: Interpretive Dance

Background: Historians use multiple authentic formats to make their arguments, including dance. Many professional dance choreographers have used ballet, jazz, and modern dance (among other genres) to make a historical argument. For example, the Alvin Ailey Dance Company, one of the premier New York City ballet companies, performs an important piece called "A Dance Tribute to Civil Rights."

Deliverable: Use your dance to develop an argument that answers your compelling question, exploring the key content and ideas that support your claim.

Requirements:

- ◆ You may do a solo or group performance.
- ◆ The dance must be five to ten minutes long.
- ◆ You should carefully consider and choose one or more songs to serve as background music.
- ◆ Consider how your dance genre, characters, story, movements, interactions, expressions, tempo, wardrobe, and style all function as evidence to support your historical argument.
- ◆ You must practice and prepare for the performance and treat it as a real artistic show.

Considerations

- ◆ Who are your characters? What do they do and how to they gesture and express themselves? How does that help their characterization?
- ◆ What is the story? Is there a conflict in the story?
- ◆ What dance style (ballet, modern, folk, etc.) do you want to use to depict the story? What is the background music?
- ◆ How do you want to depict the characters' clothing?
- ◆ How do you portray your argument through the dance?

Artist Statement

Include a one-page artist statement, written in the first person. You should describe:

- ◆ Why you chose to create this dance.
- ◆ What is your historical question and argument.
- ◆ What historical choices you made in creating it.
- ◆ What artistic choices you made and what symbolism you included.
- ◆ What the piece represents about the event.

Music

Real-World Context

We know that music can be, and often is, political. Rap burst onto the national stage in the 1980s with socially conscientious songs like Public Enemy's *Fight the Power*, and the drive to continually critique social injustice or to imagine a better world can be found in countless hip-hop songs. 2Pac's "Changes" sought to bring to light America's indifference or outright hostility toward young black men by purposefully shipping drugs and guns into black neighborhoods. More recently, Beyoncé's "Run the World (Girls)" has served as a possible feminist anthem when she declares that women are bright enough to achieve wealth and powerful enough to birth the next generation. I wish I was cool enough to be able to add in something about Kendrick Lamar here.

Long before hip-hop challenged conventions and contemporary inequities, folk and rock musicians in the 1960s protested the Vietnam War, misogyny, racism, and the hypocrisies of American culture. In my classes, we have analyzed Creedence Clearwater Revival's symbol-laden diatribe against the ruling class. The band's ironic juxtaposition of "silver spoons" with a home that looks like a rummage sale when the IRS arrives sends a message about patriotism and hypocrisy during war. Of course, during that time period we have Bob Dylan's "Blowin' in the Wind," a plea for change and compassion, for seeing injustice rather than turning one's head. Sam Cooke's tragically hopeful "A Change is Gonna Come" sets his own biography into the larger Civil Rights Movement. He teaches the listener about segregation and resistance when he is prevented from entering a movie theater but still has hope for change.

During this period, Helen Reddy vocalized the strength of a generation of feminists with her anthem "I am Women." She maintained that obstacles and difficulties will not destroy women, but rather make them increasingly more determined to achieve justice and more capable of gaining it.

Music is not merely political; it also helps create historical memory. The vivid combination of poetry and rhythm allows us to imbibe meaning in deep ways. We can recall lyrics to a song, years afterwards, in ways that we could never do with prose. Sometimes this is embarrassing, such as the fact that I can easily sing Aladdin's "A Whole New World" until this day. It can also be a powerful tool for learning and sharing an argument about the world or the past.

And, we ought not forget, long before any of those songs I mentioned, America was reminded of brutal lynchings in the Jim Crow South by Billie Holiday's haunting 1939 ballad, "Strange Fruit." The song is both historical and political, reminding the listener of the past and urging him or her to change the future. The fruit is strange because it is a black body rocking back-and-forth in the wind, hanging from a tree after a lynching.

There was no ambiguity in Neil Young's historical argument when he sang, in 1975, of Cortez' role centuries earlier in the destruction of a great indigenous civilization. In "Cortez the Killer" Young depicts the indigenous women as beautiful and the men as standing ramrod straight and powerful, only until they meet up with Cortez who arrives dancing across the ocean to kill them.

Similarly, by 2006, Neil Young was already participating in the historical conversation about the meaning of the Iraq War. Again, Young eschews nuance in favor of straight-on argument and a bit of irony and playful teasing by crooning about the overconfidence of the "shock and awe" campaign and the "mission accomplished" banner.

We know that music is often decidedly political. It is important to remember that it can also be superbly historical.

Bringing Music into the Classroom

Like many of the art forms I have discussed, working with music requires multi-dimensional thinking. Students must consider word choice, meter, symbolism, and rhythm in the same way they would do with poetry. Additionally, they need to take into account the melody, instruments, beat, and musical genre. A song must be performed or it is not truly a song. Hence, students who choose music to make a historical and political claim must be willing to make a video to share with the teacher and show up for their gig in front of 25 of their peers.

For this reason, music and dance occur a bit less frequently than more individual and private forms of art like painting. Students are more likely to compose a song and perform if they are in groups or pairs; the support of a friend can be crucial to beat down the stage fright.

Students can pick from any musical genre: rock, country, hip-hop, folk, soul, pop, oldies, salsa, etc. It makes sense for the musicians to consider how the genre might connect to the theme of the piece. For example, a song about the Civil Rights Movement probably works better in folk, rock, hip-hop, or soul than it would in salsa or country.

There are also different levels at which the students can produce the piece. A beginning step, which is most likely to happen, is for the budding musicians to take the "Weird Al" Yankovic approach: choose a piece of music with the right beat and style and change the words to make their argument. Students are not required to mimic his hairstyle. I remember when two students of mine, who were avid fans of the musical *Hamilton*, transformed one of the epic cabinet battles into an ideological rap battle between Martin Luther King Jr. and Malcolm X. Their parallel worked really nicely, as in both cases the songs were about competing views of the future of America. In this vein, the students' argument essentially became that MLK and Malcolm X were continuing a long tradition of political debate about values in America.

In the excerpt below, it is clear how the students take the structure of a *Hamilton* cabinet battle and use it to develop an argument about MLK and Malcolm X's competing views on the right path for the Civil Rights Movement.

Last night (August 13, 2019), a friend reminded me that I once wrote and performed this type of song. He asked me jokingly if I was practicing a rap for his wedding toast, which made me recall a musical nightmare that I had suppressed for about a decade. One year, at Facing History School, I volunteered to teach a geometry class so that we could overcome a shortage that would have left a class with 40 students. At some point in the year, I gave an assignment to the students asking them to create a rap about one key idea

[MLK]

You must be out of your goddamn mind
If you say
That violence is going to be the most effective way
Of making changes after years of racial segregation,
In this nation,
Marches make peaceful demonstrations
I think our followers would rather be in jail than in a casket,
I served my time, no need to mask it
Sit-ins in Greensboro and boycotting the bus
Were both successful and in peace. Don't dare disparage us.
Enough is enough, it does not matter who is right.
Malcolm X
We're too fragile to start another fight
We should unify not start a Civil War
I have a dream: you make me question what it's for.

MALCOLM X:

The people are leading!

MLK:

The people are rioting! There's a difference!
Frankly it's a little disquieting you would let your ideals blind you to
brutality!
Malcolm. X?

MALCOLM X:

Sir

MLK:

It seems you've sacrificed morality.
[MALCOLM X]
Did you forget Emmett Till?
[MLK]
What?
[MALCOLM X]
Or Jimmy Lee Jackson?
With every man that faces death another needs us to protect
Yet in their hour of need, you forget.

in geometry. I thought it would inspire them if I modeled the approach, so I wrote my own rap about geometry and math called "Nuthin' but a Math Thang" to the beat of Dr Dre's "Nuthin' but a 'G' Thang."

With my nascent understanding of authentic assessment, I then did the only logical thing: I performed the song at a school assembly. After all, my family had asked me not to sing at a Passover Seder but they never said anything about rapping. My heart was beating intensely, I took the stage to a grand applause, the background music started, and I began, "one, two, three, and to the four ..."

Within moments, I lost the beat and found myself hopelessly stranded somewhere in Snoop Dogg's part. It must have been quite a sight; one of the dorkiest members of the faculty flailing helplessly to a hip-hop oldie that the students probably didn't even know. It didn't matter: they kindly cheered and applauded and gave me high-fives afterwards.

Later in the year, my colleague Bishop Sand recorded me rapping "Ain't Nuthin but a Math Thang" to apply for some math teaching contest, which somehow I lost. The video is on YouTube, and I saw it again for the first time in years. My wife described it as "cute and painful at the same time." The best part is definitely when I try to rock the stapler to the beat, only to miss it time after time.

My students have generally done this art form much better. One of my students composed a classical orchestral piece about the Indian Independence Movement using a computer program that then played the song. She arranged the notes and instrument selection. The use of classical music, with no lyrics, forced her to think on a symbolic level to make an argument, to consider the meaning of different instruments, as well as changes in volume and tempo.

A more advanced step is for a student or a group to write the instrumental music and lyrics, and to play it all on their own. I'm still waiting.

Keeping It Real Tips

Apprentice	Individual students use the "Weird Al" Yankovic technique of modifying lyrics to an existing song and performing karaoke style
Samurai	Students write the instrumental music and the lyrics
Jedi	The entire class puts on a history concert

Authentic Assessment: Song Compositions

Background: Music has always been used as a medium to express historical and political arguments. We can look at Neil Young's "Cortez the Killer," Billie Holiday's "Strange Fruit," and Shostakovich's "Symphony No. 11" (about the Russian Revolution) as wonderful examples of musicians making a historical argument.

> **Deliverable:** Use your musical composition to develop an argument that answers your compelling question, exploring the key content and ideas that support your claim.

Requirements:

- You may do a solo or group performance. Make a video in addition to the performance.
- The song and performance must be between four and ten minutes long.
- Consider how your harmony, melody, progression, instrument choices, volume, tone/mood, and lyrics all function as evidence to support your historical argument.

Considerations

- Who or what is the song about? Who is narrating the song? A character or a narrator?
- What is the story of the song? Is there a conflict? Does anything change throughout the song?
- What genre (rock, hip-hop, country, soul, folk, pop, salsa, etc.) do you want to use to depict the story? What instruments will you use?
- How will you prepare for the performance? Will you memorize the lyrics?

Artist Statement

Include a one-page artist statement, written in the first person. You should describe:

- Why you chose to create this piece.
- What is your historical question and argument.
- What historical choices you made in creating it.
- What artistic choices you made and what symbolism you included.
- What the piece represents about the event.

Artful History Rubric

	Jedi	Samurai	Apprentice
Argument	– Establishes and develops a compelling, elegant, or very original claim and message – Overall evidence/symbolism and analysis strongly supports a coherent and complex argument	– Establishes and develops precise, knowledgeable claim and message – Overall evidence/symbolism and analysis supports a coherent argument	– Establishes claim and/or message – Overall evidence/symbolism and analysis somewhat supports a coherent argument
Historical Context	– The work of art successfully captures and teaches complex facts and ideas about the historical content and makes the viewer understand AND want to learn more	– The work of art captures and teaches some complex facts and ideas about the historical content	– The work of art teaches some facts and ideas about the historical content
Accuracy	– Correct and specific factual accuracy that demonstrates a deep understanding of the complexity of the historical content	– Correct and specific factual accuracy that demonstrates an understanding of the historical content	– Mostly factually accurate, demonstrating a general understanding of the historical content

Artistic Voice	– Produces a creative, artistic, original piece that stuns the viewer with the quality of the imagery and symbolism – The artist uses complex symbolism to advance the argument	– Produces a creative, artistic, original piece that very much impresses the viewer with the quality of the imagery – The artist uses symbolism to advance the argument	– Produces a piece that communicates to viewer with the quality of the imagery – The artist provides obvious images to advance the argument
Artist statement	– Artist statement demonstrates highly thoughtful choices of subject matter, tone, portrayal, imagery, and symbolism	– Artist statement demonstrates choices of subject matter, tone, portrayal, imagery, and symbolism	– Artist statement demonstrates logical choices of subject matter, tone, portrayal, imagery, and symbolism
Artist statement	– Clearly and thoroughly explains and analyzes how evidence presented supports, extends, or challenges each claim and reasons	– Clearly explains how the evidence presented supports, extends, or challenges each claim and reasons	– There is some basic explanation of how the evidence presented supports, extends, or challenges each claim

Notes

1 Kaphar, T. (2018, October 4). Behind the myth of benevolence, 2014. Retrieved from https://kapharstudio.com/behind-the-myth-of-benevolence/.

2 Kaphar, T. (2017, April). Can art amend history? Retrieved from www.ted.com/talks/titus_kaphar_can_art_amend_history?language=en.

3 Gordon-Reed A. & Kaphar, T. (2019, July 4). Are we actually citizens here? (2019, July 4). Retrieved from https://onbeing.org/programs/annette-gordon-reed-and-titus-kaphar-are-we-actually-citizens-here/.

4 Kehinde Wiley: A New Republic. (n.d.). Retrieved from www.brooklynmuseum.org/exhibitions/kehinde_wiley_new_republic/.

5 Mount Rushmore National Memorial (U.S. National Park Service). (n.d.). Retrieved from www.nps.gov/moru/index.htm

6 Rothstein, E. (2011, August 25). A mirror of greatness, blurred. Retrieved from www.nytimes.com/2011/08/26/arts/design/martin-luther-king-jr-national-memorial-opens-in-washington.html.

7 Presidential: A podcast about the character and legacy of America's presidents. (n.d.). Retrieved from www.washingtonpost.com/graphics/business/podcasts/presidential/.

8 Bildner, P. (2014). *The soccer fence: a story of friendship, hope, and apartheid in South Africa*. New York, NY: G. P. Putnams Sons, an imprint of Penguin Group (USA).

9 Floca, B. (2013). *Locomotive*. New York: Atheneum Books for Young Readers.

10 Getz, T. R., & Clarke, L. (2016). *Abina and the important men: a graphic history*. New York: Oxford University Press.

11 A Dance Tribute to Civil Rights. (2018). Retrieved from www.youtube.com/watch?v=usp0v6ChJJM.

12 Flames de Paris. (2017). Retrieved from www.youtube.com/watch?v=HwdMQjIG_F4.

7

Digital History

Computers, the internet, and smartphones have revolutionized the way we acquire information. The days of the travelling salesman going door-to-door to offer World Book Encyclopedias are long gone. I now regale my students with tales of me heading to the library to use the card catalogue. I am more of a Luddite than an early adapter and none of my activities or assessments involve social media. I do prefer school to be an opportunity for students to learn and communicate face-to-face and for the classroom to be a dynamic environment of interaction.

Nonetheless, we ought not deny digital tools and what they allow our students to create. We all gain knowledge from computers and now we have the chance to easily use these programs to become producers and to participate in the intellectual conversation of history and politics. In this chapter, I will examine how students can use digital tools to create testimonials, websites, documentaries, newscasts, and films. We begin by looking at digital history that individuals can produce relatively easily and move on to more complex group endeavors. There are other options for digital history out there, such as making video games or producing social media campaigns that I did not include, either because they involve a really specific and complex skill set or because the medium is one we really don't need to encourage students to spend more time on.

After reading the chapter, use the following chart as a plan to "keep the learning real"

In which unit(s) of your course could you integrate digital history projects?
Would your students work individually, in groups, or as a full class?
Which format of digital history would your class pursue? Or, would you provide choice?

Testimonials

Real-World Context

The National Constitution Center and iCivics produced a series of short online videos called "Why I Love the Constitution." In those clips, a wide array of famous individuals declare their undying love for the Constitution as if it were a wedding vow.

In her video, Ruth Bader Ginsburg explains, "The genius of our Constitution, I believe, is that over the course of more than two centuries, those words – 'We the People' – have become ever more inclusive." Congressman John Lewis, a Civil Rights icon, declares, "The vote is precious. It is almost sacred. It is the most powerful, non-violent, instrument or tool that we have in our democratic society." Senator Susan Collins of Maine says:

> What I love most about our Constitution is its first three words: "We the People." Those simple words powerfully describe our responsibilities as citizens. They tell us that, in America, the government is not an all-powerful ruler over us – it is all of us. The fate of our nation lies in our hands.[1]

All of these are historical arguments about the founding document and its importance.[2]

On the National Constitution Center website, we also find a series of videos in which a leader scholar sits behind a desk, looks at the camera, and speaks to us directly. It is sort of like a YouTube video reviewing a vacuum cleaner, or showing how to make a chocolate mousse, except in this case the product being reviewed is the Fourteenth Amendment. There are no special effects; there need be no animation or music or even video editing. It is just one person talking to another. Professor Eric Foner, of Columbia University, sits behind a desk in front of a shelf of books, wearing a black sweater over a buttoned dress shirt, sleeves pulled up, looking every bit relaxed and professorial. He argues in the testimonial that the Fourteenth Amendment "tries to deal with the consequences of the Civil War," namely the abolition of slavery and the preservation of the union. Here, we see how one of the most esteemed professors of American history stretches beyond the conventions of the written word by using a video testimonial and the internet to spread his knowledge and claims.[3]

A TED talk video is, to some degree, a testimonial. In this case the speaker is talking to a live audience but also, we know, to the camera and a larger internet audience. There are rarely special effects in the videos. Really, we care about the conversation, the ideas, and seeing and hearing the speaker. Take Latvian historian Maria Golubeva's talk on "Why medieval Europe was nothing like Game of Thrones." She does show a few PowerPoint slides but mostly she just talks and explains the important role of institutions in the Middle Ages.

Bringing Testimonials into the Classroom

I just missed my chance for fame in 2017. That year, a play by Heidi Schreck premiered, which then reached Broadway in March 2019. It was called *What the Constitution Means to Me* and it became a finalist for the Pulitzer Prize. Jesse Green, reviewing the play for the *New York Times*, remarked that "it is not just the best play to open on Broadway so far this season, but also the most important."[4]

One of my students rushed up to me a bit later in the spring of 2019. "Mr. Sherrin," she said, "you have to see this new play on Broadway; it is exactly what we did in class and it was amazing!" This was the assignment I had given her class in the fall of 2017 before the premiere of Scheck's play:

Constitution Assessment

Read the "about" section of the website "We Love the Constitution." Then, read the "participate" section. Watch a couple of the videos of individuals discussing why they love the Constitution. Then, create your own thoughtful video explaining what the Constitution means to you. Speak to me through the camera. Consider whether you want to explain:

  a. Why I love the Constitution?
  b. Why I have mixed feelings about the Constitution?
  c. Why I actually dislike the Constitution?

Recently, Heidi Schreck had a public conversation at the 92Y in New York City called, of course, "What the Constitution Means to Me" along with Harvard University Constitutional Law professor Laurence Tribe. Professor Tribe has actually helped write the constitutions for a number of countries, including South Africa. The juxtaposition of those two figures demonstrates the extent to which we now recognize the fluidity of intellectual mastery. The right to expound on the nature and value of the Constitution, and to participate in the public conversation, is not limited to those in the ivory tower. In fact, during the talk, Laurence Tribe declares that Schreck's work "is a sophisticated Con-law class on Broadway."[5]

Clearly, if I had channeled my inspiration into writing a brilliant Broadway play rather than a social studies assignment, I would now be touring the country as a Broadway superstar and giving talks at the 92Y.

When I was in high school, the only type of oral presentation involved standing in front of the class and the only way we communicated our ideas to the teacher was through writing. Now, however, the incredible ease of recording means that we can offer other ways for the students to talk to us and share their knowledge and arguments orally – and a simple testimonial video is one of the best ways to make that happen.

Most students record a direct "face-the-camera" speech. It is important for them to plan what to say and to use notes, if needed, but they should speak rather than read. A few add in some twists, such as a surprising wardrobe or setting choice. One particularly artistic student didn't appear visually in the film. Instead, she drew out her ideas and filmed her hand actually drawing, then used time-lapse to speed up the drawing time. This allowed her to do a voice-over to narrate what she was drawing.

We can ask students to record an oral argument, an informal testimonial video on basically any historical question. It can be a formative assessment following a homework assignment, rather than asking them to write a paragraph or a reflection. Or, we can use it as an end-of-unit summative project for almost any topic. My Holocaust unit asks the straightforward (but difficult) question: What caused the Holocaust? This is a great option for this type of video. It can also work for a "what should we do?" assessment. For example, what should we do about the Syrian Civil War? Just letting students talk to us really opens up an opportunity for them to express themselves more naturally and, importantly, for us to get to know them better as students and people.

This is a wonderful assignment for taking a Facing History and Ourselves approach by inserting any historical event or era into the blank of the following question: "what does _____ mean to me?"

Keeping It Real Tips

Apprentice	Student(s) film a basic testimonial speaking to the camera about their historical argument
Samurai	Student(s) film a testimonial speaking to the camera about their historical argument, paying careful attention to the background setting and using props to make their point
Jedi	Students put-on a TED talk video series about a particular theme

Authentic Assessment: A Testimonial Video

Background: Using digital tools as a way to record a simple presentation is a relatively new form of communicating history. Essentially, we can speak into a camera, record it, and share our knowledge. The National Constitution Center takes this approach by providing testimonials of important historians and other public figures who speak about the Constitution.

> **Deliverable:** Use your testimonial video to develop an argument that answers your compelling question, exploring the key content and ideas that support your claim.

Requirements:

- ◆ Record yourself speaking to the camera for four to six minutes.
- ◆ Introduce yourself, the topic, and your question.
- ◆ Pay careful attention to argument, specific evidence, detail, and historical accuracy.
- ◆ Give thoughtful attention to volume, setting, and any props.
- ◆ Wrap up your testimonial with a few concluding sentences.

Websites

Real-World Context
As teachers, we must admit that websites are not only our main destinations to find primary sources, but also the places we often look to for the big ideas or specific tidbits of information we require for a lecture. Certainly, Wikipedia

is an invaluable reservoir for background knowledge. A few other key websites serve the history community for general tertiary research, such as history.com, Teaching American History (TAH), Gilder Lehrman, and the BBC.

When I used to teach ancient history, I adored the Pyramid Challenge and Mummy Maker on the BBC Ancient Egypt site. The combination of interactivity, photographs, and articles written by historians like Joyce Tyldesley provides an excellent balance for teachers looking to diversify units.

When we think about using the internet for learning about more specific topics, we can identify a range of stellar sites. For the Holocaust, among others, we have access to the "German History in Documents and Images" (GDHI) website as well as the incredibly rich website of the United States Holocaust Memorial Museum, which provides an informative "Holocaust Encyclopedia" as well as access to testimonials and other primary sources. George Mason University created one of my favorite French Revolution websites called "Liberté, Egalité, Fraternité: Exploring the French Revolution." The site includes, in its own words, "12 Topical Essays, 250 Images, 350 Text Documents, 13 Songs, 13 Maps, a Timeline, and a Glossary."[6]

For understanding the Cold War and international politics, we can now benefit from the work of the Woodrow Wilson International Center for Scholars, which developed an incredible website "Digital Archive: International History Declassified." The site has collections on the Soviet Invasion of Afghanistan and North Korean Nuclear History. Similarly, the "National Security Archive" at George Washington University allows us to access a wealth of formally classified documents on events like the Chilean military coup of 1973, the Brazilian coup of 1964, and the United States' role in each.

Those who are interested in African-American history, culture, and contemporary politics can learn from the creation of professors Keisha N. Blain and Ibram X. Kendi, author of National Book Award winner *Stamped from the Beginning: The Definitive History of Racist Ideas*. Their site, "Black Perspectives," includes articles, interviews, and book reviews on topics ranging from "Overseer Violence on 18th Century Plantations" to "Radical Hospitality and the Beauty of Black Queer Kinship."

My own creative contributions have largely fallen in this arena. Two years ago, I developed an online Iranian Revolution choose-your-own-adventure book for my students, utilizing Google Sites. Students navigate the 26-page story about a young Iranian girl living in Tehran in 1979, discovering secrets about her family and country's past, the 1953 coup of Mohammad Mossadegh, and the hidden brutalities of SAVAK. Throughout the game, readers must make choices, avoid SAVAK, and successfully weave through the chaos of the revolution.

Last year, I sought to meld the various strands of my teaching about the Holocaust: my grandfather's testimony, arguments about causation from leading historians, and incredible primary sources from GDHI. I had posted many of the source links before, for students to access, on our school's internal page, but I decided to use the visual and navigational power of the internet to create a student-centered virtual unit in which students could choose what interested them and read or watch those sources. Not every student would have the same experience, but all would learn crucial content.

As a result, I created and curated the "Joseph & Myra Brandman Virtual Holocaust Memorial Museum," which can be found at brandmanmuseum. com. The site functions as a museum experience by including suggested music, audio guides that read the text (for struggling readers), and 12 exhibits that take the visitor from Jewish Life before the Holocaust to Justice after the Holocaust. Each exhibit includes narratives about my grandparents' stories (taken from my own interviews and research), images of actual artifacts from their lives, as well as the best historical videos, background readings, and primary sources that I selected from the rest of the internet. The students used this museum to learn for the past two years, and for many the individualized experience made for the best unit of the year.[7]

Bringing Website Creation into the Classroom

Students can create websites about any topic in human history; the internet, after all, covers everything. Given the multi-layered nature of websites, whatever topic they choose they should consider how to integrate text, images, and videos into the final product. Websites work best when they avoid overloading the reader with the amount of text on any page or the number of internal pages to visit. Look for a simple, sophisticated website that allows for easy navigation and interaction.

I have only offered website creation as one option in a menu approach; I've never done a full-class assignment, although I see no reason not to. When I choose that "click" approach of matching a particular medium to the topic, I like there to be a reason I'm choosing a website. As such, it makes particular sense for students to create a website on contemporary issues, such as climate change, human rights, or globalization. In fact, I developed my first website in 2002 while taking a college course on globalization. A website works well, in that sense, to be part of a civic action project raising awareness about a contemporary issue.

Students do not need to know code to develop a site, as we enjoy access to a number of excellent free web design programs. Google Sites is particularly easy to use, although limited in options. I utilized wix.com to create my JADE learning site as well as the Brandman Museum. Students of mine have also used Weebly and Squarespace to create sites on a range of topics, from the French Revolution to the Constitution.

Websites make it easy to get distracted by the process and the story, thereby forgetting to include an argument. Be sure to remind students that somewhere in their homepage or on a specific subpage they need to advance and support a claim about the topic or question.

Keeping It Real Tips

Apprentice	Individual students create simple sites about a historical topic
Samurai	Students work in groups to create multi-page sites
Jedi	The whole class works together to create a website about a topic or an idea

Authentic Assessment: Web Design

Background: Historians use multiple authentic formats to make their arguments, including websites. There are countless websites that disseminate information, primary sources, and arguments about the past. Web designers need to consider their layout, information, and argument, paying particular attention to the homepage.

Deliverable: Use your website to develop an argument that answers your compelling question, exploring the key content and ideas that support your claim.

Requirements:

   ◆ Beautiful homepage.
   ◆ At least three internal pages plus an "about" page.
   ◆ Vivid layout with easy navigation.
   ◆ Consider how your text, images, resources, and layout all function to support your historical argument.

Artist Statement

Include a one-page artist statement, written in the first person. You should describe:

- Why you chose to create this website.
- What is your historical question and argument.
- What historical choices you made in creating it.
- What design choices you made in developing the site.
- What the site represents about the event.

Suggested Website Builders

- Wix
- Weebly
- Squarespace
- Google Sites

Documentary

Real-World Context

Documentaries have long been a mainstay of the historical record. When I was in school, documentaries often meant substitute teachers, and the soft, monotonous voices that made my eyelids almost instinctively heavy. The traditional PBS and History Channel documentaries mostly involved plodding paces, with voice narration over scrolling images, and the occasional expert brought on screen to provide snippets of wisdom.

The 1985 ground-breaking documentary *Shoah* took over a decade to make and nearly as long to watch, clocking in at nearly ten hours. In the same vein, the remarkable 14-hour television series *Eyes on the Prize* became one of the most comprehensive histories of the Civil Rights Movement; it is fair to say that snippets of the documentary have been used by teachers across the country in the decades after its release. The integration of original video footage in *Eyes on the Prize*, in addition to its sophisticated and wide-ranging coverage that reaches far beyond the classic stories of Rosa Parks and Martin Luther King Jr., has made the series a treasured teaching tool. Ken Burns probably became the most famous historical documentary filmmaker with his Emmy Award winning *The Civil War* and his various Academy Award nominations for films, such as *Brooklyn Bridge*.

I began teaching in 2004, at about the same time that the technical quality and entertainment value of documentaries took off. When teaching the Ancient World, one of my prized resources was the History Channel's series *Engineering an Empire*, especially the episodes on Egypt and China. This new generation of historical storytelling added computer animation and graphics to the usual narration and talking heads. The pace is quicker and the storytelling more dramatic. A newer generation of filmmakers uses more live footage and emphasizes the human dramas and stories. Few fictional films, for example, can match the emotional impact of documentaries on Syria like *The White Helmets* and *A Syrian Love Story*. Currently, famous filmmakers, such as Spike Lee, also produce riveting documentaries like *4 Little Girls* and *When the Levees Broke*. There has never been a better time to learn history from film.

As a teacher, I also began to appreciate the expertise of the scholars brought in to discuss the history; my students can't read much of UCLA historian Lynn Hunt's scholarship, but they can certainly take in her knowledge when she speaks in the History Channel film *The French Revolution*. We read a bit of *Avengers of the New World*, Duke historian Laurent Dubois' seminal book on the Haitian Revolution, but it certainly adds even more when my students can see him and hear his insights in PBS' *Egalité for All: Toussaint Louverture and the Haitian Revolution*.

The internet, and especially YouTube, has added new dimensions and new genres to documentary films. YouTube provides what we could essentially call "documentary shorts." They are quick, five to seven minute teachings or tutorials about key topics in world history or important events in contemporary politics. Many of these documentary shorts include animation, and the extra visual layer adds to the viewer's comprehension. The dynamic nature of the animation seems superior to the somewhat static scrolling of images in traditional documentaries.

Documentary shorts are now crucial tools in the history teacher's toolbox; my analysis of student learning and student feedback shows that nothing is more effective in producing immediate content comprehension. The dynamism of these videos, combined with the use of narration, text, and animation, provides for a rich learning resource.

For over five years, my students have learned about the Syrian Civil War. The essential resources in providing the necessary context for understanding the complex causation of the war is the *Guardian*'s "The War in Syria in Five Minutes" and Vox's "Syria: Who is Fighting and Why." The latter, for example, has a timeline that scrolls on the bottom throughout the video, and a map animation in which images of important players, such as Assad, Erdogan, and Ali Khamenei pop up above their respective countries, color-coded to show whose side they're on in the proxy war's complex web.

In this same vein, John Green's *Crash Course World History* uses ten-minute documentary shorts to, literally, teach the history of the world. The animation is very helpful for comprehension, as is John Green's vivid, dorky, and playful personality (he is almost like a funny Mr. Rogers). He provides some of the traditional scrolling over images and paintings for visual stimulus. His humorous comments like "unless you're over 60, and let's face it internet, you're not, you've only known a world of nation-states," keeps us all engaged. And no student can resist his point, after mentioning that Robert Mugabe used to be a high school teacher: "let that be a lesson to you, your teachers might have dictatorial ambitions." For any teacher and learner looking for a quick background primer, few resources can beat Green's series. I've used his episodes on "Imperialism" and "Decolonization and Nationalism" in my modern world history course.[8]

My colleague, Nicola Minchillo, organized a summer collaboration day between English and social studies teachers to look at the concept of video essays as a form of assessment. She pointed to the work of the Nerdwriter as an example of a video essay. What I love about the Nerdwriter's videos, such as "Why This is Rembrandt's Masterpiece," is that he is making an argument and using the visuals of the video, in this case the painting *The Night Watch*, as evidence. He focuses specifically and analyzes the painting as evidence to support his larger point. He's not just telling a story, which can sometimes be the case in a documentary; rather, he is making a historical assertion. We then used his example to collaborate and think about how we can support students in producing sophisticated and thoughtful video essays.

Bringing Documentaries into the Classroom

YouTube provides a wealth of documentary models for students to consider, ranging from the traditional talking heads and image scrolling to Vox and John Green's animation narration to the Nerdwriter's video essays. I've only taught a handful of students who had the technical skills early in high school to produce high-quality animation. One of them, Jason Merrin, was a student in my class in my first year of teaching, which, unfortunately, was well before I had the outlook and tools to let him loose to produce historical animations. Now, he is an accomplished filmmaker whose incredible animation can be found on his website.[9]

Nonetheless, without too much technical prowess, students can use relatively simple editing tools to make a documentary film. Even I have learned how to scroll images, add background music, and insert some talking heads. My first and only documentary short, actually, was a film I put together with my students in Brazil, former street children, about the impact of learning to use computers in our computer lab. It was called *Portao Virtual* (virtual gateway) and it featured the music of Toquinho, a great Brazilian singer, and the wisdom of beautiful young people trying to build better lives. I made that in 2004 when it was much harder to edit such films. Currently, most students use either iMovie or a free online program, WeVideo, to stitch together their films. Fortunately, at this point, students who choose to make a movie normally have the technical skills to figure out the basic steps on their own, especially since the sophistication of a basic documentary need not be extraordinary.

When you do a documentary or film with students, think about how much you care about the aesthetics and production and how much you care about the argument. Make that clear to students so they have guidance on whether to focus on the style, the substance, or both. If it is the substance that counts, this is another medium where it is worth stressing the inclusion of argument in addition to story.

This type of project is perfect for groups, especially since students can take on the roles of different scholars commenting on the history, or they can act out scenes as if it is original footage. Given the contemporary feel of the medium, documentaries work particularly well as a way for students to grapple with contemporary social issues and communicate their findings, such as racism, sexism, climate change, immigration, and more.

Keeping It Real Tips

Apprentice	Individual students or groups develop traditional documentaries that feature voice narration, scrolling images, and background music
Samurai	Individual students or groups develop traditional documentaries that feature voice narration, scrolling images, and background music; additionally, students add-in animation, real video footage, and/or talking head commentary from scholars
Jedi	The entire class works collaboratively to film a documentary and/or groups film separate documentaries and the class screens their film(s) at a schoolwide events, such as a historical film festival

Authentic Assessment: a Documentary Film

Background: Historians use multiple authentic formats to make their arguments, including documentary films. Documentaries use a variety of audio-visual tools to convey information and arguments. Some great documentaries include *4 Little Girls*, John Green's *Crash Course World History*, PBS' *Egalité for All: Toussaint Louverture and the Haitian Revolution*, and the Nerdwriter's "Why this is Rembrandt's Masterpiece."

> **Deliverable:** Use your documentary to develop an argument that answers your compelling question, exploring the key content and ideas that support your claim.

Requirements:

- ◆ A creative, relevant title.
- ◆ Five to ten minutes.
- ◆ Vivid visual style and sharp, relevant audio.
- ◆ Consider how your choice of style, pacing, and narration work to convey information, keep the audience interested, and support your historical argument.

Considerations

- ◆ Who is your narrator? What is the narrator's style? Does the narrator appear visually in the documentary?
- ◆ Are there scholarly "talking heads?" If so, who? What do they say?
- ◆ What images or animation will you use in the background?
- ◆ How do you portray your argument in addition to telling the story?

Artist Statement

Include a one-page artist statement, written in the first person. You should describe:

- ◆ Why you chose to create this documentary.
- ◆ What is your historical question and argument.
- ◆ What historical choices you made in creating it.
- ◆ What artistic choices you made in the film.
- ◆ What the piece represents about the event.

Newscasts

Real-World Context

I'm never a fan of fake or apocryphal quotations, but I do rather like the statement, attributed to *Washington Post* publisher Philip Graham, that journalism is "the first rough draft of history."

If history is the story of the past, then history only ends with yesterday. Or, in the era of social media, what is now history is the moment when I typed the word "word." If history is our conversation about the meaning of the past, then programs like "Meet the Press" are already engaging in historical meaning-making.

YouTube makes for a useful and fascinating clearing house of old newscasts; at the time, they were reporting recent history. Now, we can use them as primary sources to get a sense of what the period looked like and how people responded to particular key events. I'm sure that, like me, many other social studies teachers show clips of newscasts from the 20th century in their classes.

I love watching, with my students, a short ABC news broadcast on day six of the 1979 Iranian hostage crisis. Frank Reynolds dramatically passes the baton to the American journalist in Tehran who speaks alongside footage, naturally, of burning American flags and arm-pumping Iranian youth. The newscast involves an interview with a former hostage, a young female Iranian interpreter at the embassy, who calmly relates, "they took us, blindfolded us, and tied our hands behind our back."[10]

We watch a November 9, 1989 ABC report, where Peter Jennings sits behind his desk and tells the viewer that "the Berlin wall doesn't mean anything anymore."[11] Or, we can study Tom Brokaw's broadcast, from NBC news, as he reports live from the Berlin Wall. Brokaw is attempting to talk over the cheering, gleeful crowd as water cannons spray in celebration behind him.

News has been happening every day in history, but we can really begin accessing television broadcast news reports only from the middle of the 20th century until today. Within that time frame, you can view any of the momentous historical reports: the Apollo 11 landing, the assassination of Martin Luther King Jr., the Challenger disaster, the September 11 terrorist attacks, and the 1986 Mets World Series victory.

Bringing Newscasts into the Classroom

Students love creating group newscasts, even today when far fewer of them have the nightly news playing in their homes in the evening. The fact that newscasts must really function as a group task increases the complexity a bit.

There was a time when so many households had the nightly news as background during dinner; now, ironically, just as it is so easy technologically for students to film, they really don't have the same familiarity with television journalism. Still, students find inherent joy in taking on the generic broadcast roles (anchor, reporter, interviewees, and live-action subjects). They tend to be over-serious in a playful way when reporting and pleasantly silly when acting out the events. This seems to be what Denise Pope means when she talks about adolescent play in *Overloaded and Underprepared*.

All students, however, can grasp the basic outline of a standard newscast if they watch Charlie Brooker's hilarious clip "How to Report the News," which my Scarsdale colleague Nicola Minchillo shared with me. Charlie Brooker begins at the newsdesk, pans to a landscape shot, then walks slows toward the camera, describing exactly what he is doing, before "posing a question, what comes next?" The clip includes a few ordinary people talking, including one man opening letters at his kitchen table who mumbles "unless there's a person talking to me, telling me what's going on, I don't really listen to what they are saying." It is sort of a humorous meta-analysis of news reporting, satirically showing us exactly what normally happens through a format that is, actually, fake news.[12]

Since every event we study in history was once news, really any event can serve as the focus of student newscasts. That being said, to increase the "click" on authenticity, I encourage broadcasts that take place in the post-1945 era.

My first experience doing a newscast with a class was in my "Sports, Fashion, and Politics" course at Harvest Collegiate. We had been studying the cultural diffusion of cricket and soccer through British colonialism. In the assignment below, you can see how I deviate a bit from historical accuracy in the setting, as I place "Sportscenter" back in 1932, but I do provide as a context a real historical event.

Assignment

The year is 1932. You are a team of Sportscenter reporters. You have decided to travel abroad to England to interview a team of Indian cricket players who have just played their first test match in England (and lost).

Your film should interview athletes about their experiences playing sports in a British colony and then in travelling to the "mother country" to compete. Your final product must be a well-edited and thoughtful film that puts together a Sportscenter broadcast of the interviews. Some questions to think about:

- Who are the athletes?
- What does it mean for the Indian athletes to play these sports in England?
- How do they view the "mother country" and how is this reflected in their sports?
- What feelings and emotions would the players describe? What questions would the reporters ask?

The field trip we took to a local park was one of the most enjoyable experiences I'd ever had with my students. One quiet student loved building things so much that he worked with one of our science teachers, Paul Huseman, to build an actual cricket bat. They researched the dimensions and then did some woodworking magic to make it, sand it, and paint it with the colors of the Indian flag.

When we got to the park, students threw the ball, hit it with the paddle, and generally tried to do what we all imagined cricket to be. I'm sure it was far from the real thing. I had an additional assignment option about a Nigerian soccer team that also travelled to England to play there, and ended up victorious. I still remember filming that soccer match; one of the players was supposed to score, and no matter how many times the defenders helplessly fell to the ground to allow him to pass, he still couldn't get the ball in the goal. It was one of those joyful, hilarious moments of camaraderie and laughter that I can still remember nearly a decade later. The students' newscasts then intertwined the footage with interviews with "players" and "fans" who talked about the games and their meaning in the colonial context.

One group of students filmed a newscast about Gandhi's independence movement. Without having seen Brooker's clip, they still nicely followed the pattern: news anchor, clips of action, interviews with reporters on the scene. There is a reason we call theater a "play." The kids just love doing it. Watching it, you can tell that they enjoy putting one of their colleagues in jail. The best part, however, was the Salt March, in which the actors simply marched around one of the student's yards for about five minutes of seemingly endless video. It did culminate, however, in the students using actual salt as a final prop in the report, which they lift off the ground and raised to the sky.

Keeping It Real: Tips

Apprentice	Students conduct a video interview with one person involved
Samurai	Students in groups put together a broadcast about an event with a variety of scenes including the anchor, footage, and interviews
Jedi	The class puts together a series of newscasts from different channels, thereby showing multiple perspectives on the event

Authentic Assessment: Video News Broadcast

Background: Journalism is sometimes considered "the first rough draft of history." We can look back at television newscasts to understand what happened in the past and how people reacted to and grasped events from their time. Newscasts use anchor coverage, video footage, reporter coverage, and in-person interviews to tell their stories. Some great newscasts from the past include ABC News' coverage of the 1979 Iranian hostage crisis and NBC Nightly News' coverage of the 1989 Fall of the Berlin Wall.

Deliverable: Use your video news broadcast to develop an argument that answers your compelling question, exploring the key content and ideas that support your claim.

Requirements:

- ◆ Six to ten minutes.
- ◆ A careful attention to detail and historical accuracy.
- ◆ Consideration of roles, action, and interview subjects.
- ◆ A thoughtful attention to speaking and volume, setting, props, characters choices, visuals.

Tips:

- ◆ Make your historical question and argument/thesis clear.
- ◆ Ensure that the character identities are evident.
- ◆ Do not attempt to adopt a foreign accent.

- ◆ Consider how to ensure your work is respectful to the individuals and cultures involved in the story.
- ◆ Plan out how your newscast might combine action, dialogue, and analysis.

Artist Statement

Include a one-page artist statement, written in the first person. You should describe:

- ◆ Why you chose to create this newscast.
- ◆ What is your historical question and argument.
- ◆ What historical choices you made in creating it.
- ◆ What directorial choices you made and what symbolism you included.
- ◆ What the piece represents about the event.

Film

Real-World Context

What is the first question that students ask when I say that we are going to watch a film?

"Is it a real movie or a documentary?"

It doesn't matter how engaging documentaries have become, in most minds they are still no match for the real thing: the feature film. There was once a time when most films set in the past strayed shamelessly from historical accuracy; nowadays, we learn tremendously from historical films. Films often allow students to deepen their visceral, aesthetic, and empathetic sense of events and the people who lived through them. The *American Historical Review* recognized films as works of history. The April 2018 issue reviewed four films, including the Liberian film *The Land Beneath our Feet*.

There are a few types of "historical films." First, we have historical fiction; these are stories that could have been true, but they are not based on real people or accounts. A few examples of historical fiction films include *The Last Samurai*, *Les Misérables*, *Gladiator*, *Titanic*, *The Boy in the Striped Pajamas*, and *Gone with the Wind*. Each of these films give the viewer a sense of the time period to various degrees of accuracy. Second, we have films that are based on a true story, which take liberty with dialogue and a few details, but overall try to tell something close to a true account; movies like *Lincoln*, *Ray*, *The King's Speech*, *Schindler's List*, *Iron Jawed Angels*, *Hidden Figures*, *12 Years a Slave*, *Bohemian Rhapsody*, and *Glory*. Lastly, we can look at films that were set in the present when they were made, but now are primary sources that reveal much about the past: Charlie Chaplin's *The Kid* or Cold War films like *The Manchurian Candidate*.

I usually show only about one full movie a year to my class, although whenever possible and relevant I try to play clips from Indiana Jones. Here are a few of my favorites that I've integrated into my curriculum: *Troy*, *Luther*, *Gandhi*, *Long Walk to Freedom*, *Defiance*, *John Adams* (HBO miniseries), and *Kundun*.

It is hard to oversell the extent to which films have shaped our historical understanding and the public's historical conversation. I grew up in the 1980s and never much liked Queen, but now if you asked me the most important band of that era I'd be hard pressed to put anyone above Queen after having seen *Bohemian Rhapsody*. Similarly, our use of terms like "Gandhi's independence movie" to some degree result from the somewhat problematic hagiographies of historical biopics. Some of those films, mentioned above, were based on books, but arguably the film versions have done much more to shape the historical record.

Bringing Film into the Classroom

Most students love making films for the same reason they enjoy newscasts: it is play. The difficulty with any real filmmaking is the amount of time it takes, the technical expertise needed, and the number of students who need to be involved in the cast or behind the scenes. Certainly, for a film short, the technical ease of using iMovie or WeVideo allows students to do the necessary editing to get their ideas across.

Where I've had most success is in "clicking" a film project into an early 20th-century American history unit on urbanization, innovation, and the progressive era. During this unit, I normally include some clips from Charlie Chaplin and Buster Keaton's black-and-white silent films. Students are normally surprised with how much they can grasp from a silent film, which they attribute to the over-acting of the cast.

Many years ago, one of my American history classes at the Facing History School produced a silent film that they wrote and directed about factory life. Here, the film style matched the time period and the topic. I still remember the factory boss, played by a student who was quite short, jumping on a chair and backhand slapping his best friend, who then sprawled to the ground. Back then, we were editing and stitching together the movie with Windows Media Player, which was not a very user-friendly program. But still we were able to integrate some of Scott Joplin's ragtime music as well as the visual word slides that serve as dialogue.

Two of my American history students took a screenplay assignment I had given to the next level: they filmed their screenplay. It was about an inventor trying to make it big. They also used ragtime music to set the tone, and really hammed up the acting with that silent film pizzazz. I think one of the reasons students particularly enjoy making silent films is because they can unabashedly over-dramatize, which is just a whole lot more fun.

Turn of the 20th Century Film Project

Job Description: A Hollywood producer recently contacted you as she is interested in producing a period piece about the early 20th century. She's not sure what to call it, or what she really wants, but she knows it should be set between 1890–1920 and she wants three to four main characters who represent the spirit of the times, a gripping plot, and realistic historical settings. She has contacted you and four other writer/directors to send out a pitch.

Here's what you need to do to get the job:

- Title the film. A suggestion is starting with something like "A Time of …" or "The Age of …" and including a word or two that really captures this period in American history.
- Create three to four characters (with a one to two paragraph description for each) who represent important archetypes from the period. Remember, identities can be complex and one person can represent more than one "group." The description tells the producer everything she needs to know about the character and her/his identity.
- Provide a one to two paragraph plot synopsis. Here, you need to explain what happens to the characters. You must introduce at least one internal or external conflict *related to the time period* and how the character(s) resolve the conflict. In your plot synopsis, make sure to make some direct references to "historical details" that will surround the characters in their setting.
- Create a movie poster or some other type of advertisement for the film OR a graphic storyboard that portrays one scene. A graphic storyboard is basically a comic book depiction of the scene.

Keeping It Real Tips

Apprentice	Students write out a film script
Samurai	Students in groups write scripts, film the movies, and edit them
Jedi	Students in groups or as a whole class write script(s), film movie(s), and screen the productions at a school film festival.

Notes

1 The National Constitution Center and iCivics launch initiative to unite Americans around their love for the U.S. Constitution. (2017, January 18). Retrieved from https://constitutioncenter.org/images/uploads/news/WhatILoveAboutTheConstitutionPressRelease.pdf.

2 The National Constitution Center and iCivics launch initiative to unite Americans around their love for the U.S. Constitution. (2017, January 18). Retrieved from https://constitutioncenter.org/images/uploads/news/WhatILoveAboutTheConstitutionPressRelease.pdf.

3 14th Amendment with Eric Foner. (n.d.). Retrieved from https://constitutioncenter.org/learn/hall-pass/scholars-edition-eric-foner.

4 Green, J. (2019, April 1). Review: can a play make the Constitution great again? Retrieved from www.nytimes.com/2019/03/31/theater/what-the-constitution-means-to-me-review.html.

5 What the Constitution means to me: Heidi Schreck & Laurence Tribe with Dahlia Lithwick. (2019). Retrieved from www.92y.org/archives/what-the-constitution-means-to-me-schrek-tribe-lithwick.

6 Exploring the French Revolution. (n.d.). Retrieved from http://chnm.gmu.edu/revolution/.

7 Joseph & Myra Brandman Holocaust Memorial Museum. (n.d.). Retrieved from http://brandmanmuseum.com.

8 Decolonization and Nationalism Triumphant: Crash Course World History #40. (2012). Retrieved from www.youtube.com/watch?v=T_sGTspaF4Y.

9 Jason Merrin. (n.d.). Retrieved from www.jason-merrin.com/.

10 Iran Hostage Crisis 1979 (ABC News Report from November 11, 1979). (n.d.). Retrieved from www.youtube.com/watch?v=A8bC1DEYbI4&t=228s.

11 November 9, 1989: The Berlin Wall falls. (2009). Retrieved from www.youtube.com/watch?v=jnCPdLlUgvo.

12 Charlie Brooker's How to Report the News – *Newswipe* – BBC Four. (2010). Retrieved from www.youtube.com/watch?v=aHun58mz3vI.

Part 4

Civic Action Assessments

8

Civic Action Assessments

Most schools teach "social studies" rather than "history" because the discipline includes a wider array of topics, such as geography, psychology, philosophy, current events, politics, economics, and civics. In New York State, one semester of senior year must be a civics course. Social studies is about more than teaching content and skills; it is about preparing our young people to be active and productive citizens* in the future. In civic action, voice and choice are essential. One objective ought to be to develop empathy so that the students care enough to want to act. Additionally, students must have enough understanding of the complexity of the content and political process to identify multiple possible avenues for action and multiple possible outcomes, thereby allowing them to truly choose what they want to see happen (the goal) and how they want to try to get there (the action plan).

How do we get students to do meaningful civic action in school? This chapter will examine a variety of authentic assessments that allow students to engage with issues that matter to them, whether globally, nationally, or locally: a letter to a representative, leading a school teaching, planning a historical civic action, organizing a conference, advocating for a cause, a United Nations conference simulation, and design thinking for local issues. Additionally, it is important to remember that many of the other JADE assessments described in this book can also be used as a means to participate in civic action, such as memorials, visual art, websites, documentary filmmaking (including PSAs), music, and more.

Given the fact that civic action is so finely embedded within a particular context, for this chapter I chose to provide sample assessments related to one

---

* I use this term loosely to refer to participants in society, rather than those who meet the legal definition of citizenship.

particular topic, rather than generic templates. I believed it would provide a better sense of what these types of authentic assessments could really look like. Once you've looked at the samples, it should be evident how to transfer the format to another context or topic. Additionally, I did not include the three levels (Apprentice, Samurai, Jedi) because, essentially, to do most of these civic action projects you really have to operate at the Jedi level, integrating a whole class toward a larger, complex goal.

After reading the chapter, use the following chart as a plan to "keep the learning real"

In which unit(s) of your course could you integrate civic action?
Would your students work individually, in groups, or as a full class?
Which form of civic action would your class pursue? Or, would you provide choice?

Contact Your Representative (Call or Letter)

Real-World Context

The letter or phone call to a congressional representative is like the scrambled eggs of political advocacy. It seems so obvious and passé, yet once you give it another try you realize it is still surprisingly satisfying.

There are many methods of influencing your representative on a particular issue. You can show up at a town hall meeting, visit his or her office, tweet, or send an email. But, as a *New York Times* article brilliantly titled "Here's Why You Should Call, Not Email, Your Legislators" explains, your best option may still be the good old-fashioned phone call. According to interviews with a group of lawmakers, "A phone call from a constituent can, indeed, hold more weight than an email, and far outweighs a Facebook post or a tweet."[1]

It is acceptable to use a script when calling, since part of what the staffers do is tally up calls or messages about each particular issue to better understand constituent concerns. However, it is far more powerful to demonstrate passion and a personal connection to the issue, especially because in those cases the staffers will realize that it may be the issue that swings your vote. A poignant message from a phone call could get relayed directly to the lawmaker, which is far more likely than from an email.

Not everyone is in agreement that there is a hierarchy of message formats. In a *New Yorker* article called "What Calling Congress Achieves," Isaiah Akin, the deputy legislative director for Senator Ron Wyden of Oregon, explained "everything is read, every call and voice mail is listened to … we don't discriminate when it comes to phone versus e-mail versus letter." According to the article, a 2015 survey made it clear that what is most important is that the message itself is personalized and not simply a standard script copied from an advocacy organization. When done in mass, telephone calls are effective because they take the most time and attention for the staff to handle.[2]

Bringing Letters and Phone Calls to the Classroom

There are a few lessons and topics that I am sometimes reticent to teach because I've done them so many times before, imagining that the students must know them by now. The problem is – it doesn't mean my current students know how to do a task just because I have taught it each year for the past decade. It is still new to them! Every year, for example, I think "uggh, do I really need to teach plagiarism again? Don't they know it by now?" The answer is "duh, no, because they weren't in your class last year."

This is how I feel about letters to Congress. It seems so unoriginal. Won't the kids be bored by doing political action that is so traditional and uninspiring? The answer here, again, is no. For teenagers, writing to an elected official is authentic, electrifying, liberating. Most of them have never done anything like it. They know they are supposed to vote (someday), but just the act of directly writing or calling a representative hits them like a civic jackhammer.

Naturally, there is a wide-range of topics and issues that students can write about when contacting their congressional representative. It is best to integrate choice and voice and allow students to direct their learning and assessment; some may choose to write about climate change, gun control, abortion, health care, foreign policy, or even education.

I took a slightly different approach early in my American History course, asking students to consider new amendments to the Constitution. The project description below shows how students can write to their representative to suggest a new Constitutional amendment.

Constitutional Amendment Assessment

Carefully read all the amendments to the Constitution and think about our society today. What is missing? What are the great issues in America that are not addressed by the Constitution and its amendments? What else do we need to achieve in order to meet the lofty goals of the Preamble? Write a letter to your

> Congressional representative arguing for the adoption of *a new amendment* to
> the Constitution. In your letter, make sure to discuss the goals of the Consti-
> tution and its evolution over time. Is it where it needs to be or can it still be
> improved to achieve the true America that you desire? On page two, write out
> the language of the amendment. Consult a few sites for drafting legislation.[3]

Most students will opt for the least personal form of communicating with
their representative because they have little familiarity and comfort with the
telephone as a tool to call strangers, and most have little to no experience send-
ing actual letters. Therefore, as the teacher, the key is to push them to do what
is hardest here. Avoid the email. Make them call or write a real letter. They will
be really nervous to call, so role-play the situation as a class and/or in pairs.
Send a student to another room to pretend to be a congressional staffer and
then have another student call him/her on speaker phone to practice in front
of the whole class. Or find some other way to do a mock call, including having
one of them call you. They will have a blast with the role-play practice and it
will give them the confidence they need to do the real thing.

Regarding the letter, how will you know if they actually send it? Here's
my trick. They submit one copy of the letter to me. I edit it and make suggestions, and then they need to send the revised version in the mail. I require
my students to send me a selfie of them putting the letter in the mail to get
credit. They are usually incredulous at first. Send a selfie? The selfie addition
is fun, and I get some really ridiculous photos, of course, since many make
goofy faces for the camera. All of this just adds to the authenticity and joy of
the assignment. Another approach to ensure the letters actually get mailed is
to fill out envelopes in class and walk together to the mailbox.

It is important to think carefully about the destination of the letter, and
perhaps to offer a few possibilities for them to choose from. The usual recipient is the student's congressional representative, although a strong civic action
project should ask students to consider whether the issue is best addressed at
the local, state, or national level. In that sense, students might choose to contact a representative in the city council, state assembly, or choose an executive
like the mayor, governor, or president.

When I taught about the Syrian Civil War at Harvest Collegiate, for
instance, the Trump administration was about to take over and I thought it
might be an opportunity for students to influence State Department policy by
writing to incoming Secretary of State Rex Tillerson. I was probably wrong as I
was unable to predict the incredible weakening of the State Department in the
Trump administration, but the idea of widening the net of possible officials
was a good one. Doing the project again, I would likely advise students to send
their letters to the traditional recipient: their congressional representative.

Authentic Assessment: Letter or Call to Representative

Background: Contacting your elected official is a crucial form of civic action. Your representatives pay attention to what their constituents care about. They especially take notice if the message is personal and shows real passion.

> **Deliverable:** Use your message to an elected official to make a clear political argument, including a concrete "ask" and the reasons, ideas, and facts that support your ask.

Requirements:

- You must either call your representative or send him/her a letter.
- Determine who is the most relevant elected official to contact.
- Make sure your introductory statement includes your "ask."
- Give reasons for why you care about the issue and why you believe a particular position is valid.
- A letter must be no more than one page, single-spaced. Follow formal letter-writing structure. Consult a source like OWL Purdue for business letter format.
- If you write a letter, send me a selfie of you putting the letter in the mail.
- If you call, record the call and share it with me.

Leading a School Teaching or Ceremony

Real-World Context

One of the most significant ways to increase the authenticity and meaning of your students' work is to look for avenues to allow them to communicate their learning outside the walls of the classroom. One of my favorite assessments for civic action, however, involves students leading a teaching, an event, or a holiday commemoration outside of their own class. It may be for other classes or even for the school and parents.

Historical commemorations, certainly, take place in the real world. We have special ceremonies and festivities for holidays such as July 4th, Memorial Day, and Martin Luther King Jr. Day. Ceremony, speeches, songs, and rituals serve as symbolic manifestations of our historical memory. In Judaism, for example, the Passover Seder is replete with symbolic objects meant to retell a collective history: the exodus from Egypt. To this day, we point to and explain the items on the Seder plate, such as the egg, bitter herb, and shank bone.

Bringing School Teachings and Ceremonies to the Classroom

When I made my big move to Scarsdale, I didn't expect to have the opportunity to put on an event like Museum Night. However, in my second year I recognized an unexpected confluence. I was teaching a "Race and Ethnicity" elective and the social studies department was searching for a new idea for our annual Martin Luther King Jr. commemoration.

The students in my Race class had led lessons for each other throughout the semester about Race in the Media and about chapters from the book *So You Want to Talk About Race*. I had modeled discussion strategies for them earlier in the year to prepare them to lead weekly in-class discussions in a way that would go beyond "presentations." I wanted the students to teach: to search out resources and to develop questions that would lead other students in the class toward a rich conversation.

It occurred to me that students in this class were uniquely prepared to lead a Martin Luther King Jr. Day learning session. Not only did the theme of the course fit perfectly with the holiday, but also the format was exactly what we had done throughout the year. And, most importantly, the kids had constantly complained that they were the only ones having conversations about these crucial issues of race and that more students needed to be thinking and talking about concepts like privilege and institutional racism.

To increase the students' buy-in and the authenticity of the project, I spent one period asking the kids to discuss what would make for a meaningful MLK Day commemoration. I had considered my students having a panel discussion on an auditorium stage in front of the school. That wasn't one of my best ideas. They nixed my proposal with such passion (and a bit of anger) and I respected them enough to realize they had a good point.

Instead, *they* proposed coming up with a lesson about race to lead in individual social studies classes. When I brought this idea to the department, a couple of teachers, Patrick Healy and Brandon Lee, had the smart alternative: having students produce four different grade-appropriate lessons on race. We moved forward with that proposal and I divided students into four groups. Each group had the responsibility to determine the topic of the lesson and then to produce it. Some topics changed over time, but they finally settled on four great themes:

What is race? Why does it still matter? (Grade 9)
Cultural Appropriation (Grade 10)
Affirmative Action (Grade 11)
Checking your privilege (Grade 12)

When you see my initial project description further on in the chapter, it is clear how each lesson's theme changed due to the student agency over the project. For example, I originally suggested "What is racism?" for the 10th grade lesson, but that group chose the topic of cultural appropriation. This is what student voice and choice is really all about.

I gave students about five to six class periods to put together the lesson. I checked in with each group repeatedly and then the week before the event, each group had the opportunity to run their lesson by the whole class and get feedback. The student feedback on the lessons was incredible: deep, thoughtful, incisive.

Students had one more chance to revise and then the day of our MLK commemoration arrived. Each group taught four class periods during the day and we met during lunch to debrief and make any necessary tweaks.

There was a lot of logistical work on my end to make this happen. I needed to work with the department to gain approval, work with the students to produce their lessons and improve them, and then to organize the day. I created a Google Form to find out which social studies teachers were able to host the student-teachers for the lesson and then I needed to organize the schedule. This type of work requires strong communication with multiple stakeholders. Also, on the day of the commemoration, I wanted to make sure to see all the groups for a short time during period one so I could see if there were any issues to address; after that, I tried to see each group teach their whole lesson over one period.

Just like with many of my own lessons, the classes improved throughout the day and also varied depending on the personality of the class they were presenting to. Some had more vigorous and rich discussions than others. I put together another Google Form for each presenter to receive feedback from the students and teachers who had experienced the lesson.

This was authentic assessment at its best. We transferred our class' work to the larger school community to honor a particular holiday and we assessed the students' ability to do what we were trying to do throughout the course: have difficult and complex conversations about race.

For your class, think about whether your students can teach the rest of the school or present their work to a larger audience. Is there a particular holiday, like Holocaust Remembrance Day, which coincides with your unit? Is there something meaningful and relevant that you can do for Women's History Month or the United Nations' Human Rights Day?

MLK Day Commemoration: So You Want to Talk About Race?

Background: We have been talking about complicated issues concerning race the entire semester. Much of our work has involved the book *So You Want to Talk About Race* by Ijeoma Oluo.[4] Now it is time to bring some of our discussions to the larger school.

Our task: In groups of three, we are going to create lessons to help teachers and students talk about race for MLK Day.

Logistical Requirements: You must create a Google Drive folder for this assignment and share the folder with me. The folder should include your lesson place, presentation, and any additional resources.

Grade and Suggested Topic (as a group, you may choose another topic)	Students
Grade 9: What is race? Is it really about race? Does race exist?	
Grade 10: What is racism?	
Grade 11: What if I talk about race wrong?	
Grade 12: Should we "check our privilege?" What does that mean?	

The Lesson Format

1   Your lesson should be about 45 minutes long. Organize your lesson for yourself and the students with a Google presentation.
2   Introduce yourselves and the purpose of the lesson/activity.
3   Begin with a warm-up question. What is a big question concerning your topic?
    a.   If students are unable or uncomfortable responding to the question, move on to the rest of the lesson and then come back to it at the end.
4   Provide students with a short excerpt of *So You Want to Talk About Race* to read. The excerpt should be no more than one page typed (single-spaced). You can use various parts of the chapter.
5   Introduce the author and provide one or two guiding questions before reading for them to think about.
6   After the reading, ask for student responses on the reading. You may consider asking one of the following:
    a.   What questions did it raise?
    b.   What surprised you?
    c.   What did you disagree with?
    d.   What did you learn?
7   Ask one to three targeted questions about the reading.
8   Provide an additional resource related to the larger topic/question. This resource may be another text, video, song, TV show, etc. You may consider using one of the pieces of media we looked at in class.
9   Debrief this additional resource. You may consider using:
    a.   Barometer Activity.
    b.   Four Corners.
    c.   Pictionation.

Leading a Lesson Rubric

	Jedi	Samurai	Apprentice
Communication	– Speaks in an articulate, clear, fluid, and confident manner – Student speaks without reading	– Speaks clearly and at an appropriate volume – Student often relies on notes	– Speaks at appropriate volume but struggles a bit to articulate ideas – Student reads a prepared script
Questions	– Establishes and develops a compelling, elegant, or very original questions for the class to consider – Overall questions strongly supports a coherent, thought-provoking and complex argument	– Establishes and develops precise, knowledgeable questions – Overall questions support a coherent argument =	– Questions are vague and/or do not fully address the core issues of the topic
Visual Presentation	– Produces a creative, artistic, organized presentation that stuns the viewer with the visual quality	– Produces a solid, organized presentation that helps the viewer follow the lesson	– Produces a presentation that has some weaknesses in layout, size, visibility, or organization
Activity	– The activity successfully leads the class into an exploration of the content and makes them want to be there – Uses relevant discussion protocols, activities, or other strategies to engage the class	– The activity leads the class into an exploration of the content – Uses an activity to engage the class	– The core of the lessons does not include an activity beyond questions to really engage the class

(continued)

	Jedi	Samurai	Apprentice
Selection of media (if applicable)	– The chosen media successfully leads the class into an exploration of the content and makes the class want to be there – Uses relevant discussion protocols, activities, or other strategies to engage the class with the media	– The chosen media leads the class into an exploration of the content – Asks thoughtful questions about the media	– The media is not fully engaging or relevant – Does not fully lead the class into a discussion of the media
Accuracy	– Correct and specific factual accuracy throughout the lesson that demonstrates a deep understanding of the complexity of the issue	– Correct factual accuracy that demonstrates an understanding of the issue	– Demonstrates a general understanding of issue with some weaknesses on details
Reflection	– Reflection demonstrates highly thoughtful choices of subject matter, process, strengths, weaknesses, and growth	– Reflection demonstrates choices of subject matter, process, strengths, weaknesses, and growth	– Reflection is vague and rarely demonstrates logical choices of subject matter, process, strengths, weaknesses, and growth

      d.   Quotation Sensation.

      e.   Silent inquiry circles.

      f.   Fishbowl.

10 Close-out the lesson by asking a big question, connecting the resources, or asking the students for their feedback and thoughts. *Make sure you make some kind of connection to MLK during the lesson.*

Planning Historical Civic Action

Real-World Context

I think it is self-evident that civic action is part of the fields of history, social studies, and politics. Most modern political history is about the civic action of ordinary people: the French Revolution, the Haitian Revolution, anti-slavery and abolition movements, suffrage, Civil Rights, feminism, anti-apartheid, etc. While often we remember only the famous leaders, we ought not ignore the role of the foot soldiers of these movements. Their actions were authentically political and consequently became essential parts of our history.

Bringing Civic Action to the Classroom

One of the many lessons I learned from teaching at the Facing History School, a small NYC public school affiliated with Facing History and Ourselves, is that we ought to make more of an effort to connect the past to our experiences in the present. The history teachers at the school consistently sought out relevant examples from students' lives to establish connections with the past. When we discussed discrimination in early Nazi Germany and the role of the press, we made connections to name-calling and bullying in school. When we studied the causes of World War I and early 20th-century European alliances we made analogies to gang behavior (which, unfortunately, was a reality in many of our students' neighborhoods).

Thus, when my classes study positive role models from the past, such as Gandhi or Nelson Mandela (to take the obvious examples) my goal is not just for them to learn what happened but also to think about the strategies those individuals and their respective organizations adopted or invented to make change. Civics does not need to be relegated to a 12th grade civics course but rather can be integrated throughout a social studies scope and sequence.

It is easiest to make a civic action plan for a contemporary topic that students can really do in real-time; for instance, a plan for action on the Syrian Civil War in a global studies class or a plan of action to get more people in the town to vote.

However, I also incorporate civic action plans as an assessment in historical units in which civil disobedience or resistance are central themes. This requires students to engage with the historical context and understand what technological, political, and social possibilities existed during that period. In other words, if a student is thinking about the Underground Railroad and developing an action plan to support fugitive slaves, the student has certain technological limitations that do not exist for a similar assessment on independence movements in the 20th century.

This type of project can be done as a simulation, in which students essentially remain as themselves but get transported through time and space so as to make the action plan. Or, even better, it can become a role-play in which students take on the role of a real individual in history and create an action plan based off of that person's philosophy, experiences, and mindset.

I want to emphasize here that creating an historical civic action plan for Gandhi's independence movement, for example, is different from *doing* contemporary civic action. When my students engage in this work during a unit on colonial India, I ask them to create a new act of protest, a new mobilization, building on Gandhi and the Indian National Congress' work and clearly embedding itself in that context, the goals, and the strategies. In the sample assessment further on in this chapter, you can get a sense of what that might look like.

Students can't plan another Salt March for the project; they can, however, identify another symbol of British rule and consider the various strategies employed by Gandhi (boycotts, marches, fasting, alternative production, etc.) in the development of their plan. This ensures the students' demonstration of their understanding of satyagraha while also making sure they are not simply replicating a famous plan. Since these campaigns need to "spread the word" I also include an advertisement of the protest as part of the project requirement. Here, I try to ensure that students use a form of advertisement (newspaper, flyer, radio program) that is feasible given the technology of the period.

I wonder whether a "social justice mindset" or "civic engagement" is an additional type of intelligence that Howard Gardner did not explore. Some individuals get so motivated by the chance to engage in real change that it almost gives them an aura of energy; authentic civic engagement sparks their thinking and creativity.

In Figure 8.1, a student's civic action plan poster, you can see how she adapts the famous satyagraha mobilizations by coming up with a new plan, a dock worker's strike, that fits within the overall philosophy of the movement by reducing British economic hegemony and simultaneously supporting local industries.

Figure 8.1 Example: Civic Action Plan Poster.

Assessment: Civic Action Plan and Advertisement

Background: Gandhi used multiple strategies to spearhead his Free India movement. Imagine that you are living in colonial India and you want to lead a new protest mobilization. Drawing on Gandhi's strategies, develop a new plan of action for a protest and an advertisement to gain followers.

Deliverable: Use your plan to develop an argument about the proper course of action that answers your compelling question, exploring the key content and ideas that support your claim.

Civic Action Plan Requirements:

◆ Two pages, single spaced.
◆ Clearly organized sections that include:
   • The problem.
   • Proposed solution (event, date(s), length of time, # people needed, strategy).
   • Reasons why this solution will be effective.
   • Ways in which this protest plan fits within prior successes and the larger goals of the Indian National Congress.
   • Potential problems you might envision.
   • Costs.
   • Ideal result of the action.

Advertisement Requirements:

◆ Use a medium available in the early 20th century (flyer, radio, etc.).
◆ Make sure to have a catchy slogan or some hook to make people want to join.
◆ Draw upon your plan to provide key information that the potential activist needs to know whether or not to join.

Artist Statement

Include a one-page artist statement, written in the first person. You should describe:

◆ Why you chose to create this action plan.
◆ What is your historical question and argument.
◆ What historical choices you made in creating it.
◆ What artistic choices you made and what symbolism you included.
◆ What the piece represents about the event.

Organizing a Human Rights Conference

Real-World Context

Most professions, whether medicine, law, or education, have annual conferences, which provide opportunities to build connections and learn from other experts in the field. Social studies teachers, for example, have the annual NCSS conference as a rare chance to gather with colleagues from across the country to complain about mandated testing and other bureaucratic nightmares (and to learn new methodologies).

Civic Action Plan Rubric

	Jedi	Samurai	Apprentice
Pitch/ Proposal	– Establishes and develops a compelling, elegant, or very original problem, solution and message – Overall explanation, understanding, and analysis strongly supports a coherent and complex argument	– Establishes and develops precise, knowledgeable problem, solution and message – Overall explanation, understanding, and analysis support a coherent argument	– Establishes general problem, solution and/or message – Overall explanation, understanding, and analysis somewhat supports an argument
Complexities	– The pitch and design successfully captures and teaches complex facts and ideas about the historical content – The proposal thoughtfully reflects the work of activists from the period while branching out and creating a new civic action plan – Very evident and thoughtful response to possible challenges of implementation	– The pitch and design captures and teaches some complex facts and ideas about the historical content – The proposal reflects the work of activists from the period while branching out and creating a new civic action plan – Evident response to possible challenges of implementation	– The pitch and design capture and teaches some facts and ideas about the historical content – The proposal somewhat reflects the work of activists from the period while branching out and creating a new civic action plan – Some evident response to possible challenges of implementation

(continued)

	Jedi	Samurai	Apprentice
Accuracy	– Correct and specific factual accuracy that demonstrates a deep understanding of the complexity of the issue	– Correct and specific factual accuracy that demonstrates an understanding of the issue	– Mostly factually accurate; demonstrates a general understanding of issue
Artistic Voice	– Produces a creative, artistic, original advertisement that stuns the viewer with the quality of the imagery and symbolism – The artist uses complex symbolism visual representations to advance the argument	– Produces a creative, artistic, original advertisement that very much impresses the viewer with the quality of the imagery – The artist uses visual representations to advance the argument	– Produces an advertisement that communicates to the viewer the plan – The artist provides obvious images to advance the argument
Artist Statement	– Reflection demonstrates highly thoughtful choices of subject matter, process, strengths, weaknesses, and growth	– Reflection demonstrates choices of subject matter, process, strengths, weaknesses, and growth	– Reflection demonstrates general choices of subject matter, process, strengths, weaknesses, and growth

Similarly, conferences are crucial venues in the human rights arena for activists and intellectuals to meet each other and exchange ideas. Typically, conferences have an opening address, a number of panel discussions or speakers, perhaps an additional keynote speaker, and possibly an award to give out.

For instance, each year the Geneva Summit for Human Rights and Democracy brings together a strong cohort of speakers who shed light on current human rights issues in the world. In 2019, after an opening address by journalist James Kirchick, the summit included panels on the "Struggle for Democracy in Latin America," "Confronting Oppression, Defending Human Rights," and "Supporting Political Prisoners," among other topics. Panel speakers represented an array of professions, such as human rights lawyers, non-profit founders, activists, filmmakers, family members of political prisoners, members of United Nations Watch, and journalists.

In the same vein, the organization "Women Deliver" held a 2019 conference in Vancouver to discuss "gender equality and the health, rights, and well-being of girls and women." Among a remarkable list of speakers were Prime Minister Justin Trudeau and Sophie Grégoire Trudeau of Canada, Tina Tchen (former chief of staff to Michelle Obama), Ziauddin Yousafzai (co-founder of the Malala Fund), and Tarana Burke (founder of Me Too movement). The conference had sessions on gender-based violence, female genital mutilation, midwifery, child marriage, womenomics, sexual and reproductive health, and more.

Bringing Human Rights Conferences into the Classroom

Probably the best thing I've ever done as a teacher is to participate in the 1st Harvest Collegiate Human Rights Conference, which was held in 2017.

In the fall of 2016, Andy del-Calvo, Daniel Marshall, and I sat down together to plan out a course on "Genocide and Human Rights." We began by discussing some overarching goals for the course and essential understandings, attempting to dig into the really meaningful structure of Understanding by Design.

Planning backwards, we wanted to think about the endpoint: the summative assessment. Andy and Daniel started throwing out some ideas, such as an essay, a piece of artwork, or historiographical work. But I nudged us to think of something that really clicked with the idea of human rights itself. This was, after all, the right opportunity to combine global history with civic action. "What is a real product of human rights work?" I asked. I suggested the conference.

I had just had my second child. I did not have the bandwidth to make the conference happen. Daniel was in his first full-year of teaching. So that left Andy to take on the endeavor, and he ran with it like the avid marathon runner he is. Andy rightly understood that in a project this big we needed all the students to participate, but we could take advantage of an "Open Honors" program at the school to get the 16 honors students in the 10th grade to do the brunt of the work organizing the conference.

Here was the main description of the conference that we prepared:

> *The purpose of the conference is to educate and connect our students to the world of marginalized communities and their rights by delving into a diverse range of topics. We strive to make an impact on our community and to help the students in our school understand ways to fight back against crimes that counter humanity. We would like you to spread awareness on not only the conference itself, allowing our names to be put out there, but more importantly, on the topics that we are covering in order to emphasize how real these issues are and to show that these problems are truly impacting everyone around the entire world rather than just the U.S. By doing this, we strongly believe, it will give our students that extra push they need to physically take action on all that they have worked so hard for in the time leading up to the conference.*

The conference began with an opening ceremony in the cafeteria. One of the student co-chairs gave an opening address. As part of her speech, she declared:

> *Human Rights on their own, however, don't have power. Alone, they are just guidelines on paper to try and make sure none of us go out there and start committing mass genocide without being punished severely. Human rights are* nothing *if we as a community don't try to actively try and ensure our rights aren't being violated.*

Ingrid Laslett, of the United Nations, gave the keynote address on her work trying to stop the use of chemical weapons in Syria. Then, we moved into breakout sessions led by honors students on the following topics: refugees, women, indigenous people, the LGBTQ community, and education. The audience for each session consisted of one class of students. Each breakout session also included an expert from the field who sat in and provided advice, but did not lead the discussion. For example,

Noah Gottschalk of Oxfam and David Ponet of UNICEF participated in the refugees sessions.

We called the second half of the breakout sessions "crisis committees." The guest experts in each session along with the student moderators (the honors students) presented the audience with a typical real-life crisis to resolve and students needed to work collaboratively to come up with the best solution.

The closing ceremony was an opportunity for breakout groups to share their crisis resolutions with the larger conference community and for a closing address from two of the co-chairs. In her closing remarks, one student reminded the audience that:

> *No matter if you are a student, a teacher, a parent, or anybody in this world, for if human rights are not protected, we will have nowhere to turn to. It is our job to protect our fundamental rights as humans, and hopefully this conference has aided you in realizing this.*

It is difficult to describe the amount of work that went into planning and executing the conference, especially since we, the teachers, refused to do the work. Andy met weekly with the honors students to brainstorm topics, nominate and vote on students for major roles, consider the format of the conference, organize the panels, determine what the student moderators would do, divide up roles, contact any outside speakers, promote the conference, and more. Like a real conference, students would be both presenters and audience depending on the session. We called in some outside speakers, but ultimately this conference was really about the students. As the planning progressed, I sat in, occasionally, to provide a bit of support and I gradually increased my presence as we got closer, but ultimately the conference was Andy and the students' triumph.

Authentic Assessment: A Human Rights Conference

Background: Human Rights Conferences bring together activists and intellectuals to discuss problems in the world today and possible solutions.

Deliverable: As a class, organize and execute a Human Rights Conference.

Requirements:

- ◆ Development of a theme and title for the conference.
- ◆ Identification of a keynote speaker.
- ◆ Identification of five topics for breakout sessions.
- ◆ Organize the structure of breakout sessions.
- ◆ Decide on an opening and closing speaker.

Considerations

- ◆ Who are the two to three chairs of the conference?
- ◆ What experts will you invite as guests to the breakout sessions?
- ◆ Who is in charge of advertising and promoting the conference?
- ◆ Who is in charge of creating the schedule?
- ◆ Who will contact and invite experts?
- ◆ Who is in charge of the logistics (space, food, etc.)?

Advocating for a Cause/Global Citizenship Conference

Real-World Context

I'm a sucker. When I walk through Union Square, it is like I have a target on my head for two groups of people: the Chabad-Lubavitch youth who ask me if I'm Jewish and want to lay tefillin and the non-profit street fundraisers who call me over to tell me about their organizations. No matter how much I try to look down and walk quickly, I can't seem to lie and say I'm not Jewish, and I can't walk past the charity asks.

For those who haven't been accosted by really kind, compassionate youth on the street asking for donations to support kids with cleft lips, refugees, or climate change, let me explain: it is a brutal experience to even attempt to turn down the request. The fresh-faced activists look you in the eye, ask your name, and then give a very short pitch about why their cause is essential to justice. Fundamentally, they are making an argument about the social importance of their organization's work. They obviously have the pitch perfected because in a few moments they have tugged at your heartstrings, your sense of justice, and your image of yourself as a moral and empathetic human being.

I'm signed up for monthly donations to a number of wonderful charities because of the great work of these citizen activists, but the truth is, many of them never would have made my list if someone hadn't spoken to me on the street. I still remember the day I had to go home and sheepishly tell my wife that we were now proud supporters and protectors of bumblebees (to be fair, I now recognize much more clearly the importance of bumblebees and the threat that their extinction poses to agriculture).

Advocating Causes in the Classroom

For many years, I have closed-out global history with the study of a contemporary human rights issue, most often Syria, and a corresponding civic action piece. One of the best projects in this vein is the United Nations Conference that I describe in the next section.

Last year, however, I became even more interested in the idea of student choice and getting the students to envision themselves as current and future citizen activists. Conference role-plays are excellent at helping students understand competing perspectives and the complexities of action, but I'm not sure they push teenagers to think about what *they* care about and how *they* can support their cause. My hope is to push them to consider the possibilities of what *they* can do, rather than what powerful government officials ought to be doing. After all, as Howard Zinn once said, "whatever progress has been made in this country has come because of the actions of ordinary people, of citizens, of social movements."[5]

I created an assessment that asks students to role-play as themselves, six years in the future. That might be a bit confusing. A role-play is when we take on someone else's role or persona. While by definition we normally can't role-play as ourselves, people change significantly over time. Becoming ourselves in the future is, essentially, a role-play. Thus, when high school students role-play as the 22-year-old adult version of themselves about to enter the real world, they gain the opportunity to think about what really matters to them and how they want to eventually participate in society as adults.

I remembered that crucial time in my own life, as a senior in college, when I tossed aside law school in favor of working as a street educator in Brazil. I used my own story to frame the assessment, and then asked them to really consider what matters in our world today and how they could advocate for that cause. My pledge to donate my own money to the winning non-profit added a greater sense of authenticity to the assignment; it was like they really were citizen activists on the street asking for support.

They also had to frame the pitch as if they were going to work for the organization next year. I wanted them to envision that they could do more than give money. They *could* dedicate their life and work to a cause. It is an option for their future.

Day one of this futuristic role-play conference consisted of the two-minute pitches. The pitches were remarkable, both for their quality and for the ways that, at the very end of the year, they gave me an even better sense of who the students were and what mattered to them. Their pitches advocated for an array of organizations: environmental, educational, health care, animal welfare, and mental health non-profits.

Day two began with open time for students to walk around the room and discuss their vision with others individually or in small groups. It was informal, chaotic, and wonderful. It was as if Union Square were filled with activists talking to people strolling by and to each other! After about 15 minutes, I asked each student to declare where he or she would donate an imaginary $1000. We tallied up the top six recipients, who then got to sit at a long panel table. They had another shot to give a quick pitch and then they answered questions about their cause from the audience and from me. Each participant had to explain what his or her cause could achieve with $1000. This gave us the opportunity to really think about impact and what non-profits can and can't achieve with regards to their mission. We considered whether it is better to donate to an organization tackling a major global crisis, such as climate change, or one that tackles a more localized problem like malaria through the dissemination of mosquito nets.

Finally, everyone had the chance to send their imaginary donation to one of those six final causes, and then we tallied up the winner. I opened my computer and, as the students watched on the projector, I donated to the winning organizations. In my two classes, the winners were Amazon Watch and, ironically, the Honeybee Conservancy.

Thus, this project combines civic action with oral literacy, communication, concise argumentation, and a consideration of current global issues and the value of (and drawbacks of) non-profit charities. Taking the experience a bit further, students can reflect on the nature of global problems and the complexities of addressing them through governmental and non-governmental means.

Authentic Assessment: Global Citizenship Conference Role-Play

Background: In 2001, I was a college senior deciding what to do with my life and how to try to make the world a better place. I looked at the world around me and its problems as well as my own skills and interests. I decided that a major problem was poverty and inequality, and that what I could do to help was to use my Portuguese language skills and my education to help street children in Brazil. It was then that I decided to join Projeto Axé. Now it is your turn to make that evaluation and choice.

Role-play Description: The year is 2019 and you are a college senior. *You are you*, but you are six years older than you are now. You think about the world around you and its problems. You think about what you care about and where you would like to make an impact. You realize you have education, privilege, and power and that this is the chance to start an adult life in which you give back and try to make the world better.

Part A

- ◆ Choose a global problem of major importance that affects the lives of ordinary people. Choose something that is of personal importance and significance to you … something you care about.
  - Examples: computer surveillance, social media, political tyranny, refugees, child marriage, child soldiers, human trafficking, rainforest destruction, LGBTQ persecution, girls' education, climate change, street children, nuclear weapons, anti-Semitism, freedom of speech, privacy, authoritarianism.
- ◆ Identify a place where this problem is happening.
- ◆ Read about the issue using at least five quality sites: newspaper articles, NGO websites, governmental briefings, etc.
- ◆ Make sure you have a deep understanding of:
  - The nature of the problem and its manifestations … how it hurts people.
  - The causes of the problem.
  - Possible solutions + reasons why solutions are difficult. *What solution do you advise?*
  - Groups (NGOs) that work on resolving this problem. *Which non-profit will you work or volunteer for?*
  - What is the job you will do for this organization next year?
  - Possible opposition to this work

Part B – Global Citizenship Conference for Young Leaders

You have been invited to participate in a two-day Global Citizenship Conference for Young Leaders. The goal of this conference is to raise awareness of global issues and to obtain support for your cause. Each participant will have the opportunity to make a TWO MINUTE pitch about the above-mentioned information. After that, there will be time for open discussion in large and small groups to try to influence people to support your cause. All participants will be given an imaginary $1000 to donate to one other cause besides their own. *At the end, I will donate $50 of my own money to the cause that raises the most money.*

Mock United Nations Conference

Real-World Context
The real-world context for the United Nations is the United Nations. I hope I do not have to explain what the United Nations is.

Bringing the United Nations to the Classroom
One of the most popular clubs at Scarsdale High School is Model UN, run by a charismatic young teacher named Patrick Healy, who I consider young because he is my age. Model UN, one of the most popular clubs at Harvest Collegiate, was run by an excellent math teacher and knitter, Laura Maurino, who formerly worked at the United Nations. Students just seem to love Model UN! And I love the gorgeous blanket Laura made for my daughter!

At Scarsdale High School, a team of 10th grade teachers – Patrick Healy, Brendan Lee, Andrew Morgan, and Chris Paulison – put together a tremendous end-of-year Model UN conference on climate change. They achieved such a degree of collaboration that they even coordinated to have their classes that meet the same period face off against each other. I went to see the event, and the energy was palpable. All the students in a room of about 100 students were engaged and actively participating in the role-play.

I avoid the term "Model UN" in my assessments because I do really stripped down versions of the club format, which is why I call them "Mock United Nations Conferences." Despite the fact that I wrote a book about role-playing, I've never had so much interest in Model UN. I think it is because the technical rules seem a bit convoluted and the experience appears overly focused on procedure. That being said, what counts is that students love it and learn tremendously from the experience. I'm a bit less interested in the procedures and drafting of resolutions and more in the use of the setting to get students to discuss and debate crucial contemporary issues.

Over the past few years, my classes have put on mock United Nations conferences on the 1980 Soviet invasion of Afghanistan, the ongoing war in Afghanistan, and the Syrian Civil War. UN conferences are perfect assessments to click with the study of current social and political problems in global history, and I want to emphasize here that students must have a deep and nuanced understanding of the issue going into the role-play, otherwise the result will be superficial. When studying a global human rights crisis like the Syrian Civil War, my main questions are both simple and difficult:

What is happening?
Why is it happening?
What can we do about it?

One factor that was great about the Syria conference (the assignment is on the next page), which I put together in collaboration with my friend Noah Gottschalk, Oxfam's Senior Policy Advisor on Syria, was the inclusion of NGOs as voices in the discussion.

When we did this project at Harvest Collegiate, I brought the students to the Kings County Courthouse to have a more formal experience for the conference. Even though the courtroom wasn't the perfect setup for a conference, it added a sense of gravity to the proceedings. We followed the format on the assignment sheet, with the student playing the UN Special Envoy acting as the moderator. I gave him some tips to introduce the conference, to call up the representatives to speak, and then to moderate the discussions. The speeches showed students' abilities to understand the perspectives of the countries and organizations as well as the connections between them. We laughed so much when the representatives from Turkey and Greece began arguing with each other and when one student began accusing another of lacking humanity. Most importantly, when they got down to figuring out an actual course of action they became stumped since the various interests of the security council and the Syrian representatives made any kind of consensus impossible. This added to their sense of the complexities of the conflict.

Authentic Assessment: A United Nations Security Council Meeting on the Syrian Crisis

Briefing

World leaders, members of NGOs, and members of the Syrian government and opposition have gathered in Geneva, Switzerland to try to establish a resolution to the Syrian crisis.

The Question: How do we stop the crisis in Syria?

Supporting Questions:

- ◆ What is the crisis?
- ◆ What are its causes?
- ◆ What are our options? What are the consequences of each option?

Your Mission

Each of you will take on the role of someone with stakes in the crisis. Some of you are on the UN Security Council, which means you can decide the United Nations' policy. Others have been called to give opinions and advice based on your perspective.

- ◆ Research and learn about your country or organization's policy related to the Syria conflict. What are your interests, goals, and concerns?
- ◆ You must write a one-page brief stating your position on the conflict and its resolution. Consider the questions above as well as the perspective, interests, and goals of your particular role. You must be prepared to give a two-minute speech outlining your position.

The Format

- ◆ Each diplomat will give a one to two minute briefing speech.
- ◆ Open time to walk around, meet with other delegates, converse, and attempt to use individual conversations to bring people over to your position.
- ◆ We will have 15 minutes for open debate and Q&A moderated by Staffan de Mistura.
- ◆ Members of the Security Council plus the Syrian government and opposition have 15 minutes to achieve consensus and a resolution. Moderated by Staffan de Mistura.

The Roles

Security Council: US, Russia, France, UK, China, Jordan, Egypt.

Central Figures: Staffan de Mistura, United Nations Special Envoy for Syria; Salim al-Muslat, Opposition High Negotiations Committee; Bashar al Jaafari, United Nations Syrian ambassador.

Others: Turkey, Israel, People's Will Party (Qadri Jamil), 13th Division, Free Syrian Army, Saudi Arabia, Iran, Oxfam, Germany, Greece, SAC – Syrian American Council, Kurdish representation, Iraq, Doctors Without Borders, Mercy Corp, The White Helmets, UNICEF.

Design Thinking for Local Issues

Real-World Context

Design Thinking is a human-centered problem solving strategy used in a variety of arenas to generate innovative, empathetic, and practical solutions. Design Thinking helped Oral-B develop a better electric toothbrush, improve sanitation systems in Cambodia, and Airbnb to reinvent itself and avoid bankruptcy. Tim Brown's article "Design Thinking" in the *Harvard Business Review* explains that the process "uses the designer's sensibility and methods to match people's needs with what is technologically feasible."[6]

Doug Dietz, of GE Healthcare, used Design Thinking to create an improved MR scanner experience for children. He realized that the MR process was terrifying for children, partly because of the danger signs and other aesthetic warnings surrounding the machine. So, he did something new: he asked them what they would like to see to improve the experience. The result is astounding and it emerged from those interviews: by using paintings, games, and storytelling, Dietz turned the MR process into an adventure. According to GE Healthcare's online newsletter *The Pulse*,

> *In the variety of adventures, which include aromatherapy, calming decorations and in some cases, disco-ball bubbles, children are transported to another, more imaginative world where simple commands to get the scan done accurately become part of the adventure. In one of the Adventure Series, children have to get into a canoe, and are made to lie down inside.*[7]

A *New York Times* article called "Design Thinking for Doctors and Nurses" also demonstrates how the problem-solving strategy has helped the medical field. The author, Amitha Kalaichandran, explains that the trauma area in her hospital had often been a bit chaotic, with countless doctors and nurses working simultaneously and sometimes disjointedly over gunshot victims, for example. This raised a problem: who was in charge? No one knew. Using Design Thinking, a nurse came up with the idea of having the trauma team leader wear a bright orange vest. Similarly, including patients in medical design has led to great innovations, such as a cloud-based diabetes monitoring system that allows parents to track their child's glucose levels on a mobile app.[8]

My former colleague and Design Thinking guru, Maggie Favretti, is using the process to help students and schools recover from the hurricane in Puerto Rico.[9]

Bringing Design Thinking to the Classroom

The Design Thinking process has a few variations, but we teach it in Scarsdale High School as follows: (1) empathize; (2) define the problem; (3) ideate; (4) prototype; (5) test and revise.

I am not a Design Thinking Jedi. In fact, when compared to everything else in this entire book, Design Thinking is the topic in which I have learned completely from others. I am still at the Apprentice level. That being said, I believe in the value of Design Thinking and thus wanted to share it here.

Design Thinking has a relatively lengthy history at Scarsdale High School and is utilized in a variety of courses that make up a three-level STEAM sequence, including a social entrepreneurship course taught by Lisa Yokana and Brian McDonald. In the social studies department, we have a senior class called City 2.0, which was created about five years ago by Maggie Favretti and Fallon Plunkett. Students in Lisa's class have done incredible work developing innovative designs to solve real social problems, and last year a student team won a national award for their product: a shirt for students who can't dress themselves vertically, instead opening horizontally like a book. It also is made with conductive fabric that alerts caregivers if the child has slipped and moved into an uncomfortable or unsafe position.

Maggie and Fallon created the City 2.0 class to transform the notion of what a civics class could be. They discarded rote memorization and quizzes, opting instead for getting students to use Design Thinking to solve local problems, whether in New York City or in the village of Scarsdale. Different teachers who have taken up the course, including Emily Block and myself, have added new twists depending on teacher and student interests. Maggie's civic engagement was heavily invested in having students get out of a "Scarsdale bubble" to learn about New York City and design concrete solutions to real problems. Other teachers have emphasized going really local and using Design Thinking to understand and attempt to resolve some of the actual problems facing Scarsdale, despite its affluence.

Problems in a town like Scarsdale that emerge out of Design Thinking often relate to modern social and environmental ills, such as the lack of walkability, the lack of community engagement, excessive loneliness, and stress. Students find it empowering to use Design Thinking to really tackle what seem to be minute issues, such as the paucity of sidewalks or multi-use spaces in town; however, much of the gleanings about civics and Design Thinking is that achieving resolutions for even what seem to be really small issues turns out to be a complex, difficult task.

One project in this urban design City 2.0 course asks students to redesign something in their own town. Many of them have lived there for 18 years; now it is time for them to think civically and leave it in a better place before they go on to college.

Authentic Assessment: Redesigning Your Town's Living Experience

Background: The purpose of this project is to use the problem solving mindset you have developed throughout the year to find solutions to real, human-centered problems: *DESIGN Thinking*.

The task: Imagine your town council has commissioned your group to devise a way to improve the town's livability and sustainability. How can you redesign a neighborhood in your town to make it better? Or, how can you change one thing in your town to make it a better place to live?

Step 1: Research/Empathy – What is it like to live in this town or neighborhood?

◆ Interviews.
◆ Spend 10 minutes observing in four different places in the neighborhood (per group). Take notes. How many different people do you see? What are they doing? What is your feeling while you are there? Track one person … watch as she enters and leaves the space. What does s/he do in the space?

Step 2: Define the Problem – What is the problem with the living experience? Consider your interviews + your readings + observations + your own experiences.

Step 3: Ideate – What are possible ways to make those improvements?

Step 4: Prototype – Which idea should we move forward with? Make a prototype of the neighborhood or design change! Possible prototypes include maps, online drawings, 3D models of blocks, etc.

Step 5: Pitch – What do our fellow townspeople think about our redesign? What feedback can they offer?

Step 6: Reiterate – How can we incorporate people's feedback to improve our solution?

Design Thinking Rubric

	Jedi	Samurai	Apprentice
Oral Pitch	– Establishes and develops a compelling, elegant, or very original problem, solution, and message – Overall explanation, understanding, and analysis strongly supports a coherent and complex argument	– Establishes and develops precise, knowledgeable problem, solution, and message – Overall explanation, understanding, and analysis support a coherent argument	– Establishes general problem, solution, and/or message – Overall explanation, understanding, and analysis supports a basic argument
Written Pitch	– Establishes and develops a compelling, elegant, or very original problem, solution, and message – Overall explanation, understanding, and analysis strongly supports a coherent and complex argument	– Establishes and develops precise, knowledgeable problem, solution, and message – Overall explanation, understanding, and analysis support a coherent argument	– Establishes general problem, solution, and/or message – Overall explanation, understanding, and analysis somewhat supports a basic argument
Test and Revision	– Reworking of pitch and prototype demonstrates a significant incorporation of new knowledge emerging from prototype testing and interviews	– Reworking of pitch and prototype demonstrates incorporation of new knowledge emerging from prototype testing and interviews	– Reworking of pitch and prototype demonstrates little incorporation of new knowledge emerging from prototype testing and interviews

	Highest	Middle	Basic
Complexities	– The pitch and design successfully captures and teaches complex facts and ideas about the historical content and makes the viewer understand AND want to learn more – Very evident and thoughtful response to possible challenges of implementation	– The pitch and design captures and teaches some complex facts and ideas about the historical content – Evident response to possible challenges of implementation	– The pitch and design capture and teaches some basic facts and ideas about the historical content – Some evident response to possible challenges of implementation
Accuracy	– Correct and specific factual accuracy that demonstrates a deep understanding of the complexity of the issue	– Correct and specific factual accuracy that demonstrates an understanding of the issue	– General factual accuracy that demonstrates a basic understanding of issue
Artistic Voice	– Produces a creative, artistic, original prototype that stuns the viewer with the quality of the imagery and symbolism – The artist uses complex symbolism visual representations to advance the argument	– Produces a creative, artistic, original prototype that very much impresses the viewer with the quality of the imagery – The artist uses visual representations to advance the argument	– Produces a prototype that communicates the main idea – The artist provides obvious images to advance the argument
Reflection	– Reflection demonstrates highly thoughtful choices of subject matter, process, strengths, weaknesses, and growth	– Reflection demonstrates choices of subject matter, process, strengths, weaknesses, and growth	– Reflection demonstrates an overview of choices of subject matter, process, strengths, weaknesses, and growth

Notes

1 Victor, D. (2016, November 22). Here's why you should call, not email, your legislators. Retrieved from www.nytimes.com/2016/11/22/us/politics/heres-why-you-should-call-not-email-your-legislators.html.
2 Schulz, K. (2019, July 9). What calling congress achieves. Retrieved from www.newyorker.com/magazine/2017/03/06/what-calling-congress-achieves.
3 https://legcounsel.house.gov/HOLC/Drafting_Legislation/Drafting_Guide.html. www.law.com/thelegalintelligencer/almID/1202794475598/?slreturn=20171003080041.
4 Oluo, I. (2019). *So you want to talk about race*. New York: Seal Press.
5 Zinn, H. (1993). *Failure to quit: reflections of an optimistic historian*. Monroe, ME: Common Courage Press.
6 Brown, T. (2015, August 28). Design thinking. Retrieved from https://hbr.org/2008/06/design-thinking.
7 From terrifying to terrific: the creative journey of the adventure series. (2014, January 29). Retrieved from http://newsroom.gehealthcare.com/from-terrifying-to-terrific-creative-journey-of-the-adventure-series/.
8 Kalaichandran, A. (2017, August 3). Design thinking for doctors and nurses. Retrieved from www.nytimes.com/2017/08/03/well/live/design-thinking-for-doctors-and-nurses.html.
9 https://www.designed4resilience.org/.

Conclusion

The Frankfurt Barkeep and Other Heroes

Somewhere in Frankfurt, near the airport, there is an average hotel. Inside that hotel, there is a very average bar.

Inside that average bar, in 2008, I stumbled upon a very extraordinary bartender.

My wife and I found ourselves in the bar, the night before our flight home, because the hotel offered a free drink to guests. It had been one of the best trips of our lives; we had visited really good friends who we had not seen in years and had a chance to tour some of the great cities in Central Europe: Prague, Vienna, and Munich. In Austria, we even got to watch a marionette show of *The Sound of Music*.

When my wife and I wax nostalgic about this unforgettable summer trip, the memory that pops up most frequently is about this bartender. We don't remember what we drank in the bar and I actually don't know if he makes a great cocktail.

Instead, we reminisce about the way he dried the wine glasses.

I've dried wine glasses before. I rub a towel this way and that; after a few moments, there are always some drops left over. He had a different system. He dried and shined each glass with infinite care and pride; he washed them with something bordering on love. We watched mesmerized, silently, as he swiped and rubbed the towel across the stemware, before holding the glass up to the light to study it as if he were a Super Bowl quarterback sizing up the defense. There was no braggadocio; there was only concentration. It was like I was viewing a walking meditation or a tutorial with Zen Master Thich Nhat Hanh on how to mindfully eat an orange.

That day, he became one of our heroes.

The world is made up of heroes like our favorite Frankfurt barkeep. They are the people who find a particular vocation and make the world better, in sometimes miniscule ways, by practicing their craft with integrity, purpose, and care. They turn the everyday into an art; the mundane into moments that sparkle. Sometimes their vocation comes out of a passion. Sometimes it comes out of a calling. As David Brooks said to the Dartmouth class of 2015, it comes by asking: "What is life demanding me to do?"[1]

My small world has been made better by a few people with impressive academic degrees, law and medical diplomas, and occasionally by someone who holds public office. More frequently, I have grown to appreciate the people who practice their vocation as if it were an art and who go beyond the typical ceiling to achieve excellence regardless of the prestige of the task.

My heroes are people like Nick Caragiulo, of Transcend Construction, who took care of unexpected snafus while renovating our home, met his bid price and timeline, and never asked for anything more to do the job right. When your home is in hands you trust, little in life is more comforting.

There is our friend Gladys, who helps us take care of our house as if it were her own, scrubbing and rinsing and cleaning with determination. Her hard work and commitment, in a world that has denied her the opportunities to follow her dreams of nursing, allows my wife and me a little extra time to parent our young children.

A person whose vocation repairs the world is Maria, the Portuguese owner of a pastry shop in Tarrytown. Not only does she make delectable apple and marble cakes; she's also the type who knows her customers' names and makes them feel as if the bakery exists for them. She gives my oldest son a small slice of carrot cake when he is with me and she asks about our family. The shop is a gathering of local elderly who sip on coffee and discuss their aches and joys. Going there is like seeing a live episode of *Cheers* in which everyone is sober and all the characters are about Coach's age.

My heroes are a number of exceptionally skilled and dedicated flight attendants on LATAM who made a 10 hour flight from JFK to Santiago with three children doable for us (and the other passengers).

One of my heroes was my grandfather, Joseph Brandman, who took incredible pride in his work as a barber. He often told me about how he had cut the hair of important state officials in Albany so that they could look dignified while doing their work.

Of course, there are also the many people who use their traditional academic education and their passion to better the world, such as my friend Noah Gottschalk. Noah took his degree in international affairs to heart. He lived in

Egypt, Uganda, and South Sudan, and now in Washington D.C., advocating on behalf of refugees for Oxfam and the International Rescue Committee.

We need people who find joy, meaning, and dignity in the incredible panoply of vocations that makes our world and our lives run smoothly. As Ambassador Omar Saif Ghobash of the United Arab Emirates remarks in his book *Letters to a Young Muslim,*

> *Life is diverse. Living is to live with difference. Anyone telling you that difference should be stamped out is stamping out life. Those people insisting that there are black and white answers to the difficult questions are stamping out the diversity that is inherent in life.[2]*

A healthy society depends on creating opportunities so that people can find a suitable match with a vocation that brings meaning to their lives and goodness to the world, whether as doctors, teachers, artists, construction workers, farmers, or preachers.

David Brooks, in his poetic book *The Second Mountain*, calls the match with vocation an "annunciation moment." It is

> *the moment when something sparks an interest, or casts a spell, and arouses a desire that somehow prefigures much of what comes after in a life, both the delights and the challenges ... every once in a while, a new passion is silently conceived. Something delights you and you are forever after entranced by that fascinating thing.[3]*

It is much more difficult to have an annunciation moment and to discover that fascinating thing if we never encounter it and never have the chance to engage with it.

We find our vocations by understanding the patterns of joy and meaning in our lives. I realized I needed to become a teacher only deep into my work as a street educator in Brazil. There, I took stock of my activities over the past five years and I realized that every time I made a choice about how to spend my productive time, I ended up working with children, whether tutoring elementary school kids or working at the Latin American Youth Center in Washington D.C. And, I realized, those experiences brought me great joy. As Nietzsche writes in "Schopenhauer as Educator,"

> *What have you truly loved thus far? What has ever uplifted your soul, what has dominated and delighted it at the same time? Assemble these revered objects in a row before you and perhaps they will reveal a law by their nature and their order.[4]*

One role of schools is to help young people find that match and to unlock their creativity and passions, to give students enough meaningful experiences that later on, in college or afterwards, they can arrange them in order to find a pattern: the pattern of who they are. Schools most likely will not give every young person their annunciation moment, but we can certainly try.

I am not teaching students like Jake, Emma, and Mariana so that they become bakers, flight attendants, barbers, historians, or contractors, although I certainly would be thrilled if more students felt a calling to bake brownies and bring them to class. I am teaching them social studies so that they can figure out who Jake, Emma, and Mariana really are and so that they have the skills and experiences to become those people. The goal of education cannot be to bury young people's individuality under an avalanche of formulaic learning but rather to give them skis, snowshoes, or, God forgive me, a snowboard so they can find a path down the mountain.

When I began this book, I wrote the introduction with the conception that while I am not artistic, I am cultivating possibilities for students of mine who are. Indeed, one of the first things I put down was the sentence, in the introduction, that "I am writing this book because I can't paint it, sing it, or film it. I am not actually 'artistic' other than having written a few mediocre poems and one good enough to get a second date."

During the process of writing all that I know about authentic assessment, however, I began to recognize how much creativity lies within me. Only while composing this book did I realize that, in addition to "The Mariner's Gaze," in the past few years I had written a picture book and a historical fiction novel, created a virtual museum, designed role-plays, and even performed the worst math rap in human history. The creativity is there, even if it does not float up to the level of brilliance. But it took me a really long time to even figure out that there is a creativity in there.

Both writing and education are paths of discovery; discoveries about the world and about ourselves. I must wonder: to what extent did my own traditional education stifle my understanding of who I am and what forms of creativity may be within my grasp? School may not function to teach us creativity or to find our calling, but it can at least do its best to not get in the way.

Writing this book has also shown me that I have a long way to go to reach the highest levels of authentic assessment. There are many times when I have settled for landing only a few rungs up the ladder, falling short of a performance, a showcase, or a collaboration that could have boosted the students to get to the top. There are forms of art, such as filmmaking or graphic design, that I should study on my own so as to be able to support students in learning some of the techniques. And I really want to figure out how these authentic assessments translate to English, Science, and Math classes.

One thing I knew before I started this book is that I am a teacher and I can't escape being a teacher: that is why I structured this conclusion using my RICE format so that you have one more example to take with you into your own classroom.

Notes

1   Brooks, D. (2015, June 14). 2015 Commencement Address. Retrieved October 7, 2019, from https://news.dartmouth.edu/news/2015/06/david-brooks-commencement-address.
2   Ghobash, O. S. (2018). *Letters to a young Muslim*. New York: Picador.
3   Brooks, D. (2019). *The second mountain: how people move from the prison of self to the joy of commitment*. New York: Random House.
4   Brooks, D. (2019). *The second mountain: how people move from the prison of self to the joy of commitment*. New York: Random House.